FEMINIST AGENDAS AND DEMOCRACY
IN LATIN AMERICA

# Feminist Agendas

---

## and Democracy

---

## in Latin America

EDITED BY

JANE S. JAQUETTE

*Duke University Press*

DURHAM & LONDON 2009

Printed in the United States
of America on acid-free paper ∞
Designed by Jennifer Hill
Typeset in Minion Pro by Tseng Information Systems, Inc.

Library of Congress
Cataloging-in-Publication data
appear on the last printed pages of this book.

In memory of Ruth Cardoso,
who devoted her life to
social justice through both
thought and action.

W hen I took an extensive trip to Chile, Brazil, Argentina, and Peru in the spring of 2006, I was not thinking of putting together a book on what has happened to women's movements in Latin America. I had not done field research in the region since the mid-1990s, and from a distance it seemed that women's movements had declined and that women were no longer considered political actors of any consequence. Instead of focusing on women, I therefore joined my husband in a series of interviews on political and economic conditions, eager to see at close range how these democracies were evolving in general and to assess the effects of globalization.

Yet as I conducted interviews in Brazil, attended Michelle Bachelet's inauguration in Chile (and returned to Santiago for several weeks during the height of the debate on gender quotas), caught up with Peru in the period between the first and second rounds of the 2006 election, and wrestled with the Kirchner phenomenon in Argentina, I came to realize that a new book was necessary. Women's movements were not moribund, as some I interviewed had suggested, but were instead undergoing major shifts in strategy, and their agendas had changed. This book aims to capture the new directions of feminist activism and their implications for democracy and gender justice.

It would be impossible to thank all the individuals who helped along the way. My greatest debt is to the authors themselves, who were enthusiastic from the beginning, grappled with the issues, and responded with good spirit to my editorial blandishments. Augusto Varas, then at the Ford Foundation, and Claudio Fuentes of FLACSO-Chile, provided support that made this project possible.

I also thank those whose insights I have repeatedly sought over several years: Maruja Barrig, Julio Cotler, Celso Lafer, Cecilia Blondet, Jacqueline Pitanguy, María Elena Valenzuela, María del Carmen Feijoó, Alex Wilde, Anne Perotín-Dumon, Augusto Varas, Sergio and Kenny Bitar, Genaro and Ana María Arriagada, and Manuel Antonio Garretón. Elisabeth Friedman helped connect me with feminists in Venezuela; Cynthia McClintock provided helpful feedback on an essay I wrote on Bachelet; Joan Caivano kindly included me in a conference on women's political leadership in Latin America, cosponsored by the Inter-American Dialogue; Susan Eckstein, Kevin Gallagher, and Scott Palmer invited me to present the introductory chapter of *Feminist Agendas* at Boston University.

In Latin America, many others were generous with their time and knowledge: In Brazil, Ruth Cardoso, Eva Blay, Sonia de Avelar, Danielle Ardaillon, Norman Gall, Fatima Jinnyat, Maria Herminia Tavares de Almeida, Lidia Periera, David Fleischer, and the helpful staff of the Secretaria Especial de Politicas para as Mulheres. In Chile, María de los Angeles Fernández, Antoineta Saa, Lorena Frias, Sonia Montesino, Victoria Hurtado, Steve and Chris Reifenburg, María Elisa Fernández, Javier Couso, and Soledad Falabella. In Argentina, Elizabeth Jelin, Diana Maffia, Catalina Smulovitz, Laura Pautassi, Santiago O'Donnell, and Dora Barrancos. In Peru, a special thanks to Sandra Vallenas for her invitation to talk about this project at La Católica, and to Jane Henrici, a U.S. scholar doing research in Peru.

At Duke University Press I received sustained support and encouragement from Valerie Millholland, senior editor, and enjoyed the capable assistance of Miriam Angress and Pam Morrison. The book's arguments were sharpened by the work of two anonymous readers, and the final version was much improved by my student research assistant, Elizabeth Cutler, who energetically tracked down sources. My sister, Beth Von Voigt, helped me with the index.

Finally, I am deeply grateful for the ongoing intellectual stimulation and personal support I receive from Irene Tinker and Kathy Staudt, on this project as on so many others, and from my husband, Abe Lowenthal, my companion in travel, research, and life.

# Introduction ⟨

Jane S. Jaquette

Latin American women's movements played important roles in the democratic transitions in the Southern Cone (Argentina, Chile, Uruguay, Brazil) and Peru in the 1980s, as well as in the civil wars and peace processes in Central America in the 1980s and 1990s. They put gender-equity issues on political agendas throughout the region, reforming discriminatory family and labor laws, criminalizing violence against women, and introducing gender quotas for elections to national legislatures in several countries. Democratic governments established offices or ministries within the executive branch to design legislation, monitor progress, and carry out specific programs for women.

Yet women's movements in Latin America appear to have lost momentum, unable to sustain their initial successes. The issues that mobilized women over the past few decades—equality in family law and violence against women—have been addressed by constitutional reforms and new laws in virtually every country, but the new laws are rarely adequately implemented. Women's issues are now institutionalized in government ministries, but these often remain underfunded and lack strong connections to women's organizations. Women's political representation has been promoted by quotas that require political parties to nominate women, but the laws are often evaded or ignored. Social norms have shifted markedly in favor of women's rights and toward equality for women; rural women have asserted demands for property rights (Deere and León 2001); and rising indigenous movements have produced powerful women leaders. But persistent machismo and the opposition of the Catholic Church and of other conservative sectors of society have made it difficult to change laws regarding sexual preference or women's reproductive rights.

The essays in this book show that the need for political activism on women's issues has not diminished. Democratic politics, new constitutions and laws, and the changing international environment suggest the need for new strategies to achieve gender equity. The authors of this volume, as activists and researchers, document the ways in which feminists are pursuing their specific agendas in the Southern Cone, Peru, and Venezuela, as well as in international forums, and on the Mexico–United States border. They explore the implications of these changes for democracy in countries that are becoming more differentiated from each other in many ways—in response to economic and political crises, persistent economic inequities, underinvestment in human capital, and frayed safety nets. Trends toward decentralization, the growing political power of marginalized groups (the indigenous and the poor), and the continuing activism of environmental, human rights, and women's movements are creating a more pluralist—but also a more fragmented—politics. At the same time, the opening of Latin American economies to global forces of economic change and dramatic advances in communication technologies have created new arenas for feminist activism, with important consequences for citizenship and democracy.

Globalization, Neoliberalism, and the Democratic Deficit ⚜

Although the democracies in postauthoritarian Latin America have not been overthrown by military coups, as was so often the case during the twentieth century, there is widespread concern that many Latin American democracies are facing a "democratic deficit" and that the quality of democracy is being undermined.[1] Heightened presidentialism and a failure of checks and balances among the executive, legislative, and judicial powers—a lack of horizontal accountability—is accompanied by a lack of vertical accountability as political party systems and labor unions in many cases have weakened, lessening their ability to mediate between citizens and the state (O'Donnell 2007). Parties and politicians are held in low esteem, with legislatures in opposition and often gridlocked. Clientelism and patronage politics have not diminished, and corruption scandals have further sapped the legitimacy of democratic administrations. In many countries, indigenous groups are seeking recognition and greater autonomy from the state. Levels of state capacity vary dramatically.

Globalization has intensified all these challenges. The so-called Washington Consensus among northern industrialized countries pressed for the adoption of market-oriented economic reforms in many Latin American countries, where the debt crisis of the 1980s had weakened traditional economic nationalism. In part because they brought down inflation and attracted foreign investment, the reforms gained many adherents among the new technocratic elites in the region. They ushered in an unprecedented (but unsustainable) period of ideological accord in the hemisphere, which was reinforced by international changes that favored market-oriented development and diminished the appeal of Marxist alternatives.

The Washington Consensus promoted markets over states and trade over protectionism, which amounted to a frontal attack on the nationalist model of import-substitution industrialization that had guided development in most countries of the region from World War II until the mid-1970s. Only in Chile, however, did the prescribed economic ("structural adjustment") reforms produce robust rates of growth, or produce them rapidly enough. Macroeconomic policies provided the greatest success: by matching government expenditures more closely with government revenues, they succeeded in reducing inflation to historically low levels. However, the privatization of government-run industries and the reduction of government budgets meant cutbacks in social services, which increased poverty and postponed needed investments in education and health.[2] When growth did occur, the divisions between rich and poor grew wider. Opening Latin American markets to foreign investment made them more vulnerable to international forces beyond their control, leading to a series of economic crises that shook public confidence.

A range of so-called second-stage reforms—designed to strengthen the rule of law, give legislatures greater research and policy capability, and increase investments in social capital—recognized the need for capable states. But these reforms were slow to take hold, and their effects remained diffuse or ambiguous, increasing the gap between the hopes many had during the transitions—that democracy and markets would address long-standing inequities in political representation and social justice—and the economic and political performance of elected governments.

In South America several presidents ran on populist platforms in the late 1980s and early 1990s, campaigning against neoliberal policies imposed by the economies of the North. Once elected, however, presidents like Fernando Collor de Melo in Brazil, Carlos Menem in Argentina, and Alberto Fujimori in Peru soon reversed themselves, coming to terms with the International Monetary Fund (IMF) and foreign investors, maintaining tight controls on government budgets and promoting foreign investment and trade.[3] This pattern of "bait and switch" (Stokes 2001) kept the reforms in place during the 1990s, but it put severe strains on the processes of democratic consolidation.[4] During the so-called lost decade of debt restructuring in the 1980s, and well into the 1990s, growth rates remained feeble. A series of financial crises in the latter half of the 1990s, capped by an economic meltdown in Argentina at the end of 2001, further undermined popular support for the reforms (Mainwaring and Pérez-Liñán 2005).[5]

Although several countries were headed by social democrats during the 1990s, including Fernando Henrique Cardoso in Brazil and the presidents of the center-left Concertación in Chile, these governments largely worked within the Washington Consensus rather than challenging it. Voter discontent thus increasingly drew electorates toward more radical candidates. But when the Brazilian Workers' Party won the presidency in 2002, their candidate, Luiz Inácio Lula da Silva, a leftist with working-class origins and immense charisma, surprised analysts by maintaining Cardoso's economic policies, although his government moved more decisively to reduce poverty (Santiso 2006).

The first serious challenge to the Washington Consensus began with Hugo Chávez's election as the president of Venezuela in 1998. Chávez had led an attempted coup in 1992 against a government that had tried, unsuccessfully, to impose neoliberal reforms, leading to riots in several cities. Since 1998, or more accurately, since 2003 (when oil prices began to rise and Chávez began to promote his "Bolivarian" agenda more aggressively in the region), several presidents have been elected on so-called populist platforms, including Evo Morales in Bolivia (in 2004), Rafael Correa in Ecuador (2006) and Daniel Ortega in Nicaragua (2006). Néstor Kirchner's government in Argentina (since 2007 led by his wife, Cristina Fernández de Kirchner) adopted some populist economic measures in response to the country's economic crisis of 2001–2, which put over 40 percent of Argentina's population below the poverty line. His government cultivated a close relationship with Chávez, and Venezuela bought billions of dollars worth of Argentine bonds. These facts, combined with close defeats of populist candidates by moderates in Peru and Mexico in 2006, prompted some analysts to ask whether Latin America was veering toward the left (Vilas 2006; Castañeda and Navia 2007). With the exception of a few NACLA *Reports*, however, there has been little attention to the feminist implications of this trend.

Women's Movements from the 1970s to the Present:
From Visibility to Fragmentation ·⸙

Catalyzed by the United Nations (UN) Decade for Women (1975–85), feminist and women's groups formed during the 1970s and 1980s and became involved in the resistance to military authoritarian regimes in the Southern Cone and Peru. Along with other "new social movements" (Cohen 1985; Slater 1988), women's movements helped legitimize democracy, in part by shifting the agenda away from the class politics that had polarized the region during the previous decades. However, the return to democracy meant a return to government by political parties, which pushed social movements off center stage as sources of new ideas and as arbiters of the political agenda. Conflicts between women's movements and political parties formed part of a broader pattern of disenchantment that replaced the euphoria of the transitions.

Because they originated under repressive regimes, as Maxine Molyneux (2001b) has observed, women's movements "identified themselves as oppositional and anti-state," and for many women's groups, "autonomy became a principle of political organization" (174). The state's often inconsistent gestures toward institutionalizing women's interests within the government (in the form of gender units with varying degrees of policy influence and resources) were in some cases rejected by women's organizations as elitist and bureaucratic, sharpening conflict between "insiders" and "outsiders."[6]

In the posttransition period groups that had been united in opposition to the military (and who were often recipients of material as well as moral support from foundations, foreign assistance agencies, and transnational NGOs) were now divided by class, race, and ethnic divisions, as well as by partisan differences. As international donors turned their attention to other issues and to other parts of the globe, women's NGOs found themselves in competition for scarce resources. Although many feminists, largely urban professional women, had participated in cross-class alliances during the transitions and were committed to social justice, they found it increasingly difficult to maintain these cross-class connections. Working-class and poor women, who had originally rejected any association with feminism, began to see that their "practical" gender interests had "strategic," feminist implications, but the trend toward fragmentation continued.[7]

Many of the policies prescribed by the Washington Consensus in the 1980s and 1990s, including the privatization of state-owned industries, the reduction of tariffs and barriers to foreign investment, and balanced budgets, could be justified in macroeconomic terms, as import-substitution industrialization had lost its dynamism and many countries were experiencing hyperinflation, with very negative consequences for the poor. But these measures had severe microeconomic effects, particularly for women, as government expenditures in the areas of health, education, and welfare were cut back to balance the budget (e.g., Elson 2003; Aguilar and Lacsamana 2004).[8]

As men lost their jobs, women's participation in the labor force increased, but not on the terms women wanted. Privatization, international competition, and reductions in state spending increased male unemployment and forced many women to join the labor force to support their families. They often had to take low-wage or part-time jobs, working in the maquilas in Free Trade Zones, or in the informal sector, or doing piecework at home. Reduced social spending meant that women had to fill the gaps (Bakker 2003; Bonería 2003). Structural adjustment policies came under attack from women's movements, both locally and internationally. The World Bank and other foreign aid agencies turned their attention from women and development programs to ameliorating the effects of structural adjustment on women and children.

Women's movements today are not seen as significant actors in Latin American politics. But that is not to say that women's—or feminist—activism has ceased. Rather, progress on women's issues has depended on the concerted actions of a few: feminist and/or grass-roots groups, both urban and rural; women in political parties; elected women; and so-called femocrats in government bureaucracies. They rarely achieve the level of coordination and consensus that the term *movement* implies. Parties have not made addressing women's issues a high priority, although many have adopted voluntary gender quotas, and several legislatures have passed gender quota laws (Htun and Jones 2002; Krook 2007). The Argentine quota law passed in 1992 became a model for the rest of the region, but it depended critically on the support of the Argentine president, Carlos Menem, who actively opposed other goals of the women's movement.

Women's movements have also suffered a loss of momentum as a result of their successes. Cultural beliefs concerning gender relations have undergone a sea change. The legal subordination of women is no longer taken as natural or just, and there is solid support for policies ending discrimination and for criminalizing violence against women. Surveys suggest that many Latin Americans think that women make more honest and even more capable political leaders than men (Htun 2001:13). Attitudes about women's reproductive rights are also changing, and it is increasingly possible to engage in public debate on the issues of abortion and sexual preference (NACLA 2007; Mongrovejo 2006; Mariner 2005), topics once taboo.[9]

Although women's movements are no longer as visible as they were during the transitions in the 1980s, women continue to organize and press for change in a variety of local and national arenas. Feminist activism has also gone global, a shift made possible by changes in communication technologies and by three decades of UN conferences that brought women together to debate, share experiences, and build networks. Latin American women's movements helped create a transnational feminist movement, a process that began during the first UN conference on women in Mexico City in 1975 and grew steadily through the fourth conference in Beijing in 1995 (Meyer and Prügl 1999; Lebon and Maier 2006). Latin American feminists have met in regional meetings (*encuentros*), held every two or three years since 1981 (Sternbach et al. 1992), and there have been several subregional and national feminist conferences on a variety of issues.

Under the aegis of the UN Decade for Women (1975–85), new international norms emerged to promote women's equality by ending discrimination in employment, education, and family law, while also recognizing that women are different due to their reproductive roles and in their vulnerability to certain forms of violence. This norm-setting process gained additional momentum in the 1990s as women's NGOs from many countries participated actively in a series of UN conferences on global issues ranging from the environment (Rio de Janeiro, 1992) to human rights (Vienna, 1993), population (Cairo, 1994), and sustainable development (Copenhagen, 1995). The documents produced by the decade and other UN conferences, as well as the Convention on the Elimination of All Forms of Discrimination against Women (CEDAW), signed in 1979 and subsequently ratified by all Latin American states, commit governments to make specific reforms to their laws and to adopt proactive policies (Winslow 1995). Drawing on European models, many Latin American countries adopted gender quotas for elections, and gender was increasingly seen as an appropriate criterion for appointments to cabinet posts and other executive positions (Krook 2007; Craske 2003; Del Campo 2005; Schwindt-Bayer 2006; Htun and Jones 2002).

The commitments made by Latin American countries at UN and regional conferences have become an important basis for feminist initiatives. Like organizations that promote changes in human rights or environmental practices, women's groups have been able to use their governments' international obligations as leverage to change laws and establish new policies. Regional institutions and conventions have also played a role, particularly the Inter-American Commission on Human Rights, the Inter-American Convention on the Prevention, Punishment, and Eradication of Violence against Women (known as the Convention of Belém do Pará), and the UN CEDAW Committee, which regularly produces country reports (Barrig 2001:31; see also the essays by Kohen, Piovesan, and Valdés and Donoso, this volume). Regional offices of the UN Development Program and the International Labor Organization have provided research and policy recommendations to improve the conditions of women's employment and political participation.

## Feminist Activism and Democracy ⚕

The authors of this volume were asked to look at how women's movements have adapted to the political and economic changes outlined above and at how feminists are pursuing their agendas in the Southern Cone, Venezuela, Peru, and internationally. They were asked to assess what strategies work, what impact they have in terms of feminist goals, and how feminist activism affects the dynamics of democratic change.[10] Their essays can be grouped under three broad topical headings: women and the state (part 1), legal strategies (part 2), and the international arena (part 3), although the categories overlap in significant and interesting ways.

### FEMINISMS AND THE STATE: CHILE, VENEZUELA, ARGENTINA AND BRAZIL

In the opening essay Marcela Ríos Tobar explores the reasons why Michelle Bachelet, a divorced mother of three, a militant socialist, and a declared agnostic, was elected president of Chile, a country known for its political and religious conservatism, as well as the impact of her election on gender equity. Ríos analyzes the problems the women's movement faced after the transition to democracy in 1990. Although the government has been run by a center-left coalition (the Concertación) since 1990, the agenda developed by the women's coalition within the Concertación has met with strong resistance from the Christian Democrats, which for several years was the strongest party in the governing coalition, with close ties to an increasingly conservative Vatican. The government did establish a women's ministry, the Servicio Nacional de la Mujer, or SERNAM, but it was unable to act decisively on issues relating to family law and reproductive rights. Efforts to reform the divorce law, for example, met with stiff resistance in the Chilean congress.

During this period women's activism became more decentralized, moving outside of Santiago to other cities in Chile. SERNAM's attempts to address issues of poverty, adolescent pregnancy, and the plight of rural women soon came under attack from popular women's groups who felt excluded from decision making and from feminist and women's groups critical of the idea that the leftist governing coalition would continue to follow a neoliberal economic agenda. A national *encuentro* organized in 2004 (after a ten-year hiatus) brought together over five hundred participants, but it did not succeed in creating a new consensus and did not agree to endorse Bachelet.

Bachelet made gender parity an important part of her campaign, and she fulfilled a number of her promises early in her term. As president, however, Bachelet faced harsh criticism for the way she dealt with a series of crises. During these times of trial, Ríos observes, Bachelet has not been able to call on the support of the women's movement, which remains divided.

Although women put gender issues on the political agenda during the transitions (Jaquette 1994; Waylen 2007), few women were elected to national legislatures or appointed to cabinet positions once democratic institutions were again in place. Over time, however, political leaders and popular opinion came to accept the argument that gender quotas would be good both for women and for democracy.

Gender quotas address gaps in political representation, an important element of democratic quality (Hagopian 2005). Feminists who have studied the issue tend to favor quotas, but with reservations. Having more women in positions of power is critical to the consolidation of women's rights and the achievement of their social agendas. However, there is concern that quotas may ghettoize women representatives and relieve men of the responsibility of taking up women's issues. There is also no guarantee that women who are elected will be sympathetic to feminist concerns (Phillips 1995).

Jutta Marx, Jutta Borner, and Mariana Caminotti, authors of an in-depth study comparing gender quota laws in Argentina and Brazil (2007), analyze why the 1992 Ley de Cupo Femenino in Argentina has been so much more successful in increasing the number of women in Congress than the quota laws passed in Brazil.

The comparison is instructive, and it depends on features of both electoral systems, loopholes in Brazilian law, and the strict enforcement of the requirement that women be placed in winnable decisions on party lists in Argentina, which now has one of the highest levels of women's legislative participation in the world. By contrast, Brazil's quota laws have only marginally increased the percentage of women elected to the national legislature. Ironically, the authors note, during their study a higher percentage of women served in the Senate, where quotas did not apply, than in the Chamber of Deputies, where they did.

But Marx, Borner, and Caminotti do not think the Argentine experience is an unqualified success. Drawing on interviews with women deputies in both countries, they note that, after a decade and a half of experience with the quota law, women are still largely excluded from the critical process of candidate selection. Their finding is consistent with recent research showing that, despite quotas, women are excluded from powerful committees and leadership roles in Latin American legislatures (Escobar-Lemmon and Taylor-Robinson 2005; Heath, Schwindt-Bayer, and Taylor-Robinson 2005). The relative success of the Argentine quota proves, however, that women's family responsibilities are not an insurmountable barrier to increasing women's formal representation. Rather, the costs of campaigning and the unwillingness of the parties to actively recruit women discourage Brazilian women from seeking political office.

Gioconda Espina's essay shows how changes in the Venezuelan political system under Chávez are shaping feminist options. She reviews the history of feminist activism in Venezuela, noting the role of a "flexible core" of women who, although divided by principles and party loyalties, have repeatedly united to support legislation for women. Recounting the periods of polarization and political mobilization from Chávez's election in 1998 to the present, she observes that although tens of thousands of women have gone to the streets as supporters of or in opposition to the Chávez government, they have not done so as women or to demonstrate for women's rights. Indeed, she argues, most women in Venezuela are unaware of their rights and even of the policies the Chávez government has formally adopted with regard to women.

Espina is an active member of the core group of feminists, which has been shaken by the degree of polarization and the pace of political change in Venezuela, as well as by the challenge of dealing with a government that has become increasingly centralized and personalist. Nonetheless, the government is giving long overdue recognition and voice to the poor and the marginalized. Venezuelan feminists are cautious, cooperating when possible with those in the government and in the coalition of *chavista* parties who care about feminist issues. They have begun to seek new alliances, especially with groups supporting the rights of gays and lesbians. Although Chávez lost a December 2007 referendum, which would have allowed his indefinite reelection, he achieved this goal in a second referendum in March 2009. It is not clear how much space there will be for independent feminist activism in the future.

These three chapters show that the state proves critical to feminist advocacy, but also that national political contexts differ significantly in the opportunities they present, and the barriers they offer, to feminist activism. Brazil, Argentina, Chile, Peru, and Venezuela are moving along different paths of democratic change. Analyzing how feminist and women's groups interact with the state can provide an important indicator of how well democratic institutions are working in each country—and where they are falling short.

## LEGAL STRATEGIES IN ARGENTINA, BRAZIL, AND PERU

The essays in part 2 address the use of litigation to address feminist goals. Beatríz Kohen, the cofounder of the Latin American Group on Justice and Gender (Equipo Latinoamericano de Justicia y Género, ELA), analyzes the progress made using litigation to improve the odds that women can actually enjoy the rights granted to them by domestic law and international agreements. Although Argentine democracy has survived a series of economic and political crises, it is, in Kohen's view, under stress. Political parties and unions no longer prove very effective in mediating among conflicting interests and channeling popular demands. This has led to the judicialization of conflict, as people turn to the courts to resolve issues that in the past would have been negotiated in the legislative or executive branches of government.

Kohen argues that the litigation strategy is more powerful than many assume because, although cases do not set precedents in the same way under the Argentine legal system as they do under the common law system in the United States, decisions in one case can influence legal discourse, affect the views of legislators, and shape public opinion. She then analyzes a range of gender-equity cases, from family law to violence against women, reproductive rights, and the gender-quota law, noting that pro-life and other antifeminist groups have also begun to use the courts to press their agendas. Kohen believes that the greatest barrier to the litigation strategy is that most women in Argentina do not know their rights. Many women resist the idea of legal confrontation, while others who might be willing to take their cases to court lack the financial resources to do so.

Flávia Piovesan is a feminist activist and law professor; her essay describes how the women's movement used a legal strategy to strengthen Brazil's law on violence against women. Although the legal and cultural environment for gender equity has changed dramatically in favor of women's rights, many laws remain weak or unenforced. The women's movement in Brazil chose the case of Maria da Penha to push for more effective laws against domestic violence. Penha's husband abused her and twice attempted to kill her, leaving her a paraplegic at age thirty-eight. Although a local court convicted him, the husband was not imprisoned, a sign, as Piovesan notes, that Brazil did not take the issue of violence against women seriously. Several groups in Brazil and internationally joined in an initiative to take the case to the Inter-American Commission on Human Rights (IACHR), and in 2001 the commission found the Brazilian state guilty of "negligence and failure to take action against domestic violence."

The judgment provided the impetus for passing a new law that changed the definition of violence against women from a minor offense to a human rights violation with serious penalties. The law makes sexual orientation irrelevant, thereby accepting a broader definition of "family" than has customarily been the case and establishing integrated prevention measures.[11] The Penha case provides an example of how the litigation strategy can be used successfully to pressure states to make good on the international commitments they make. Piovesan emphasizes that the international feminist and human rights communities gave Brazilian feminists the additional leverage they needed.

Julissa Mantilla Falcón served as an advisor on gender issues to the Peruvian Truth and Reconciliation Commission, established to document human rights violations after the civil war between the Peruvian state and Sendero Luminoso (Shining Path), a Maoist guerrilla group. The Peruvian case differs from the Southern Cone cases of Argentina, Brazil, and Chile in that the violence leading to a repressive response did not occur under a military authoritarian regime, but under the civilian democratic governments of Alan García and Alberto Fujimori. The leftist military government of General Velasco Alvarado implemented an agrarian reform, but its economic plans failed and elections were held in 1980. The return to democracy coincided with the rise of the Shining Path (Gorriti 1990) and later of the MRTA (Túpac Amaru Revolutionary Movement). Sendero's Maoist ideology, its violent, even grisly treatment of its enemies, and its increasing ability to terrorize Lima led civilian governments to encourage the armed forces to do whatever necessary to stop the insurgency. Sendero collapsed in 1992 when its leader, Abimael Guzmán, was captured in the Peruvian capital by an elite intelligence unit of the police, then imprisoned, and publicly humiliated by a triumphant President Fujimori. But it was not until the Truth and Reconciliation Commission carried out its work several years later that the shocking extent of the killings emerged: sixty-nine thousand people had died in the conflict.

Although the international public has become increasingly aware of the use of rape as a weapon of war, Mantilla points out that truth and reconciliation commissions rarely take gender into account. The Peruvian Truth and Reconciliation Commission found several cases of sexual mutilation, sexual molestation, sexual humiliation, forced prostitution, forced pregnancy, and forced nudity. The commission's work not only shone a strong light on the human rights violations committed by the army and the guerrillas during the war, it highlighted the kinds of torture and abuse to which women, particularly women from racially or ethnically marginalized groups, are especially vulnerable.[12]

The essays in part 2 suggest that litigation can prove an effective strategy for feminist activists who can bring cases to ensure that the laws women's movements have often worked hard to pass are publicized and enforced, and that the gendered biases of the legal system are challenged. Although the state may sometimes take the initiative, in Latin America gender justice often depends on women's groups who have the motivation, expertise, and financial resources to pursue cases with a broad impact. The use of legal strategies also marks a shift from popular mobilization to the professionalization of social movement advocacy.

INTERNATIONAL AND CROSS-BORDER ACTIVISM

Ever since the first UN Conference on Women in 1975, feminist activism has had an international dimension. Part III begins with Virginia Vargas's essay analyzing feminist participation in the World Social Forum (WSF), where Vargas has served as a member of the International Council and is one of the organizers of the Articulación Feminista Marcosur (AFM), a Latin American–based caucus within the forum.

Because the UN has been weakened by the rise of new global economic powers and by U.S. interventionism, Vargas believes that there is a strong need for a new international forum to develop emancipatory strategies against the hegemonic power of neoliberal capitalism and its privatizing and consumerist ideologies. The WSF has been a learning process for feminists. Although Latin American women came to the forum with experience gained during the UN Decade for Women, regional *encuentros*, and at UN conferences in Vienna, Cairo, and Beijing, they had not faced the kinds of challenges that the pluralist environment of the World Social Forum presents.

Participants in the WSF are united in their opposition to globalization, but they remain divided in many other ways: by age, political experiences, gender and sexual orientation, and regional and cultural differences. These differences are vital to the pluralist dialogues of the WSF, Vargas argues, where many reject older ideological approaches and seek new visions. Feminists have organized into various *articulaciones*, or caucuses. They have had to fight for space, but gender panels, marches, and proposals for action now form an integral part of the WSF.

Recent meetings of the WSF have begun to attract participants opposing feminist agendas, however, including so-called pro-life groups. Using some examples of their attacks on feminists at the WSF meeting in Nairobi, Vargas asks whether an organization committed to pluralism can exclude those who wish to exclude others.

The essay by Teresa Valdés and Alina Donoso describes a very different form of international feminist activism. Valdés played a critical role in designing a project that would enable women's organizations in various countries to create a national *Indice de Compromiso Cumplido* (Indices of Commitments

Fulfilled), or ICC. Valdés and her team drew on earlier work that assembled and analyzed sex-disaggregated data for Latin America to develop a project that would give women the tools to hold their governments accountable for the promises they made in Cairo and Beijing (Valdés et al. 2005, 2007). The concept of "active citizenship," which "places a high value on rights, but also on the responsibilities individuals have to the political communities to which they belong," is at the core of the project. In creating ICCs, women's organizations become "political subjects" who can make "realizable" demands and who are capable of "developing practices that are autonomous, deliberative, and participatory." The ICCs provide a way to grasp complex social processes and to track outcomes shaped by multiple actors: governments, corporations, the media, and individuals and groups in civil society. By 2005 eighteen Latin American countries had participated in the project, and Valdés and Donoso here present and review the results obtained in three different cases: Brazil, Venezuela, and Mexico.

The ICCs do not challenge powerful global actors with new visions or attack global capitalism, but they suggest a different kind of radical approach: giving women the resources to hold their governments accountable. Using quantitative methods for progressive purposes runs counter to much contemporary feminist and postmodern theory, which rejects "empiricist" social science.[13] But as Valdés and Donoso observe, having a political strategy to change laws and policies is not enough. "It is necessary to proceed with an idea of rights that will enable the state to express popular sovereignty beyond its own technocratic and bureaucratic dynamics," that is, by actually meeting the commitments it has signed onto and that have consequences for women's lives.

The ICCs and the WSF offer contrasting responses to the challenges of globalization and to changing concepts of citizenship, but both follow logically from the experiences feminists gained during the UN Decade for Women and the UN conferences of the 1990s. The WSF follows the dialogic tradition of the NGO forums at UN conferences, which were highly charged with intense debates and cultural clashes as well as with the excitement of making new connections and planning new strategies. The ICCs, on the other hand, build on the experiences many feminists had in the national and regional preparatory meetings that took place prior to each UN conference. These brought women's groups and experts together, created cross-party and cross-class coalitions and regional networks, and improved the collection of sex-disaggregated data to develop new policies and demands. Together, these two kinds of efforts made the last thirty years an unprecedented era of women's mobilization and feminist advance on a global scale.

Kathleen Staudt and Gabriela Montoya are both active in groups that link women across the border between El Paso, Texas, and Ciudad Juárez, Mexico, to deal with domestic violence. They argue that the notorious femicides in Ciudad Juárez should be understood in the border context. El Paso–Ciudad Juárez constitutes an important gateway for North-South trade, as well as for trafficking drugs and people. The border is permeable: people from both sides cross every day to work, shop, and connect with family and friends. But it is also a harsh environment, especially for women migrants, who are often isolated, lack education, and do not know their rights or are afraid to demand them.

The problems faced by the organizations trying to assist victims of domestic violence do not arise, as might be expected, from cultural, language, or class differences, but from the structural difficulties of working in two different political, legal, and law-enforcement systems. Rising sentiment against unauthorized immigrants in the United States has made their task more difficult. As Staudt and Montoya observe, the murders that have received so much international publicity are the ones that involve some form of sexual mutilation, about a third of the total. There has been much less concern, however, for women who die from "ordinary" domestic violence, or for the thousands of women who have disappeared, perhaps voluntarily, or perhaps because their bones "have not yet been found in the desert."

The essays in part III illustrate the rich variety of forms international feminist activism has taken and, along with the articles in part II, they show how such efforts complement what women are doing at national and local levels to change constitutions, write new laws, press for their implementation, and engage in ongoing debates about social values and changing gender roles. They show the connections between the global and the local, yet they also underline the roles that only states can play, bringing us full circle to the theme of part I, women's representation in the state. The essays in this volume make it clear that feminist activism is alive and well, and they offer concrete examples of successes and barriers as feminists try new strategies, rethink their goals, and seek new allies. The process of changing norms and institutions to promote gender justice in Latin America is often frustrating and has become largely invisible to those outside the region. But feminist activism continues, and it has achieved important successes, often against great odds.

## Notes ⁜

1  President Fujimori's *auto-golpe*, or self-initiated coup, in Peru in 1992 was not a military coup in the classical sense; with military support, Fujimori closed the Congress from April to November 1992, when a new Congress was elected and a new constitution was approved by referendum in 1993 (Tanaka 2005:263). Coups and *auto-golpes* (presidential coups occurring with the support of the armed forces) were successfully blocked by regional pressures in Paraguay and Guatemala, through the Organization of American States.

2  However, as Frances Hagopian observes, the worst cutbacks occurred in pensions and transfer payments; health and education spending were less vulnerable, but not high enough to begin with. Latin American publics are generally supportive of more state involvement (2005:339). There are some signs that market policies are beginning to produce higher rates of growth, lower levels of poverty, and small improvements in income distribution, although much of this is due to high global demand for commodities.

3  Venezuela is an important exception. Although Carlos Andres Pérez tried to bait and switch, austerity policies produced riots and looting in Venezuelan cities, as well as a coup attempt, led by Hugo Chávez, in 1992. Between 1994 and 1998 the party system collapsed, and Chávez easily won the presidential election of 1998. Increases in the price of oil gave him abundant resources to back his "Bolivarian" alternative to neoliberal policies and U.S. dominance (McCoy and Myers 2004), but oil prices fell again in 2008.

4  For a detailed analysis of public opinion and democracy in Latin America, see Hagopian 2005; Stokes 2001; and Kurtz 2004.

5  Particularly devastating were the currency crises in Mexico, Russia, and Asia, the Brazilian devaluation of 1998, and the crisis in Argentina in 2001–2 that wiped out middle-class savings and more than doubled the rate of people living in poverty, to over 40 percent. Although short-lived, the drop in Argentina's economy was dramatic and produced a political crisis but did not provoke a military response. The U.S. dismissal of Argentines as incompetent, and the U.S. refusal to provide short-term assistance, as provided to Mexico in 1998, has had long-term effects. A 2007 survey by the Chicago Council on Global Affairs poll shows that 69 percent of Argentines think the United States "cannot be trusted at all" (Chicago Council on Global Affairs 2007:30–31).

6  The case of SERNAM in Chile has been widely debated (see Valenzuela 1998; Schild 2000; Franceschet 2003). Insiders run the risk of being or appearing co-opted, while bureaucratization and elitism, perhaps both inevitable results as institutions mature, have repeatedly drawn criticism from feminists and women's

movement activists. But see Pribble 2006 for a comparative study of women's participation and social programs in Uruguay and Chile. Fiona Macauley (2006) argues that, in Brazil, the relative lack of interest shown by the Cardoso administration had the effect of strengthening the institutionalization of the women's movement at the provincial and municipal levels; today the Secretariat for Women's Policies is a very effective gender unit with national reach.

7   The terms strategic and practical gender interests are taken from Molyneux 1985. She replies to her critics in Molyneux 2001a.

8   There was popular tolerance for austerity policies in part because they dramatically reduced inflation, a factor rarely emphasized in feminist analyses (see Wise and Roett 2003). As Martín Tanaka observes, the presidents who were able to reduce hyperinflation (Cardoso in Brazil, Fujimori in Peru, Paz Estenssoro in Bolivia, and Menem in Argentina) were able to lead a "profound reconfiguration of the statist, national populist social and political order" (2005:263).

9   In fact, abortion restrictions are being challenged in several countries, including Mexico and Colombia, but Nicaragua has recently passed the most restrictive antiabortion legislation in the hemisphere. See LaRamée 2007.

10  The focus here on *feminist* activism distinguishes between activism that addresses issues of gender equity and women's issues more broadly, such as poverty and the effects of globalization. This is not to deny that women's mobilizations for practical goals often have strategic consequences, but rather to understand the priorities, strategies, and barriers facing women whose activism is explicitly feminist.

11  Brazil pioneered integrated police stations (*delegacias*) for the treatment of rape and violence against women. See Alvarez 1990, 1994.

12  Although most scholars would now agree that Sendero did not represent an indigenous revolt, but rather a war led by young people educated in provincial universities (which helps explain Sendero's Maoist rather than indigenous ideology), the fact that many civilian and *senderista* women in Peru's highlands were viewed by soldiers as racially inferior added a racial dimension to the abuse. See Barrig 1998.

13  The antiscience position has a long history. For a succinct discussion of critical theory and anarchist and Marxist views, see Eckersley 1992. The feminist anarchist position claims that the state is always repressive and that increasing its capacity only increases its ability to control and repress. Mary García Castro and Laurence Hallewell write from this position when they say that "suddenly, gender and feminism have ceased to be the adversaries of the authorities and have become their darlings, the subject of official speeches, policies, and statistics—things that smack of authoritarianism and social perversity as far as the living conditions of the poor and working class are concerned" (2001:32).

# ❧ FEMINISM AND THE STATE ❧

# Feminist Politics in Contemporary Chile ⸙

## FROM THE DEMOCRATIC TRANSITION TO BACHELET

*Marcela Ríos Tobar*

The election of Michelle Bachelet as president of Chile on January 15, 2006, sparked unprecedented interest in the developments of gender relations and women's political roles in the country. Her election was undoubtedly a historical milestone. The mass media and international observers alike emphasized the seeming paradox that her election constituted in what was perceived as one of Latin America's most conservative countries.[1] The result of the presidential election was deemed particularly puzzling in light of who the female candidate was and what she represented politically. She was no "ordinary" woman, but a longtime socialist militant, a recognized agnostic, and a divorced mother of three whose father had been imprisoned and killed during the military dictatorship and who had herself, together with her mother, survived torture, imprisonment, and exile. Moreover, Bachelet had followed a trajectory distinct from that of other women who had reached similar posts in the region. She was elected at the ballot box following an independent political career: she was not the widow or close family member of a notable male politician.

The debate that surrounded the presidential election positioned Bachelet's life story and personal traits as the point of departure in tracing the evolution of political culture over the past two decades after the formal transition to democratic rule. Issues such as the significance of this event for the correlation of forces between the political left and right in the country, its relationship to more substantive cultural transformations, and the place of women in society became subject to heated debate before, during, and after the elections. Also passionately discussed were the impact of the women's movement and the ideology of women's rights and gender equality on electoral politics. Despite the influence and visibility of the women's movement during the struggle to regain democracy, neither the mainstream media nor the male political establishment had ever paid so much attention to questions of women's political representation, women's leadership, and gender relations as they did during this election.

It is difficult to assess whether Bachelet's election was the product of significant political and sociocultural transformations in Chilean society or of the particularities of a close and contentious electoral competition. Nor is there any consensus regarding the role played by feminism and the women's movement in Bachelet's election or in the development of her pro-women policy agenda. While some have argued that her election and platform directly resulted from three decades of feminist activism (and thus support the "cultural transformation" argument), others see only indirect and sporadic connections between an increasingly weak and relatively silent women's movement and recent political developments.

This article addresses some of the above questions and tries to explain what made the election of a woman committed to gender equity possible in a country in which a once vibrant women's movement has lost the preeminence it had during the transition from military rule. It does so by tracing the trajectory of feminist organizing and gender politics since the transition to democracy in 1990, including the transformation of feminist movement politics, as well as by analyzing the policies pursued by four consecutive center-left governments on gender issues. It argues that the latest victory of the leftist coalition, the Concertación de Partidos por la Democracia (Coalition of Parties for Democracy),[2] represents both continuity and significant changes in the way in which social democratic governments, which have generally taken a distant and demobilizing policy toward civil society actors, have related to feminist demands and organizations.

The policy agenda on gender issues has shifted and been invigorated by the election of a socialist woman to the presidency. But, contrary to what others have argued, this analysis suggests that feminist political mobilization had only an indirect influence on Bachelet's election, largely through the long-term process of changing societal and cultural attitudes in ways consistent with Chile's economic and social modernization. More egalitarian attitudes and interests have thus made it easier for women to run for office and gain the support of the electorate. Chilean feminism and feminists have had little impact on specific political developments and outcomes, however, with consequences for Bachelet's presidency. Inequalities in the distribution of power and resources have left feminists to face major opposition from conservative forces with little support from progressive political actors such as left-wing parties. Moreover, internal divisions, professionalization, decentralization, and specialization, as well as a tenuous autonomy vis-à-vis the state and political parties have all played a role in weakening feminist voices in the political debate.

This weakness has left the initial efforts of the Bachelet government with little support from civil society in its efforts to promote gender parity against the resistance of entrenched conservatism. As a result, incumbent political elites have managed to defend their privileges while casting doubt on the president's leadership capacity and failing to support the government's efforts to move forward on issues of women's sexual and reproductive rights and other gender issues.

The Political Opportunity Structure: Chilean Social
Democracy and the Women's Rights Agenda ⸙

The electoral triumph of left-wing candidates in several recent Latin American presidential elections—in Ecuador, Venezuela, and Nicaragua in 2006, and in Bolivia in 2005—constitutes one of the most significant political shifts in the region since the restoration of democratic rule. The latest electoral triumph of the Concertación in January 2006 is the fourth consecutive victory of this center-left coalition, which has won every single election since the 1988 plebiscite that marked the end of the Pinochet regime. Thus the recent election in Chile is not part of a new wave of leftist victories. Bachelet was elected not by the left per se but by a center-left coalition, in which the Christian Democratic Party has historically played a strong role. Further the Concertación did not significantly modify macroeconomic policies after the transition to democracy, continuing with a neoliberal agenda strongly criticized by the traditional left at home and abroad.

The fact that the government included a substantial part of the left in its governing coalition had an impact on feminist politics in Chile. The relationship that developed between the successive Concertación governments and women's organizations was not a product solely of the success of the left, but part of a broader process of democratization that deeply affected the opportunities and barriers faced by civil society organizations and influenced the decisions of many feminist activists to become involved in democratization processes. The sheer length of the Concertación's rule has magnified its effect on society, on state-society relations, and on civil society's capacity to organize and negotiate vis-à-vis a strong and stable state and political party system. After seventeen years of uninterrupted rule, the Concertación has held power as long as the military regime under Augusto Pinochet.

Yet unlike the social democratic government under Luiz Inácio Lula da Silva (Lula) in Brazil, or under Hugo Chávez in Venezuela, the ruling Concertación is not a strictly left-wing coalition. In the current government led by Bachelet, as well as in those led by the previous presidents Patricio Aylwin, Eduardo Frei, and Ricardo Lagos, the Christian Democratic Party has played a central hegemonic role, especially during the first two presidential terms, when it was the largest electoral party within the coalition and two of its members (Aylwin and Frei) held the presidency. The presence of a political party that identifies itself as a confessional organization that follows Catholic social doctrine and maintains close relations with the church hierarchy has limited the kinds of policies that Concertación governments could pursue to advance women's rights and gender equity, especially those perceived to be connected to "moral values" such as reproduction and family legislation. Indeed, the survival of the alliance that the traditional left has established with the Christian Democrats has been largely contingent on their mutual agreement to leave these divisive issues outside the policy agenda.

Despite this arrangement, small groups in all of the parties within the coalition have supported the demands put forward by the women's movement during and after the transition. They were most successful in the first years after the return to formal democratic rule in the early 1990s. Responding to a demand posed by the women's caucus within the Concertación de Mujeres por la Democracia (Coalition of Women for Democracy),[3] the government created the Servicio Nacional de la Mujer (SERNAM), which soon drafted a national Plan for Equal Opportunity for Women, designed and implemented specific social programs aimed at improving the living conditions of highly vulnerable groups of women, and supported legal changes to comply with the demands of the women's movement, most notably a law that penalized domestic violence against women and legislation to eliminate formal discrimination against women in different spheres of life.[4]

Advances did occur in women's living conditions, most notably a sharp reduction in the level of poverty. Chile is the only country in the region that has been able to significantly reduce its poverty levels in the past two decades, lowering the percentage of the population that live under the poverty line from 38 percent in 1990 to 13.6 percent in 2006.[5] In addition, maternal mortality rates have been cut in half and rank among the lowest on the continent; women's average schooling has surpassed that of males, and women represent over half of all elementary, secondary, and university students. Most formal legal impediments to inequality have been eliminated from civil, criminal, and labor legislation. Specific social programs have been implemented to address the needs of specific groups of women, such as heads of households and agricultural seasonal workers. The original law criminalizing domestic violence was reformed in 2005 to increase penalties and better assist victims.

Despite these important advances, the pace of change on more controversial issues was glacial after the initial posttransition period. Fourteen years passed before Chile approved a new divorce law, in 2004, and most of the other major changes called for by the women's movement during the struggle for democratization have not yet been met. Both feminist groups and intergovernmental organizations have called attention to the lack of progress toward gender equality in areas such as abortion, sexual education, teenage pregnancy, women's political representation, labor-market participation, and affirmative-action measures to combat these and other problems of gender exclusion. The lack of progress is also evident in the Chilean state's continued resistance to ratifying the Optional Protocol of the International Convention on the Elimination of All Forms of Discrimination against Women (CEDAW), as the majority of other Latin American countries have done.[6]

This deadlock in Chile was evident in 1999 during the CEDAW's twenty-first session. The United Nations committee set up to monitor progress on the goals set out in the convention found that "Chile's women had played a leading role in the battle against the dictatorship and for human rights, yet they had no divorce law, were under-represented in decision-making positions and faced severe constraints in reproductive health."[7] A member of the committee also commented that "the Government of Chile was modern and thriving, so it should have no problem providing certain contraceptives, such as emergency measures, to women and girls who became pregnant, through rape, for example." Abortion had been permitted for health reasons before 1990, but a few days before the formal transition to civilian rule, the military regime declared abortion illegal under all circumstances. This restrictive legislation remains in place.

Social democratic administrations have also had a problematic impact on women's political organizing capacity. Concertación governments have failed to promote or strengthen civil society actors in general and women's groups in particular. They have tended to privilege technical exchanges with intermediary organizations such as professional NGOs or academic experts, rather than engage in political interaction with social movements and other forces in civil society (Ríos Tobar 2003). This has further accentuated the internal divisions and fragmentation of feminist organizations and contributed to the growing isolation of grass-roots women's groups, which are rarely invited to participate in professionalized exchanges between civil society and the state.

The relative stagnation of a women's rights agenda that characterized Concertación governments before the election of Bachelet cannot be attributed solely to the governing coalition's unwillingness to act or to the inability of the feminist movement to mobilize society in support of its agenda. Both of these factors have indeed played a role, but they might have been overcome had there not been strong conservative opposition to policy advances on gender issues. Mala Htun (2003b) has emphasized the role of the Catholic Church in opposing such change through its close relations with Latin American governments. She observes that in the case of Chile, the ties between the church and the opposition—which later became the government—were strong, a situation that closed opportunities for action on the part of progressive actors on contentious moral issues such as abortion and divorce. Merike Blofield (2006) has also looked at the influence of the Catholic Church, but has highlighted the role income inequalities play in creating power differentials between feminists and their opponents. She argues that the political system in Chile is "status quo-oriented" due to the existence of a "high number of veto points (points at which legislation can be rejected or changed)." The economic and cultural resources at the disposal of conservative actors, the close links between the church and economic elites, and the lack of power and of support from progressive sectors received by feminists have all had a negative impact on the possibility of change.

The electoral institutions inherited from the authoritarian period have also had the effect of overrepresenting the political right and traditional political actors in key political institutions like Congress. This together with a system of legislative quorums makes it extremely difficult for the government to pass legislation without previous negotiation and compromise with the opposition. Add to this situation internal divisions within the Concertación and the power and policy preferences of the Christian Democratic Party, and it is clear why the scope for action on gender policies was limited to areas of high-level consensus. Despite this difficult scenario, sectors in the feminist movement continued to collaborate with Concertación governments to achieve goals that would have been impossible had the political right held power instead.

Thus the track record of center-left governments is not predictably progressive. On the one hand, Concertación governments have made formal and explicit commitments to eliminating discrimination against women and to promoting women's rights, social security, and equal-opportunity policies. That SERNAM continues as one of the biggest, best-funded, and most highly ranked gender units in Latin America stands as a testament to this commitment.[8] On the other hand, there has been little progress in areas linked to women's political, sexual, and economic empowerment, areas that have continued to face open and organized opposition from the Catholic Church and from right-wing parties who have veto power not only over legislation but also over setting the agenda for national debate. Together these actors have a wealth of material resources that they have used consistently to block change. Yet opposition has also come from within the governing coalition, and parties that might be expected to support feminist issues have given only sporadic assistance, restricted to very specific, noncontentious issues. Meanwhile, the traditional political left (both within and outside the governing coalition) has not given centrality to feminist demands, and as we will see, the feminist movement itself has confronted this very adverse scenario internally divided and with few links to broader society.

The Reconfiguration of the Feminist Movement
after the Transition ⸙

An in-depth study of feminist organizations in postdictatorship Chile concluded that the return to democratic rule and the consequent transformation of the political opportunity structure had a significant impact on women's organizations and the feminist movement. Many feminist and women's groups survived as organizations well beyond the transition, but the close links among them that had been forged during the struggle for democracy progressively weakened and, in many instances, disappeared. Moreover, the connections between feminist groups and NGOS, on the one hand, and base-level women's organizations (especially poor women's groups), on the other, became increasingly distant and pragmatic, centered on the organization of specialized events or projects, but with little long-term continuity or political impact beyond immediate goals.[9] The struggle for democracy had been the single most important mobilizing goal that kept a very diverse set of groups and individuals politically united; once that objective had been achieved, the alliance between feminists and the broader women's movement withered away at the same time that feminists began to collide over ideological and strategic issues (Ríos Tobar, Godoy, and Guerrero Caviedes 2004).

As elsewhere in the region, the transition to democracy produced a dramatically new set of challenges for feminist activists: for the first time in decades they were confronted with having to interact with the state, state actors, and professional politicians, and to negotiate their political role with respect to the political parties now dominating the public sphere. The creation of SERNAM, the debate over a law to regulate domestic violence, and other legislative initiatives that had long been central banners for the women's movement, together with the inauguration of several social programs and policies aimed directly at women, forced feminists to transform their previous oppositional, antistate stance into a more dialogue-driven strategy.

International developments, such as changes in donors' objectives and the organization of a series of UN global conferences that welcomed and encouraged civil-society participation, coincided with this internal process of return to "politics as usual." Their combined effect brought about a transformation of Chilean feminism, diversifying its priorities, spheres of action, and interlocutors. A once socially and ideologically homogenous core group of activists lost its central focus as the number of women involved in pursuing feminist goals expanded. Our 2004 study found that while the majority of active feminist groups were located in Santiago in the 1980s, by the late 1990s there were women's NGOS, feminist collectives, and women's studies programs at universities throughout the country (Ríos Tobar, Godoy, and Guerrero Caviedes 2004). Concepción, the second largest city in the country, for example, had only three feminist groups before the transition; by 2000 it boasted thirteen (123). Feminist antidictatorial politics was based on small collectives that sought personal empowerment and political mobilization. Today, feminists can be found in a wide variety of institutional spheres and organizational structures: NGOs, thematic networks (like the network against domestic violence), collectives, small media initiatives (radio programs, bulletins, magazines), and university programs, among others.[10]

This decentralization and organizational diversification was accompanied by thematic diversification and specialization. Feminist activists and women's groups now focus on specific issues such as domestic violence, poverty, reproductive rights, and political participation, rather than pursuing a broad political platform of gender equality. And although an important segment of the feminist movement actively participates in international and regional spheres, aiding state and intergovernmental institutions in the design and implementation of gender policies of different types, others have continued to work on base-level initiatives pursuing individual, microlevel, and cultural transformations within society instead of trying to influence policies nationally or globally.

These changes constitute responses both to the transformations in the political opportunity structure and to the internal dynamics of the movement. The experience of other countries that have gone through similar transition processes has shown that most of these challenges and transformations are intimately linked to a change of political regime and the international climate under which it occurs.[11] In the case of Chile, the transition to democracy coincided with the coming to power of (part of) the left. Among other things, this meant that many ministers, undersecretaries, and Congress members hailed from the left and that an array of lower-level and technical posts in different state institutions were filled by left-wing party members. This had a considerable impact on feminist strategies due to the widespread practice of double militancy: the majority of feminist activists were also left-wing party militants.[12] After the transition to democracy some feminists, especially professionals who occupied leadership positions in leftist parties, thus became state employees or elected officials. Even those feminists, a majority, who remained outside the state, had links to the left, reaffirming their shared political project, which was also reinforced by those in power and numerous personal, professional, kinship, and political ties.

In this context, it is not surprising that the issue of autonomy has emerged as one of the main sources of conflict among feminists since the early 1990s. The segment of the movement that cultivated close ties with the state provoked strong criticism from those who did not have those connections, including small independent groups that reject involvement in the political system on principle or with Concertación governments in particular. The feminist debate over autonomy was particularly acute immediately after the transition, but as the links between different sectors of the movement weakened, and the national and international meetings that stimulated these debates moved on to other issues, the question of autonomy has slowly become less central.[13]

The changes experienced by the feminist movement after the transition did not occur overnight, nor did they follow a linear path. On the contrary, there have been different phases and trajectories. The immediate aftermath of the transition saw a marked interest in and concrete initiatives toward making the most of the momentum of the struggle against the dictatorship to consolidate a broad-based women's movement with the active participation of feminists. During this period feminists organized the first national Feminist *Encuentro* in Valparaíso in 1991. Despite good intentions, however, ideological and partisan divisions made unity impossible.[14]

By the mid-1990s, these internal conflicts became public as several groups clashed with the feminists working with SERNAM and the Concertación government to prepare the country's participation in the Fourth UN Conference on Women to be held in Beijing in 1995, and with others who were preparing to host the sixth regional Latin American Feminist *Encuentro* in Chile the following year. The strategies, discourses, and actors involved in both processes were virtually the same, reducing the possibilities for dialogue with disaffected groups within the movement and for mobilization toward common goals (see Alvarez et al. 2003; Ríos Tobar, Godoy, and Guerrero Caviedes 2004).

This period of ideological confrontation produced a "feminist silence" that lasted from 1997 into the new century. During this phase, few public events were organized, public mobilization remained rare, and many feminist groups disappeared. As Maruja Barrig argued eloquently at the beginning of this period, "the movement (women/feminist) does not move much, renews itself little, and congregates in the streets even less" (1997:12). Academic production, involvement in professional nongovernmental organizations, and other activities continued to flourish, but feminist issues largely disappeared from the national debate.

By 2004 this feminist silence was coming to an end. Feminists came together to organize another national *encuentro*, which took place in June 2005, a full decade after the last such gathering. Extreme polarization had given way to fragmentation and diversity, with continued differences over strategy and a growing need for dialogue and political inclusion. This was especially evident in the concerns of the large contingent of young women who attended the three-day event that convened over five hundred participants. The meeting concluded with no clear consensus on how to structure a more permanent form of political coordination among feminist groups. Nor had it managed to initiate a debate about the electoral campaigns already underway, which set two high-profile women against each other to compete for the presidential nomination within the Concertación. A vocal and well-organized contingent of activists continued to argue that feminism should have no connections with the state or the Concertación. They argued that the fact that both candidates were women was irrelevant; the issues feminists needed to focus on were socioeconomic inequalities, neoliberalism, and the transformation of patriarchy. Other participants with more moderate political views supported dialogue with the state and tried to drum up support for the socialist candidate, Bachelet, but they failed to get anywhere with this issue.[15] The document produced by the *encuentro* stated that, as an expression of a pluralist feminist movement, the meeting would not endorse any political candidate for the 2005 presidential election.

Thus by the end of the Lagos presidency, feminists were immersed in a process of regrouping and redefinition. A significant number of young women now actively claimed a feminist identity, but the movement remained politically divided, with few links to popular women's organizations, scant capacity for public mobilization, and little voice in public debates. Moreover, by failing to confront the electoral process head on, feminists in effect decided to marginalize themselves from the significant transformations of Chilean society taking place at that moment. This would have profound implications for gender relations and women's place in the political community. The election of Bachelet thus occurred with no formal ties between the socialist candidate's campaign and feminist organizations, even though a majority of feminists supported her and many of them actively campaigned for her as individuals.

Much of the excitement caused by Bachelet's campaign and election were linked to her gender and life story, which made her appear as a rarity—albeit an attractive one—in the status quo–oriented Chilean political landscape. Many analysts have tried to show that her election constituted a visible expression of Chile's modernization—one more step in a long journey toward greater progress, development, and equality. This journey is thought to include changes in the role of women in society and politics, a decline in the influence of the Catholic Church on the lives of Chileans, and the growing independence of ordinary citizen's vis-à-vis the country's political elites (Franceschet 2006).

Others have stressed that although the election of a woman committed to gender parity cannot be considered entirely independent of such cultural transformations, these alone cannot explain Bachelet's electoral triumph (Ríos Tobar 2006; Navia 2006). Cultural changes are necessarily long-term processes, occurring at a discontinuous pace and affecting distinct spheres of life to different degrees. The overall effects are often contradictory and dispersed (Güell 2004).

Comparing the attitudes of Latin Americans regarding the role of women in politics shows that although Chileans continue to move in a liberalizing direction, Chile has not advanced at the same pace or to the same extent as other countries, such as Argentina or Uruguay. This suggests that changes in cultural attitudes may not prove that useful in explaining recent electoral results. The 2004 Latinobarómetro, a multinational survey of political attitudes in the region, shows that in Argentina and Uruguay, for example, citizens display slightly less support for the phrase "men are better political leaders than women" (24 percent and 17 percent, respectively) than their Chilean counterparts (26 percent). However, 55 percent of Chileans agreed with the phrase "if women earned a higher income than men they would surely face problems," whereas only 45 percent of Argentines and 31 percent of Uruguayans agreed.[16] It is more convincing to see Bachelet's election as the result of *political* factors that converged with and were reinforced by cultural changes.

First, the Concertación was very likely to win the most recent presidential election no matter whom they nominated. The Coalition, despite the predictable exhaustion produced by fifteen years in government, had succeeded in all electoral contests—presidential, parliamentary, and municipal—since the return of democracy at the end of the 1980s; a narrow win by Lagos in 2000 marked a rough patch, one overcome, however, by the tremendous popularity Lagos enjoyed when he left office, having managed to maintain sustained economic growth, decrease levels of poverty, and make significant improvements to infrastructure and social spending, among other gains.

In 2005 the Concertación also benefited from the right-wing opposition's inability to unite behind a common project and strip itself of its ties to the dictatorial past. Many voters still consider the parties of the right heirs of the military regime, so that discontent with the governing elites translates into high levels of electoral abstention rather than support for the political opposition. As candidate Bachelet began to rise in public opinion polls, analysts became increasingly confident of a Concertación victory, despite having taken the risk of running a woman, one whose personal history contradicted Chile's conservative traditions.[17] Between December 2001 and December 2004 the percentage of people who said that they would like Bachelet to be the next president went up steadily from 0 to 35 percent.

The second set of political factors explaining Bachelet's triumph is linked more specifically to women's growing political activism. By the end of the 1980s the women who had formed the Concertación de Mujeres por la Democracia were already calling for greater female representation despite systematic opposition from the political parties (Montecino and Rossetti 1990). They pointed to the fact that in the first election after the country's return to democracy in 1990, the proportion of women in Congress was slightly lower than in the last parliamentary elections before the military coup d'état in 1973. In 1990 women represented only 2.6 percent of senators and 5.8 percent of members of the lower house. By 2006 these figures had increased to 5.2 percent and 15.8 percent, respectively (Ríos Tobar and Villar 2005).

After the transition, women increasingly played important roles in the executive branch, which gave them public visibility and allowed female leaders such as Bachelet to prove their management and leadership potential. In 1990 there was only one female cabinet member, Soledad Alvear, who was married to the president of the Christian Democratic Party and was appointed minister of the newly inaugurated SERNAM. By 2000, when Lagos became the third Concertación president, there were five women in the cabinet. Alvear continued her ministerial career as the minister of external affairs, while Bachelet began hers as the minister of health and two years later became the minister of defense.

Both women used this trajectory to launch their respective presidential candidacies; both left the government to become candidates of their respective parties within the Concertación: Bachelet of the three left-wing parties (the Radical Social Democratic Party, the Socialist party, and the Party for Democracy) and Alvear of the Christian Democrats. Their ability to secure their respective nominations in large part resulted from the high approval ratings they had consistently enjoyed in public opinion polls throughout the Lagos presidency, which put pressure on the male political establishment to accept their bids as candidates. After a short internal campaign for the Concertación primary that resulted in a seemingly insurmountable advantage in public support for the left-wing candidate, Alvear withdrew and Bachelet became the coalition's sole candidate.

As many analysts have noted, Bachelet became the candidate not because of the support of political parties or of the political elites that had dominated national politics since the transition to democracy, but *despite* them. Like other women in the Lagos cabinet, though more consistently, she maintained a high level of popular support throughout her tenure as minister.[18] This support resulted from her personal charisma and leadership abilities, but it was also nourished by persistent tendencies in public opinion: citizens' growing detachment from the traditional political parties and their most visible leaders, and the desire for changes in an apparently exclusive governing elite.

Despite its electoral and political successes, the governing coalition has appeared increasingly disconnected from citizens, and many consider its style to be technocratic and elitist, leaving little space for popular political participation. This perception was aggravated by a series of corruption scandals involving members of the government, which increased the public's rejection of the Concertación's elites. The right-wing opposition had campaigned on an "antipolitical" discourse, which resonated with the electorate. Joaquín Lavín, the candidate defeated by Lagos, ran again against Bachelet in 2005. He built his political identity and career around populist slogans that portrayed him as a political outsider, although he had long been active in the right-wing UDI (Independent Democratic Union) and maintained close connections to the military and the most conservative sectors of society. The

2005 presidential competition was thus played out in an environment hostile toward traditional political elites.

The anti-establishment climate provided added support for a woman candidate, and it helped Bachelet's campaign in particular. As a female candidate with a long political career but distant from the small group of male politicians who had governed Chile until 2005, she built her campaign on the idea of infusing the Concertación's program with a breath of fresh air. She presented herself as a candidate close to the people, as one who could listen and connect to citizens' demands in an unprecedented way. She also vowed to appoint "new faces" to her government team. In this way Bachelet was able to take advantage of the overall political atmosphere and to convincingly claim outsider status,[19] something that coincided perfectly with traditional cultural constructions of gender. Differences between women and men are regarded as common sense in public debates and public opinion. The qualities attributed to women include generosity, a commitment to service, an interest in the common good, little ambition for power or wealth, incorruptibility, and the ability to understand citizens' concerns. Ironically, traditional constructions of gender, rather than the egalitarian or modernizing ones she herself advocated, helped cement Bachelet's popular support.[20]

Bachelet thus harnessed popular support early on in the campaign by capitalizing on her predecessors' achievements but at the same time offering something new: her female identity, a new way of doing politics, and a commitment to rejuvenating government. It was precisely this mixture of continuity and change that allowed the Concertación to secure its traditional base while winning votes from other sectors who had remained on the sidelines of the electoral process or had supported the rightist opposition.[21] Although the Concertación had been expected to win, the magnitude of Bachelet's victory in the second round surprised many observers. In 1999 Lagos had defeated his right-wing competitor by a thin margin (2.7 percent), but in 2006 Bachelet's margin of victory was over seven percentage points (53.4 percent to 46.5 percent).

The difference resulted primarily from the support of two segments of the population that had previously not voted for the Concertación: women (especially from sectors traditionally leaning toward the right, such as rural and lower-middle class urban women) and voters from the traditional left who had remained outside the governing coalition. Given the numerical power of the female vote, the support of women ultimately proved decisive.[22] Public opinion surveys prior to the election (Segovia 2005), electoral results, and the massive street demonstrations following her triumph all demonstrate that Bachelet's candidacy and victory resonated strongly with women.[23] For an important percentage of women, gender identification took priority over traditional ideological preferences: "¡Vota mujer!" ("Vote woman!") took hold of the Chilean female imagination.

---

But the story does not end there. This brief account underplays the importance of Bachelet as a candidate with personal merit, charisma, and leadership skills. Bachelet showed that she was capable of going against the current and inserting herself into the heart of party power; she appealed to citizen discontent with Chile's governing elites by simultaneously presenting herself as a continuation of their success and proposing to dislodge them from the center of power. For the first time in the country's political history, Bachelet turned an electoral campaign into a debate about gender and the role of women in society; she, unlike the Chilean left to which she belongs, recognized the importance of calling on the female vote.

The newly elected president fulfilled at least two of her campaign promises when she appointed her cabinet. She used gender parity as a principle to choose high-ranking officials by appointing a cabinet composed half of men and half of women, and she selected new faces to "rejuvenate" the governing elite. Her commitment to gender parity brought an unprecedented number of women to high political positions, making this the first government not only to be led by a woman but also to boast a gender equilibrium in cabinet and regional governments. The effect that this will have on gender equity and on women's lives remains to be seen, but the attempt can only be considered a milestone for women's empowerment.

More of the Same? Continuity and Change
in the Concertación's Model ⸙

The election of Bachelet as president represents both a continuation of the Concertación's policies and its general approach to gender issues and a significant departure from them. During the presidential campaign and in her government program Bachelet expressed her deep commitment to the coalition's past achievements in terms of equal opportunities for women. Shortly before the vote, however, it became clear that she meant to make gender equality one of the key themes of her government, distancing herself from her predecessors who had never treated women's rights issues as a major political concern.

The changes have been both symbolic and substantive. Bachelet promised and successfully appointed a gender parity cabinet and extended the initiative to undersecretaries, regional governors, and high-ranking state officials directly appointed by the president. This brought an unprecedented number of women into key political positions within the state apparatus, including in the Ministry of Defense and the Secretaría General de la Presidencia (SEGPRES), the ministry in charge both of interministerial coordination and of heading the executive's legislative agenda.[24] According to a study conducted by a feminist NGO, between 1990 and 2005 women had occupied on average only 17 percent of ministerial and 18 percent of undersecretarial positions (Corporación Humanas 2006). Bachelet's appointments amounted to a significant departure from previous trends.

This measure had immediate symbolic impact. In public opinion polls, both men and women valued the presence of women in high-ranking political positions, but women proved particularly enthusiastic. A survey conducted six months after the government had assumed office showed that 73.3 percent of adults interviewed in a national representative sample approved the parity measures implemented by the government, and 86.2 percent declared that gender parity should be extended to all political institutions.[25]

There were many examples of rhetoric and symbolic support for gender equality in Bachelet's first year, but one of the most significant was the president's first annual address to Congress on May 21, 2006. As one newspaper commented the following day, the president mentioned the word *woman* thirty-six times in her speech, which began by invoking the names of two historic feminist figures, Elena Caffarena and Amanda Labarca, neither well known to the general public. She went on to repeatedly refer to herself as the first female president and to highlight the significance of this fact. Passages like the following were common in Bachelet's public addresses during her first year in office: I am here as a woman, representing the defeat of the exclusion to which we were objected to for so long. Today is the time to include in our development all those citizens that suffer other types of exclusions.

However, the rhetorical centrality of gender and women's political leadership met with strong opposition from the mainstream media, political parties (including those in her own coalition), and public figures. Perhaps because of the continued criticism, the president has slowly backed away from this overt strategy. Yet as a socialist Bachelet has continued to foster social democratic initiatives to address inequalities. She has prioritized the reform of the pension system inherited from the authoritarian period; strengthened public education; improved the quality and reach of health coverage; stimulated economic competitiveness; and improved neighborhood infrastructure and security.[26] Her government has also launched a universal day-care program for all women in the poorest two-fifths of the population and constructed shelters for battered women in every regional capital of the country. In this way this fourth Concertación government has maintained continuity with the emphasis of the previous three coalition administrations on social welfare policies focused primarily on poor women.

Bachelet's commitment to gender parity has also signaled a departure from previous Concertación governments. Initiatives to increase women's political representation are completely absent from previous government proposals. The current government has not only promoted gender parity in the executive branch but has also promoted a quota law to force political parties to increase the number of women on their electoral lists, which has triggered opposition both within the coalition and from the opposition. On economic issues SERNAM has increased efforts to put pressure on corporations and employers to confront gender discrimination in the labor force, and it is supporting legislation to make equal pay for equal work mandatory. It has implemented a program of "best labor practices" to promote gender equality and has reinaugurated a program for poor women heads of household to help them obtain paid work. Most important, the current government has moved more decisively and consistently than any previous Concertación administrations toward dealing with issues of reproductive rights, including emergency contraception and sex education.

Perhaps the best example of this has been the Ministry of Health's early approval of the Norms on the Regulation of Fertility, a mandatory guide for all public health centers. Among a broad spectrum of measures is the requirement that all primary-care facilities provide emergency contraception to all girls and women fourteen years or older who request it. No parental or spousal approval is necessary, but counseling for youth is available. Until this policy change, free emergency contraception was available in the public sector only for rape victims, although anyone who could obtain a doctor's prescription could buy it.

By universalizing access, the new policy represents an important break. Both right-wing opposition parties and the Catholic Church have adamantly opposed the measure, taking the case to every judicial and administrative body and losing the judicial battle but getting support from the Constitutional Tribunal, which ruled against distribution, although distribution was defended by the president and many of her cabinet members and approved in the lower courts. The Ministry of Health, led by a socialist female physician with close personal ties to the president, has played a leading role in this debate. Contrary to what might have been expected, most of the governing coalition has supported the policy precisely because it has been framed and advocated as an issue of social justice and equality, rather than as one concerning women's reproductive rights.

The Bachelet government has thus attempted to move forward on some of the most contentious issues blocking advances on women's rights, showing that its commitment to women's empowerment is much higher on its list of priorities than on that of previous administrations. Moreover, the president and many of her ministers have shown resolve to confront conservative arguments and to resist pressures on key gender issues. However, this greater openness to feminist demands will not easily translate into policy results. Bachelet's government has had to face more criticism and lack of political support than any other Concertación government to date. This lack of support has been evident in the difficulties the executive has encountered in passing key pieces of legislation despite the fact that, for the first time since 1990, the governing coalition controlled a clear majority in both houses of Congress. However, the majority was short-lived since two separate conflicts within the coalition produced the resignation of two senators and six Congress representatives. This has forced the Bachelet government to negotiate with individual congressional representatives, often unsuccessfully, on a wide array of legislative matters.

To complicate matters further, the Concertación experienced what all observers see as its worst political crisis since it assumed power in 1990. This is not due to a new initiative by the Bachelet government, but to a policy disaster in the public transportation sector. The TranSantiago plan was designed under the Lagos administration as an all-encompassing reform of

Santiago's transport system. Implemented in February 2007, its results provoked a firestorm of protests: massive street demonstrations, political unrest, long queues for buses, increased congestion, and a generalized public outcry from all social and political sectors. The causes of the massive failure are long and complex, but they include faulty design, bad implementation, and the failure of the private sector to fulfill contracts. The government, which initially failed to communicate with the public or deal effectively with the problem, slowly made amends but there is still a sense that the government has failed. As a result of this crisis, the president had to reshuffle her cabinet, request additional resources from Congress, and publicly apologize to the country for still unresolved problems.

The TranSantiago crisis erupted after the government had already faced criticism for failing to "discipline" the coalition. In fact, after a short honeymoon, the president and her government came under increasing fire for their lack of progress in key policy areas. The president's sex has now resurfaced as a major issue in political debates, used this time in a negative way to attack Bachelet's leadership skills and style. The tone and breadth of the criticisms attest to the still prevalent gender stereotypes and discrimination in Chilean society and among political elites. Yet what is most dangerous from the perspective of women's rights and the future of a range of important public policy measures is that Chile's fundamental political problems are reduced in public discourse to the inexperience of individuals in key political posts, or the lack of leadership on the part of the president herself.

The resort to such reductive rhetoric signals a deep resistance to the president's attempt to end the hold a small, highly homogenous group of male political elites has on the machinery of government. When Bachelet appointed her parity cabinet, she was attempting to introduce a new generation of politicians and technical experts. The "new faces" promised throughout the campaign also meant a necessary transformation of the social networks sustaining political power and a change of strategies used by those in power, away from patronage and a lack of transparency. The traditional political establishment that Bachelet sought explicitly to undermine was dominated by men, many of them of the generation that had lived through the military coup and had occupied key political positions since the transition. Most of them were from Santiago, had studied in a small group of private high schools and universities, and belonged to close social and political networks. The resistance to the "new style" has as much to do with the elites' unwillingness to accept "renovation" as it does with gender.

The problems of coordination between the government and political parties, and between the government and Congress, are not just the product of resistance to Bachelet's innovations. They are also linked to the inevitable exhaustion of seventeen years of uninterrupted Concertación government. The presidential term has been reduced to four years, which means that the two major political coalitions are already fighting over their next presidential candidate. The political turmoil within the Concertación has also invigorated the electoral aspirations of the opposition, which hopes that the administration's problems will be the sure ticket for them to gain power. They have few incentives to cooperate with a government in a context in which accusations of inefficiency or lack of progress will prove highly useful to them in an election campaign.

Concluding Remarks ✦

In this tumultuous political context, feminists face a complex set of choices. The current government has indeed moved toward incorporating some of the movement's most pressing demands, and the president seems committed to pushing a women's rights agenda to a much greater degree than any previous social democratic leader. Yet feminists have been unable to participate in the political debates or play a role either in supporting government policies or in advocating changes in the agenda because they have not confronted the historical divisions that have limited their role as a political force in post-transition Chile.

For her part, Bachelet has shown a willingness to confront the right-wing and Catholic opposition on measures long postponed by a divided and conservative-leaning Concertación. However, she must act within a very narrow set of constraints. Conservative forces continue to have veto power over legislative matters and in defining the public agenda. The coalition that supports Bachelet continues to be center-left, but the Christian Democratic Party remains a powerful voice in that segment of the governing coalition that opposes change on many women's rights issues and worries about holding onto its base. All political parties, including those of the left, have shown little interest in supporting measures that would increase women's political representation or extend sexual and reproductive rights. Moreover, the president's capacity for leadership is increasingly questioned because she has failed to enforce discipline within the Concertación, while her proposal to bring "new faces," which was popular in her campaign and offers a solution to the exhaustion of the ruling coalition and the persistent rigidities of Chilean society, now meets with great opposition that is often expressed in gendered terms. The feminist movement and women's organizations remain weak and divided, and they lack a coherent public voice in the political sphere.

The future of feminist politics and women's rights in Chile depends on the ability of women to mobilize and demand that social democracy live up to its promises of equity and solidarity for all. Strengthened women's organizations must build bridges with other progressive groups that seek to expand the limits of posttransition democratic arrangements and to confront the powerful conservative forces continuing to dominate Chilean society. The election of a socialist woman committed to gender equality and willing to confront entrenched forces on some of these issues is a historical achievement and offers unprecedented opportunities. Yet advances in the areas that continue to obstruct the full exercise of women's rights will not come only from the fact that a woman has become president. Rather, it will result from a break in the male control of government power, the appeal to women as a political base, and the courage to go beyond the timid initial measures that the country has taken to confront the problems that impede the advancement of women's rights, and the persistence of inequalities, in Chile.

## Notes ⟜

1  See, for example, the editorial in the *New York Times*, "Women's Place Revisited," from January 19, 2006.
2  This is the name adopted by the coalition of seventeen political parties that joined forces in the late 1980s to campaign against the plebiscite organized by the military regime to allow it to remain in power for another eight years. Some of these parties merged, while others left, leaving today a total of four parties: the PS (Socialist Party), the PPD (Party for Democracy), the PRSD (Radical Social Democratic Party), and the DC (Christian Democratic Party). The first three can be broadly classified as left-wing. The PS and the PPD are the most significant progressive parties, while the PRSD is a very small organization that mediates between left and center in the coalition.
3  This was a broad-based coalition of women from all the parties forming the Concertación; it also included civil society leaders from NGOs and women's

groups. It was formed to advocate the demands of the women's movement after the transition, but it dissolved soon after due to the adverse political climate for such supraparty initiatives.

4 Law 19,325 of Intra-familial Violence was approved in Congress in early 1994. Other important legal changes in this period were reforms to the Labor Code introduced to eliminate discrimination and improve women's rights, to the Civil Code to eliminate the distinction between legitimate and illegitimate children (depending on whether they had been born in or out of wedlock), and the elimination of adultery as a civil offence, until then considered a felony only when perpetrated by women (Ríos Tobar 2003:276).

5 This is official data from the CASEN survey available at www.mideplan.cl.

6 Chile and El Salvador are the only two countries in the region that have not ratified the protocol.

7 The information is taken from a press release dated June 22, 1999, www.un.org/womenwatch/daw/cedaw/21sess.htm#press.

8 Bachelet increased SERNAM's operating budget for 2007 by 13 percent compared to the previous year.

9 Two Chilean sociologists have recently concluded a study of popular women's groups in the greater Santiago area that confirms these earlier findings. See Gannon Hola forthcoming.

10 Sonia Alvarez (1998) identified this as a common trend throughout Latin America at the end of the nineties.

11 Several important volumes addressed this issue directly, including Alvarez 1990; Jaquette 1994; Jaquette and Wolchik 1998; and Htun 2003b.

12 Almost 70 percent of the feminist activists interviewed by Marcela Ríos Tobar, Lorena Godoy, and Elizabeth Guerrero Caviedas were active in women's groups and left-wing political parties simultaneously for most of their lives (2004: chap. 3). Thirty-eight percent of the women interviewed were linked to the Socialist Party, 16 percent to the Movimiento de la Izquierda Revolucionaria (MIR), and 12 percent to the Movimiento de Acción Popular Uniteria (MAPU) and Communist Party respectively (207).

13 An account of the debate around the autonomy issue (*autónomas* versus *institucionales*) is provided in Alvarez et al. 2003.

14 The divisions that resulted in a large portion of the traditional left opposing the political strategy adopted by the Concertación of confronting the dictatorship at the polls in a plebiscite first (1988), and for presidential elections later (1989), had a profound effect in the feminist movement: activists tended to side with their political sectors to the detriment of internal cross-party connections, thus impeding intramovement alliances.

15 This information is based on the author's notes and informal discussion with a wide range of participants during the *Encuentro* itself. It took place in Olmué, June 24–27, 2005.

16 For all results, see "Encuesta Latinobarómetro 2004: Una década de medi-

ciones—una década de evolución," Latinobarómetro, Santiago, www.latino
barometro.org.

17   Pepe Auth, an analyst linked to the left wing of the Concertación, predicted six
months in advance that the coalition would obtain more than 50 percent of the
votes in the parliamentary election and a landslide victory over the opposition
in the presidential race (Auth 2005).

18   By December 2003, for example, 14 percent of those interviewed by Centro de
Estudias Públicos (CEP) and registered to vote declared that they would want
Bachelet to be the next president of Chile (www.cepchile.cl). She was the first-
ranked political leader in the Concertación by far, followed by Soledad Alvear
with 10 percent, and the ex-presidents Lagos and Frei with 4 percent and 3 percent, respectively.

19   The day after her election, on January 16, 2006, *La nación* (the national newspaper linked to the Concertación) included an article entitled "When Everyone
Thought the Concertación Dead, Bachelet Reinvented It."

20   In a survey conducted in April 2006, 88.5 percent of those asked believed that
"women contributed a different perspective that was necessary in politics"
(SERNAM 2006). There were no significant statistical differences in the responses
of women and men.

21   This applied to the extreme left wing in particular.

22   Lagos received only 45.3 percent of the female vote, while Bachelet obtained
53.5 percent. This difference is even more significant if we consider that more
women than men voted in the election and that various studies demonstrate
that women are less likely to annul their ballots or abstain from voting. More
than one hundred thousand female voters that had supported other candidates
in the first round supported Bachelet in the second, as did most of those who
had originally voted for the candidate of the alternative left, Tomás Hirsh.

23   After Bachelet's triumph in the second round of voting, thousands of people
poured into the streets to celebrate, including many women wearing presidential
banners sold in the street to show that the election of Bachelet meant a triumph
for all women.

24   Unfortunately, after a first year in office, the president conducted a major cabinet
change in which four ministers were replaced, including two female ministers
then substituted by two older politicians who clearly identified with the more
traditional wing of the Concertación.

25   This information is derived from phone interviews conducted in June 2006 by
FLACSO, Universidad de Chile, and coordinated by the author.

26   See the first and second annual presidential addresses to Congress, May 21,
2006, and May 21, 2007 (www.presidencia.cl).

# 2

# Gender Quotas, Candidate Selection, and Electoral Campaigns ✦

COMPARING ARGENTINA AND BRAZIL

*Jutta Marx, Jutta Borner, and Mariana Caminotti*

During the 1990s a rising tide of demands and negotiations led, if in part temporarily, to the adoption of gender quotas for legislative candidates in twelve countries in Latin America.[1] In response to the persistence of male domination in politics and the consequent underrepresentation of women, quotas constitute affirmative action measures aimed at overcoming the obstacles women face to the full exercise of their right to hold legislative office, which can be attributed to discrimination against them within political parties and to their cultural and social subordination (Archenti 2002:31). Arguments in favor of quotas are based on a demand for justice, as women comprise more than half of the populations of these countries. But they are also defended on the grounds that giving women access to decision-making bodies will put new issues on the agenda and include questions of specific interest to women (e.g., Valdés et al. 2004:21; Franceschet 2006).

The implementation of these measures has increased the number of women in national legislatures. In 1990 the average percentage of women in lower houses (or in single-house legislatures) in Latin America was less than 9 percent (Barreiro, López, and Soto 2004). Today women occupy nearly 20 percent of the seats, and they hold 14 percent of the seats in the upper houses (authors' calculation based on data from the Inter-parliamentary Union).

However, the success of quota laws varies significantly from country to country. According to the academic literature, the effectiveness of gender-quota laws depends on the characteristics of the electoral systems, on the precise wording of the affirmative action laws, and on the existence of penalties for those parties that fail to comply with their legal obligations. From this perspective, various studies suggest that proportional representation systems prove more favorable than mixed or majority (single-member district) systems (e.g., Barreiro, López, and Soto 2004; Jones and Navia 1999; Matland 2004; Rule 1994) and that closed lists (where the party decides who will serve in the legislature by the order in which the candidates appear on the list) are more effective than open lists.[2] Closed-list systems will prove most effective if the legislation requires placement of women candidates in "winnable" positions, for example, one woman for every two men, to reach the 30 percent quota. This cannot be required in open-list systems.

This essay looks at the experiences of Argentina—a pioneer in the adoption of a legally binding female quota, considered successful internationally—and Brazil, where the achievements have been more modest to date. We begin by summarizing the relevant characteristics of the political institutions and the electoral systems of each country, noting a number of key differences in the quota laws adopted in each case. We compare the success each has had when measured by the number of women elected (although there can be other measures of success). To evaluate how quotas work in practice and how they affect candidate selection by political parties in each country, we compare candidate selection processes in both cases, drawing on interviews we conducted in 2005 with a quarter of the national female legislators in Argentina and Brazil, from across the political spectrum.[3] Finally, we look at some of the conditions under which the women we interviewed carried out their electoral campaigns in each country.

Political Institutions and Electoral Systems
in Argentina and Brazil ⚜

Argentina and Brazil are both federal countries with bicameral legislatures. The Argentine Chamber of Deputies has 257 members elected from 24 electoral districts by means of a closed-list, proportional-representation (PR) system. National deputies serve a four-year term, but elections are staggered so that half of the Chamber is elected every two years. The Senate has 72 legislators, 3 from each district, elected by a system ensuring that the party that wins the majority of votes will have two representatives, and the one that comes in second will have one. Senators serve a six-year term, and every two years a third of the Senate seats come up for election.

The Federal Chamber of Deputies in Brazil has 513 members, elected for four-year terms from 27 districts by means of an open-list, PR system. Under this system, each party or coalition presents a list of candidates in no hierarchical order. Citizens can decide to vote for a party or a coalition by voting the list as a whole (party vote), or they can vote for individual candidates (preferential vote), which is much more widely used in practice. The total of party and preferential votes determines the number of seats a party or coalition will receive, but who serves is decided on the basis of the preferential vote, so that those who receive the most votes as individuals are elected to fill the seats the party or coalition has won (Nohlen 1998).

The Brazilian Senate has 81 legislators, 3 from each district, elected by a majority system for an eight-year term. As Brazil has adopted gender quotas only for elections that are decided by proportional representation, quotas do not apply to senatorial races.

## The Origins and Characteristics of the Argentine Ley de Cupo Femenino ⚜

In Argentina, the approval of the Ley de Cupo Femenino (Gender-Quota Law) in 1991 was the culmination of a collective effort by women in political parties, who received the support of some sectors of the feminist movement. During the last few years of the military dictatorship, from 1976 to 1983, women's groups had played very visible roles in the resistance to military rule, particularly the Mothers and Grandmothers of the Plaza de Mayo. Their involvement in the electoral campaign of 1983 contrasted sharply with the low levels of female representation in executive and legislative decision-making positions under the new democratic government. As a result, women activists from the major political parties began to organize and lobby for the adoption of affirmative action measures that would ensure greater female political representation in Congress. This campaign took place in a positive environment, with support offered by international organizations (especially the United Nations [UN]), by the debates occurring in different forums, and by exchanges between Argentine women politicians and women members of European political parties who had experience with gender quotas.

Inspired by European examples, Argentine women politicians initially suggested that parties should adopt voluntary quotas. However, the unwillingness of the major parties to act made it clear that this strategy would fail. In November 1989, two draft laws were drawn up calling for mandatory quotas, one in each house of Congress, proposing that the National Electoral Law require all parties to include more women on their lists of candidates for the national legislature.

On November 29, 1991, after an intense period of lobbying on the part of women from various parties (who had agreed to unite behind whichever proposal seemed to be advancing most rapidly), with the support of women's organizations and with the decisive intervention of President Carlos Menem, the Senate approved Law 24.012, based on a proposal put forward by Senator Margarita Malharro de Torres of the UCR (Radical Civic Union). As a result, Article 60 of the Electoral Law was reformed to read: "The lists of candidates presented must contain at least 30 percent women and in proportions that will give them the possibility of election. No list will be accepted officially that does not meet these requirements." On March 8, 1993, in response to the concern of women politicians that the rule might be manipulated in ways that would distort its intent, National Executive Decree #379 was issued, specifying that the figure of 30 percent should be interpreted as a minimum (and not an upper limit) to the number of women nominated, that is, at least one woman for every two men on the list. If the party were nominating only two candidates, one had to be a woman.

In the elections held that year, many parties presented lists with 30 percent women candidates but failed to place women high enough on the lists to ensure a real chance of election for at least some of them. Faced with this situation, women politicians, regardless of party affiliation, united to address the issue. Appeals to the courts resulted in a series of contradictory rulings. These were resolved in 1999 by a decision of the Inter-American Commission on Human Rights (IACHR) to mediate on behalf of María Teresa Merciadri de Morini, a member of the moderate (despite its name) UCR (Lázaro and Fraquelli 2003:9; see also Kohen, this volume).

On December 28, 2000, President Fernando De la Rúa (from the centrist UCR-FREPASO Alliance) issued a new regulatory decree (#1246), which is still in force. It stipulates that the electoral quota for women applies to all races for deputies, senators, and National Constituent Assemblies (in the event that they are held) and that the 30 percent quota is a minimum number. A party will be viewed as in compliance with the quota law when women account for a third of those nominated for seats held by a party that are up for reelection in a given year, taking into account the number of seats formerly held by the party and not the number of candidates the party is currently putting up for election in the district as a whole. A detailed set of instructions specifies how the female quota should be interpreted in ambiguous cases.

The new decree made it clear that there would be sanctions against parties whose lists failed to comply with the law. If an electoral judge thought any of the women candidates had been placed too far down the list, the party would have forty-eight hours to remedy the situation. If the party failed to do so, the Electoral Tribunal itself would decide the female candidate's placement. Once in force, Decree 1246 greatly reduced the likelihood of a political party's noncompliance with the quota law.

Since the quota law first went into effect, there has been a sustained increase in the number of women elected to the national Congress. In 1993 the percentage of women in the lower house increased from 4.3 percent to 13.6 percent, but by 2005 it had increased to 35.8 percent.[4] All seats were up for election in the upper chamber in 2001, the first direct election of senators under the gender quota law.[5] The number of women senators increased dramatically from 5.8 percent in 1998 to 37.1 percent in 2001. In the legislative elections of 2003, the number of women senators increased to 43.7 percent, settling at 42.3 percent in 2005.

The Brazilian Quota Law ⚜

In contrast to the Argentine case, the Brazilian law was not adopted in response to a collective effort by women in political parties, nor did it involve alliances between women legislators and sectors of the women's movement.

In 1995, the initiative to establish a minimum quota for women candidates was set in motion by then Federal Deputy Marta Suplicy (of the Workers' Party, PT) after she took part in a meeting of Latin American women legislators in São Paulo as part of the preparations for the Fourth UN Conference on Women to be held in Beijing later that year. At that meeting, the Argentine gender quota law was discussed alongside examples of gender quotas adopted elsewhere (Htun and Jones 2002). The draft law proposed by Suplicy (#783/95) was endorsed by more than twenty women legislators from different political parties during a discussion of the legislation for the municipal

TABLE 1   Participation of Women in the Argentine National Congress

| CHAMBER OF DEPUTIES | | SENATE | |
|---|---|---|---|
| Legislative Session | % Women* | Legislative Session** | % Women* |
| 1983–1985 | 4.3 | 1983–1986 | 6.3 |
| 1985–1987 | 4.3 | 1986–1989 | 6.3 |
| 1987–1989 | 4.7 | 1989–1992 | 8.3 |
| 1989–1991 | 6.3 | 1992–1995 | 4.2 |
| 1991–1993 | 5.4 | 1995–1998 | 5.7 |
| | | 1998–2001 | 5.8 |
| *With the quota law in full force* | | | |
| 1993–1995 | 13.6 | | |
| 1995–1997 | 27.2 | | |
| 1997–1999 | 28.4 | | |
| 1999–2001 | 27.2 | | |
| 2001–2003 | 29.2 | 2001–2003 | 37.1 |
| 2003–2005 | 33.9 | 2003–2005 | 43.7 |
| 2005–2007 | 35.8 | 2005–2007 | 42.3 |

*Source*: Table constructed by authors based on the Dirección de Información Parlamentaria del Congreso de la Nación.

* At the beginning of each legislative session.

** Until 2001 Senate terms were for three years; after 2001, terms were set at two years.

elections of 1996. In September an amendment to the draft electoral law, then under discussion, was put forward by Deputies Suplicy and Paulo Bernardo, who proposed a minimum quota of 30 percent women for the lists of candidates (Araújo 1999:5).

Recognizing that the Brazilian electoral system would make it difficult to enforce a quota, and that the dynamics of electoral competition worked against women, the Suplicy/Bernardo proposal included additional measures to support women candidates. These included specifying that the sex of the candidate be identified on candidate lists (as candidates often use nicknames that are not gender-specific); the need for television ads and campaign information to let the public know about the new gender quota law; and funds set aside to support women candidates (Araújo 1999). Despite these efforts, the law approved on September 29, 1995 (#9.100) included only two requirements: that "each party or coalition may present candidates for the Municipal Chambers equal to 120 percent of the number of seats up for election" (Article 11); and that a minimum of 20 percent of those candidates must be women (paragraph 3).

The law not only failed to incorporate the additional measures intended to compensate for the disadvantages faced by women candidates, it also reduced the gender quota to 20 percent from the original 30 percent suggested. In addition, it allowed parties and coalitions to put forward candidates for 120 percent of the vacancies in the Chamber, not for 100 percent as had formerly been the case. This made it easier for parties to evade the quota requirement and helps explain why gender quotas have had such a modest impact in Brazil. As Suplicy herself recognized, "the law that was passed weakened the chance that the quota would make the parties invest more in the campaigns of women candidates" (see Araújo 1999:116).

The proposal "was manipulated to increase the number of candidates" (qtd. in Araújo 1999:116). As a former legislator, Eva Blay, observed, "the Quota Law passed in the Federal Chamber, after tough negotiations with male politicians, resulted in a serious distortion. To compensate for the 20 percent quota for women, the political parties demanded an increase in the total number of candidates who could be presented" (qtd. in Miguel 2004:59).

Although the initiative had the support of the cross-party women's coalition (*bancada femenina*) in Congress, and though some nongovernmental organizations participated in the public hearings held in the Chamber of Deputies and the Senate, the women's movement did not mobilize around the idea of gender quotas. As Clara Araújo (1999) has pointed out, the issue of gender quotas came up in the June 1995 preparatory meeting for the Beijing conference, which had been organized by the Association of Brazilian Women's Groups (Articulação de Mulheres Brasileiras), but the final document did not even mention quotas. In Blay's view, the lack of a broader debate in society and in the women's movement as the legislation was being drafted reduced the impact of the first quota law. "Unlike issues such as abortion, family planning, violence against women, which were and are still widely discussed in society, in state assemblies and the federal Chamber, the question of quotas was basically restricted to the legislature" (Blay 2002:59–60).

In 1997, a year after the first elections held under the new quota law for municipal elections, a new electoral law (#9.540) was passed. Article 10 allows each party to "nominate candidates for up to 150 percent of all vacant seats in elections for the Chamber of Deputies, the Legislative Chamber, Legislative Assemblies, and Municipal Chamber," adding for clarification (in paragraph 3) that "of the number of candidates on the list of each party or coalition, a minimum of one third and a maximum of seventy percent must be reserved for candidates of each sex." In practice, however, the fact that parties "reserve" a certain number of places does not necessarily mean that candidates must be nominated for all the reserved places on party lists.

The current law differs in two important respects from the previous one. Now there is no minimum quota for women, but instead minimum and maximum quotas for candidates of each sex. Although there is no consensus about the effects of "feminine" quotas versus this more "neutral" formulation, the first seems to indicate a clearer desire to redress structural gender imbalances (see Marx, Borner, and Caminotti 2007:302). The new law also extends the quota to include all elections carried out under proportional-representation rules, not just municipal elections. This includes elections to the federal Chamber of Deputies, but not to the Senate. But because parties are now allowed to run candidates for 150 percent of the vacant seats, they have a lot of room to maneuver. As Mala Htun points out, increasing the number of candidates a party or coalition can put forward works as an "escape clause" for parties in Brazil. For example, if a district has ten representatives in the federal Chamber of Deputies, each party can put forward fifteen candidates for those seats. In this case, the quota law would require that each party reserve no fewer than four of those places for either male or female candidates. But if the party does not want to nominate any women, it can put 11 male candidates on the actual ballot without breaking the law (Htun 2003a). In fact, the great majority of parties do not present lists with the maximum number of possible candidates for which they have "reserved" spaces (Samuels 2004), suggesting that most will be easily able to evade the requirement.

For these reasons gender quota laws in Brazil have produced very different results from the Ley de Cupo in Argentina. In 1998, the first year the federal law was in effect, the percentage of women elected to the Chamber of Deputies actually *fell* to 5.4 percent, compared with 6.2 percent in the election held before quotas were imposed. Women made up 8.2 percent of the lower chamber in 2002, but women continue to hold a much smaller percentage of seats in the Brazilian Congress compared to their counterparts in Argentina, and at a level dramatically lower than the minimum percentages (25 percent and 30 percent, respectively) anticipated by the gender quota laws. Thus the Brazilian quota law has features that actually diminish the chances

TABLE 2    Candidates and Elected Legislators for the
            Brazilian Chamber of Deputies, by Sex (1994–2002)

|  | 1994 (Without a quota) | | | 1998 (Minimum quota = 25%) | | | 2002 (Minimum quota = 30%) | | |
|---|---|---|---|---|---|---|---|---|---|
|  | Total No. | Women No. | Women % | Total No. | Women No. | Women % | Total No. | Women No. | Women % |
| CANDIDATES | 2,968 | 184 | 6.2 | 3,451 | 359 | 10.4 | 4,210 | 480 | 11.4 |
| ELECTED | 513 | 32 | 6.2 | 513 | 29 | 5.7 | 513 | 42 | 8.2 |

Source: Based on Luis Felipe Miguel, "Participação eleitoral e gênero no Brasil: As cotas
    para mulheres e seu impacto," paper presented at II Congreso Latinoamericano
    de Ciencia Política (ALACIP), Mexico City, October 2004.

of women's election. There have been two elections since the law passed, but the percentage of women in the Congress remains low.

The evidence presented so far suggests that the electoral laws of Argentina and Brazil differ substantially in terms of the opportunities they offer to women running for national office. The Argentine system of closed party lists, the placement-mandate requirements of the quota law, and the sanctions provided by its regulatory decree make it possible to elect the number of women anticipated by the law. In contrast, the open-list system in Brazil and the fact that parties are allowed to apply the quota to the number of candidacies they reserve, and not to those they in fact put on the ballot, make it unlikely that parties will significantly change their behavior. The results in terms of the number of women elected to the national legislature in Brazil bear this out.

## Women's Exclusion from the Candidate Selection Processes in Argentina and Brazil ⚓

In addition to nominating candidates, parties play a key role in political recruitment. Together, these processes shape the electoral choices available to citizens and set the conditions for those who wish to compete for political office. The selection process determines who will be able to get onto the party lists and therefore have a chance of being elected (Norris 1997).

In both Brazil and Argentina, only political parties and coalitions have the right to put forward candidates for national legislative posts. Parties make these decisions at the district level (state or provincial), and districts are the starting point for those who wish to begin a political career (Samuels 2004; Ames 2002; Jones 2004). In Argentina, candidacies for the national legislatures are decided at the provincial level and, in practice, each party employs its own selection process ranging from internal elections (primaries) to party conventions or — very often — closed-door negotiations among party leaders. In Brazil, parties can decide how they will select candidates (Law 9.096/95). Most hold party conventions at the state level, and the participants include delegates chosen in local conventions, sitting senators and deputies, and state party leaders.[6] In practice, the conventions usually ratify the candidates agreed on earlier in negotiations among party leaders (Mainwaring 1999).

In the process of candidate selection, the aspirants' record in party organizations is usually highly valued (Gallagher and Marsh 1988). Formal qualifications, a history of involvement in the party, previous legislative experience, political connections, and name recognition are generally seen as factors that can make a candidate more attractive, although the importance of each factor may differ depending on the country and context (Gallagher and Marsh 1988; Matland 2004).

It is not surprising that — according to the data available for Argentina (2003–5) and Brazil (2003–7) — women parliamentarians in both countries generally have high levels of education and substantial political experience (Marx, Borner, and Caminotti 2007). Almost all the women legislators we interviewed had held legislative, executive, or party office prior to winning a seat in the national Congress. Nevertheless, there are different patterns in each country that are worth noting.

According to our interviewees, the parties constitute the main avenues to political office in Argentina. Argentine parties, like the Justicialist (Peronist) Party, which used to be considered the most important mass party in Latin America (Abal Medina, Suárez Caro, and Nejamkis 2003), and the UCR, which won the presidency in the first election after the democratic transition in 1983, were formed many decades ago, and they have long served as arenas of political socialization.

In Brazil, by contrast, women legislators often developed their participation and leadership skills outside the parties — in social movements, collective associations, and labor unions, a generalization that held even when a legislator had a long history of political affiliation. This is explained by the fact that at least until the rise of the Workers' Party (PT) in the 1980s, political parties in Brazil had the reputation of being "weak, lacking in coherence, and institutionally fluid" (Araújo 2004:17), with shallow roots in society. Some of the Brazilian women legislators we interviewed had entered politics as wives of governors and municipal mayors. But for women in the PT and other parties on the left, participation in collective movements offered an important path to formal political participation. For others, particularly those in parties such at the Partido del Frente Liberal (PFL) and the Partido Progresista (PP) on the right, marriage ties were seen as an important means of entry into formal political life.

When we asked Argentine and Brazilian women legislators to speculate about the criteria they thought had motivated their parties to adopt them as candidates, most said that their political experiences in the broadest sense played an important role, suggesting that the selection of women candidates follows an electoral logic similar to that for men. However, what women legislators in both countries said about their experiences suggests that, in practice, there are still many barriers to gender equality. The findings from our interviews are compatible with those of several previous studies (De Luca, Jones, and Tula 2002; Mainwaring 1999; Samuels 2004).

Whatever the different institutional and legal arrangements, and taking into account the practices peculiar to each party, the selection of candidates for high offices is carried out primarily on the basis of decisions made by party elites, usually men. Women legislators frequently reported that they were *invited* to run by the presidents of their party at the state level (usually the governor of the state), by municipal mayors, or by officers and leaders of factions or groups within their party. A close relationship or friendship with party leaders usually made it much more likely that a woman would be chosen to run for office.

Although these mechanisms of recruitment potentially affect aspiring candidates of both sexes, they can be especially problematic for women because their participation in party decision-making circles is generally quite limited. Various women we interviewed put it clearly. To quote one Argentine legislator: "The lists are put together behind closed doors, and men who have a lot of power in the party make the final decision as to who will be a candidate" (A15, PJ).[7] Or, as a Brazilian legislator observes, "The ones who decide are the men. Women work and canvass for votes. This is what really happens. And the women are very grateful when they are asked to participate in the process" (B3, PSDB). The predominantly male-dominated process of decision making inside the parties does not necessarily imply a deliberate exclusion of women from the electoral process, but it obviously works in ways that discourage greater gender equity in politics. Our interviews show that these views—that men continue to dominate the political process despite increased representation for women—are widely held and point to the importance of candidate selection to explain why quota laws do not necessarily produce the results expected of them.

## Views of the Ley de Cupo among Argentine Women Legislators ✦

In Argentina, all the parties have complied with the quota law. The fact that gender quotas are seen as a matter of justice itself marks a considerable success. Nevertheless, given how long it has been since the law came into force, it would be reasonable to expect that women would be fully integrated into the processes of candidate selection. Yet this is not the case.

Although the legitimacy of the law is no longer an issue, conflicts between party women and their male counterparts persist. Some Argentine women have recently played important electoral roles,[8] but in general the parties tend to view female candidates solely in terms of their gender and not as individuals with particular experiences and capabilities. As one Argentine legislator put it, "In general, the men say, 'this place is for a woman—who shall we nominate?' This is what happens in all the parties" (A3, PJ). Others noted that men see the gender quota as a complicating factor in the often difficult negotiations within and among parties. When a party wants to negotiate a list or enter into an electoral alliance, the tacit but frequently followed rule is that the minority party or group has to nominate a woman: "The one who loses pays with a woman" (A11, UCR). Legislators felt that when "someone has to be taken off a list, the one who is almost always sacrificed is a woman" (A28, PJ).

That women have gained so little power in the selection process after a decade and a half of the quota law raises the question of whether the law is working as intended. Various women legislators felt that the *cupo femenino* was sometimes manipulated to position women who could increase the power of certain male party leaders. Their appraisals seem to confirm that such personalist criteria increase the dependence of women politicians on male party leaders and make collective action and cooperation among female politicians more difficult (Matland 2004). As one of our interviewees described it, "The impact of the quota law, in the case [of my party] has not generated a women's movement. The men used the quota to give places to some women who were very competent and some who were not, but no group of women legislators can claim any degree of autonomy" (A11, UCR). The apparent absence of concerted efforts to promote the participation of women candidates in any way beyond the strict letter of the law means that women candidates frequently end up competing against each other.

Several legislators felt the minimum quota for women candidates had become a maximum, narrowing their political opportunities and creating competition among potential women candidates. "It is certainly true that the spaces that the men give us are so limited that we end up competing among ourselves, and sometimes this competition may become disloyal, as we think that either another woman will have my space or that I will have hers. This is due to the fact that men give us so little room in a party structure which is still quite *machista*. This is not true just in our party, but in all parties" (A14, UCR).

The career paths and the capabilities of Argentine women politicians often are not sufficient to guarantee that they will be seen as men's equals in the political arena, although they deeply desire to be recognized for their own merits and are often ambivalent about gaining office through an affirmative action law. Quotas can be seen as discriminatory when they single out women as members of a disadvantaged group who have been given special rights, rather than as individuals with their own ideas and skills. This ambivalence may help explain why women legislators tend to regard the quota law as more of a necessary evil than a matter of justice achieved.

Despite these problems, however, the majority of women legislators we interviewed saw the quota law as helpful to becoming candidates and gaining a position within the party in their own case, and they recognized the value of the law for women candidates in general. In their view, the quota law made it possible for many capable women to gain political office who would not otherwise have been elected, and they admitted, as one of them put it, that "if the law were repealed, we would go back to where we were before" (A17, UCR). These women continue to support the law as a means of improving the quality of political and institutional life in Argentina.

## Views of the Quota Law among Brazilian Women Legislators ⟨⟩

In Brazil the implementation of gender quotas has been weakened by a number of adverse factors that hobbled their effectiveness. Since the quota law came into effect, not a single party has respected the legal quotas for women candidates in any election. This is largely due to the specifics of the law itself, as well as to Brazil's electoral system.

Open lists and the individualized nature of Brazilian electoral campaigns explain why several Brazilian women legislators thought that what is significant for potential women candidates in Brazil is not the nomination itself, as is true in Argentina, but having the resources needed to carry out a successful campaign. This makes Brazilian women legislators less worried about the parties' failure to follow the legal requirements for gender quotas and more focused on how to confront the barriers women have to overcome to run successful political campaigns.

This situation is aggravated by the fact that our interviewees felt that no political party in Brazil saw promoting women candidates as a priority. When the time comes to decide who will run, parties almost always choose someone with prior visibility, rather than being concerned about promoting women's leadership. "I don't see any discussion of qualifications. They take people who already have a good record as candidates, and the rest are chosen just to make up the numbers. I am upset that they don't organize the women, because there is no incentive for the woman to decide to run," as one deputy put it (B4, PT).

The difficult context in which gender quotas have been introduced in Brazil makes it hard to mount initiatives to ensure the quota law's enforcement. Judicial permissiveness has weakened its implementation, a major factor in the loss of momentum: "When the parties do not comply, they are not punished; they only have to convince the tribunal that there weren't enough women to fill the 30 percent quota called for by the law" (B2, PC do B). The general perception is that "the law has not been respected." Although some have pushed hard to get women candidates on party lists and to organize training activities for women candidates, most of those we interviewed agreed that they have given up trying to put pressure on their parties to act: "There is no point; there aren't enough women to fill the 30 percent quota" (B6, PSDB).

Personal ambition and the availability of opportunities are generally considered critical issues to someone who is considering running for office (Matland 2004). Potential candidates go through a process of assessing how much public support they will have and how likely it is that they can raise the necessary money for a campaign. Almost all the Brazilian women legislators we interviewed thought that the lack of women candidates was due to the fact that "they don't see any possibilities; they don't put themselves forward because they don't have the support of the party or any financial support from anyone" (B11, PTB).

As a result, fewer than half of the deputies we interviewed thought that the quota law had been important for their candidacy. If the quota law played any role, they believed, it was in terms of some additional help, but not decisive support. Like their Argentine counterparts, the Brazilian women thought that although the law had not been effective for them, it was still important for women candidates as a group. "The system of quotas is important in every party. It hasn't been given priority, but it is significant because it does make it possible for women to compete in the electoral process" (B10, PT).

Women legislators in Brazil think that the gender quota laws have not provided relevant incentives for the systematic incorporation of women. Furthermore, they are aware that the law has created resistance among party leaders. In the words of one deputy, quotas are a nuisance for party leaders, and "if the quota didn't exist, they wouldn't have to worry about looking for women to fill it" (B5, PFL).

Although most of those interviewed felt that their candidacy was due principally to their own efforts and political capital, some said they had been talked into running by particular leaders to fill the quota. In this regard, it is interesting to see how situations that seem similar acquire different significance in the context of the contrasting electoral dynamics in Argentina and Brazil. In Argentina, being placed on a list of candidates so that a party can comply with the Ley de Cupo is clearly connected to the likelihood of being elected, depending on how well the party does, as women are put in winnable positions on party lists. In Brazil, however, being included on a party list is likely to be an invitation to work on a campaign that will end up gaining votes for other candidates; it does not imply a real chance of being elected.

Given that the purpose of gender quotas is to address gender inequality in political decision making and to facilitate the systematic access of women to representative institutions, the fact that male party leaders choose women simply to fill the electoral quota, without any additional efforts to reinforce women's leadership or to nurture women in leadership positions, seems to take us back to the situation that existed before these laws were passed. It is ironic that in Brazil women achieved greater participation in the Senate, where gender quotas do not apply, than in the Chamber of Deputies, where they do. Gender quotas in Brazil are largely symbolic, intended to draw attention to the low numbers of women in the national legislature rather than remedy the situation.

It is thus important to continue to work on the issue of women's political representation. In addition to the measures mentioned earlier, many other bill proposals suggested that parties should reserve 30 percent of party funds, and a similar percentage of campaign funds, to support women's campaigns. A similar percentage of the party's TV and radio advertising should also support women's campaigns. Other suggestions include the public financing of political campaigns and the introduction of closed party lists, the latter as part of a general proposal for political reform.

Electoral Campaigns ⚜

In both Argentina and Brazil, women legislators agree that women candidates receive very limited support from political parties and that it is often inferior to that given to men. Nevertheless, the impact of the quota laws in each case, as we have indicated, differs markedly, due in large part to the way the electoral system works.

In Argentina, closed lists mean that candidates do not have to present themselves to the voters as individuals; rather, they are elected because of support for the party's platform and the appeal of its top leaders. The decisive issue is whether a candidate is high enough on a party list to win, which depends on the total support the party or the coalition receives. Once the lists are drawn up, the principal responsibility for electoral success lies with the parties. The lack of financial, advertising, or even verbal support does not reduce the chances of a particular woman being elected, because "the lists do the work" (A18, PJ). Electoral campaigns tend to focus on the candidates at the top of the list, and when legislative and executive elections coincide, on the candidates for the presidency or provincial governorships. The support a candidate receives depends mainly on the importance the parties give to the post at stake or the place of a particular candidate on the list. If less support is given to women candidates, it can be explained by the fact that there are still relatively few women heading party lists or running for executive office.[9]

In Brazil, because campaigns are highly personalized and expensive, the parties' lack of interest in recruiting women and then doing what is needed to give them a chance to win results in a clear disadvantage.[10] The open-list system with preferential voting requires that each candidate campaign as an individual, which makes the resources that a candidate can command a decisive factor. Party resources are scarce in relation to the cost of campaigns, so it is extremely important for candidates to get support from private donors, which works in favor of incumbents. One of the legislators we interviewed thinks that this explains why there are fewer female candidates in Brazil. "A campaign costs a lot, and for this reason many women cannot even consider running for office. If I were to tell you that to be elected a federal deputy you would need a million and a half *reales* [about $740,000], would you run? My financing comes from my own pocket. If you ask if I am going to stand again, I don't know, because I don't have the money. What I had is gone. It would be totally irresponsible for me to spend what I have left—my life savings. I probably won't run again" (B3, PSDB).

Another noticeable difference between Argentina and Brazil is the importance of support from groups outside the parties. Our Brazilian interviewees emphasized this factor, which further reinforces the individualized nature of Brazilian electoral politics. Support from social movements, unions, and civil-society organizations can compensate for the lack of resources offered by parties and is closely connected to the backgrounds of most of the women we interviewed. By contrast, in Argentina one's chance of winning depends entirely on the parties.

In this context, it is interesting to note the different subjective significance that the women politicians in Argentina and Brazil give to the style of their campaigns. In both countries, women see their campaigns as more frugal than men's. In Argentina, this takes on an ethical significance—women have a "woman's way of doing politics," which is seen as less hierarchical and closer to the people. In the Brazilian case, however, the fact that women spend less on campaigns is seen as a result of women's lack of access to resources, with no moral value at all.

## Some Final Considerations ❧

In light of this comparison of the experiences in Argentina and Brazil, we conclude with the following reflections that might help design future strategies to increase women's political representation.

Measures designed to increase women's representation must be formulated with care, and they should include appropriate sanctions to ensure that the rules are taken seriously. Steps taken to monitor whether parties are complying with the law are also critical. The case of Brazil shows clearly that without penalties, the adoption of gender-quota laws in itself does not suffice to increase the opportunities for women to stand for office and win elections.

Further, there is the risk that setting a *minimum* gender quota can easily be interpreted as a *maximum* in practice. It is therefore very important to address the question of what level of women's representation is considered sufficient when quota laws are being formulated and negotiated.

With regard to voting systems with open lists, and in countries like Brazil where public financing of campaigns is very limited and where individuals are largely responsible for funding their own campaigns, the success of quotas will depend on the implementation of supplementary measures to counteract the historic disadvantages of women in the political arena. The lack of such support will effectively discourage women from becoming candidates.

Despite the differences in their situations, women in both Argentina and Brazil remain almost entirely excluded from the selection process. In both cases, political parties continue as largely male-dominated arenas, and women often function as pawns in the negotiations among men. As a consequence, even in Argentina, where the quota law has been in effect for fifteen years and has achieved dramatic quantitative results, it has not succeeded in stimulating substantive changes in parties' candidate selection processes. Male elites maintain a high degree of control, as women can become candidates only if they are chosen by the male decision makers in the parties.

This suggests a deeper problem. There is a gap between the advances women have achieved in increasing their legislative presence and the degree to which they have been integrated into the internal dynamics of their parties and the legislature itself. The Argentine experience underlines the fact that an unforeseen and unintentional effect of the law has been to foster competition among women. The experiences in both Argentina and Brazil suggest the need to ensure that women are better represented in the parties' decision-making circles as well as on their ballots. At a time when the issues of the "quality of democracy" and the health of legislative bodies in Latin America are a matter of concern, it is useful to ask how the electoral reforms considered in many countries can address those issues, and what impact they will have on the political representation of women.

## Notes ✿

1  Argentina, Bolivia, Brazil, Costa Rica, Ecuador, Honduras, Mexico, Panama, Paraguay, and Peru all adopted quota laws during the 1990s. Similarly, in 1997 a quota of 30 percent for both houses of the national Congress was approved in Venezuela, but it was declared unconstitutional in 2000. In Colombia, a law adopted in 1999 established a quota of 30 percent for women in both houses of Congress, but it was declared unconstitutional in 2001. A new law, approved in 2002, stipulated a quota of 30 percent for women in high administrative and judicial posts (Quota Project Database 2006).

2  But for a critique, see Schmidt and Araújo 2004 comparing how quotas work in Peru and Brazil.

3  The interviews were carried out as part of the project Institutional Strengthening in Mercosur: Culture, Politics, Women, and Integration, funded by the Ministry of Foreign Relations of Argentina and administered by the UN Development Program. We designed a questionnaire consisting of sixty questions, most of them open-ended, formulated to reduce as far as possible the risk of shaping respondents' answers. The sample of legislators was drawn from the list of women serving in national congressional offices in February of 2005, maintaining the proportionality of party factions in Congress but also including women representatives from minor parties. Within each party, the choice of women legislators to interview was decided randomly and codes were assigned to assure anonymity. They are referred to by a letter ("A" for Argentina and "B" for Brazil), a number, and their party affiliation when they are cited later in this essay.

4  In this case, the only partial advance that women gained in the Chamber of Deputies can be explained by the partial turnover of the lower house, which meant that the Ley de Cupo only applied to half of the total number of seats in the Chamber, and the still common practice of failing to put women candidates in winnable positions on party lists.

5  According to the constitutional reform of 1994, which replaced a system of indirect election of senators by the provincial legislatures with direct elections, the 2001 election exceptionally required that all seats be contested.

6  Among the parties that select candidates through conventions are the Workers' Party (PT), the Partido do Movimento Democratico (PMDB), the Partido da

Frente Libertal (PFL); the Partido Trabalkista Brasileiro (PTB), the Partido da Socialdemocracia Brasileira (PSDB), the Partido Popular (PP), the Partido Democratico Trabalhista (PDT), and the Partido Comunista do Brasil (PC do B) (Mainwaring 1999; Samuels 2004).

7   As noted earlier, interviewees are identified by country (A or B) and party (e.g., PJ as the Justicialist Party).

8   In the elections of October 2005, the province of Buenos Aires had two women candidates: Cristina Fernández de Kirchner (wife of the president, Néstor Kirchner, and a nominee of the Front for Victory), and Hilda González de Duhalde (also a wife of a prominent political figure, from the Peronist Party), each heading their respective party's list. As a candidate for deputy, Elisa Carrio headed the list of the ARI party—Afirmación para una República de Iguales—in the City of Buenos Aires, and she won the second highest number of votes in the district.

9   For example, in the national elections of 2005, women headed only nine of the fifty-one lists of candidates for the Chamber of Deputies, and only three women headed the sixteen lists of candidates for Senate seats. In 2003–5, none of the parties represented in Congress nominated a woman to fill a governorship.

10  The efforts required for the individualized campaigns characteristic of Brazilian politics make their elections among the most expensive in the world (Speck 2004).

# 3

# Feminist Activism in a Changing Political Context ⚮

VENEZUELA

*Gioconda Espina*

It is very difficult for those who are not in Venezuela to understand that for us the days do not have twenty-four hours, but double or triple that, so that, from one day to the next, things are resolved or come apart, or both at the same time, at such a speed that it seems that more than one day has passed. It was not always like this; before 1998 the days in Venezuela had twenty-four hours as they did in the rest of the world. The pace established by President Hugo Chávez and constantly magnified by the media is responsible for this change. So readers be warned: when this text is published, it will inevitably be out of date. The only thing that the author, a feminist and an activist, can guarantee, is that this essay was finalized fewer than twenty-four hours after the December 2007 referendum in which Chávez's plan to modify several articles of the 1999 Constitution to further concentrate power in his hands lost by 1.4 percent of the votes.

Venezuelan women did not become a movement in 1998. Many began to organize immediately after the death of the former dictator, Juan Vicente Gómez, in 1935. Others became active after the return to democracy in 1958. A great deal has happened in Venezuelan history since then, but at every stage there have been women united as women, despite their political differences, to press for laws that would improve their conditions as mothers and workers and for some feminist goals (such as an end to violence against women, although not, for example, to decriminalize abortion). These efforts have continued, although the degree of political polarization in Venezuela today has made our divisions more acute. Today issues involving women's rights have been moved to the back burner, and women put their political loyalties first.

Today there is no parliamentary opposition in Venezuela's National Assembly because the opposition withdrew in protest days before the election of December 2005. Consequently, Venezuela's "national machinery," the Commission on the Family, Women, and Youth, does not have to negotiate with women's groups outside the government or work to create consensus on women's issues in the Assembly because, since 2005, the Assembly has simply proposed and passed legislation without needing to build coalitions. Three controversial laws addressing women's issues were approved in this way in 2006 and 2007: on violence against women, on the protection of maternity and paternity in families, and on the protection of lactating mothers.

Since President Chávez proposed a referendum on constitutional reform in May 2007, the only issue discussed by women in Venezuela—organized or not—was whether there should be a constitutional reform along the lines he and the Assembly stipulated (changes to thirty-three articles, made public in August 2007, and an additional thirty-six changes proposed by the National Assembly) and whether to vote at all in the referendum set for December 2. None of the proposals that came from women's groups or from sexual orientation (LGTB) groups were included in the president's proposal, and only three were later adopted by the Assembly (banning sexual discrimination, parity for men and women on electoral lists, and the inclusion of housewives as beneficiaries of social security). It was not necessary to change the Constitution to adopt those proposals, but the government followed the strategy of including changes that would benefit several groups alongside provisions allowing Chávez to remain in office for life and to establish new local government councils that he would appoint. In the end there was little that could be termed a feminist agenda in the constitutional reform package that failed on December 2.

The essay that follows discusses how women have made their demands felt in Venezuelan politics, especially since the two-party democracy established in 1958, and then documents how organized women in Venezuela have perceived and responded to the events of the past decade, one largely dominated by the figure and the vision of Hugo Chávez.

Venezuela has relied on a nucleus of feminist activists, including some who have been involved since 1936: Eumelia Hernández and others who became active after the return to democracy in 1958; and Argelia Laya, Esperanza Vera, Adicea Castillo, and Nora Castañeda (who fought for the reform of the civil code put forward by the Venezuelan Federation of Women Lawyers at the end of the 1970s). In addition there are women who, on International Women's Day in 1985, made the public aware of the many feminist collectives in Venezuela, such as Persona, La Conjura, Miercoles, MMM de Mérida, and the Liga Feminista of Maracaibo.

In 1985, to prepare Venezuela's report to the Third United Nations Women's Conference in Nairobi on progress made during the Decade for Women (1975–85), several groups joined the core, including CESAP (Centro al Servicio de la Acción Popular), Circulos Femeninos Populares,Teatro de Calle 8 de Marzo, Mujer y Comunicación, Alianza de Mujeres Médicas, Unión de Mujeres Negras, and others. These came together in what was called the NGO Coordinating Committee (CONG).

Since 1985 several important laws have been passed and legislation implemented on women's issues as a result of cooperation between organized women and women in the government and in the legislature. These include revising Title V of the labor law to assist working mothers (1990); drafting an equal opportunity law (1993); reforming the suffrage and political participation law to mandate that 30 percent of the candidates on party lists be women (1997); drafting the Law on Violence against Women and the Family (1998), and drafting chapter V of the Law on the Social Rights of the Family. They worked to make the language of the 1999 Constitution gender-sensitive, to create the National Institute of Women (Inamujer), and to replace the National Council of Women when Chávez's first chief of staff proposed eliminating it. The women's movement was also involved in drafting a revised law on violence against women after the Chávez government questioned the constitutionality of the 1998 law. The National Assembly passed a new law in 2006.

The most notable characteristic of this flexible core of activists has been its members' ability to put aside political differences to advance a women's agenda. During the writing of the 1999 Constitution, they succeeded in getting into the text almost all the demands accumulated since 1975, when the UN Decade for Women began. Even after the extreme polarization of 2002–4, this core group managed to reconstitute itself to lobby under the new *chavista* parameters for the following six-point agenda:

- Drafting the rules that would permit the immediate enforcement of the Organic Law of Women's Right to a Life Free of Violence (which had just been approved) and push for its implementation
- Substituting an article that would ratify equality and equity between the sexes based on the 50–50 rule for Article 144 of the Organic Law of Suffrage and Political Participation
- Drafting the rules to implement the new Law of Social Services to extend loans of up to the minimal monthly salary to housewives who qualify[1]
- Pushing for the implementation of laws already on the books prohibiting the use and abuse of stereotypical images of women in all kinds of publicity[2]
- Supporting the decriminalization of abortion except in cases where it is performed against a woman's will
- Replacing the National Assembly Commission on the Family, Women, and Youth with a parliamentary Commission on Women's Rights

However, the context in which the activist core can lobby for feminist goals has changed dramatically since 1998, when the traditional political parties collapsed and Chávez was first elected. To understand these changes, it is necessary to understand how Chávez came to be president, as well as the ways in which he has changed the political landscape.

The Rise of Hugo Chávez ⚜

In 1998, Lieutenant Colonel Hugo Chávez Frías was elected under the 1961 Constitution, then reelected in July 2002 under a new constitution approved by the National Constitutional Assembly and ratified by referendum in 1999. He was elected with nearly 63 percent of the votes — the first president ever to be reelected to an immediate second term in Venezuelan history.

During the 2006 campaign, Venezuela remained politically polarized between *chavistas* and anti-*chavistas*, but considerably less violently so than in the days following the short-lived coup of April 2002; or during the strike by the employees of the state petroleum company, from December 2002 to February 2003; or the period before and after the August 15, 2004, referendum on whether the president should resign, which Chávez won decisively. This level of mobilization has since declined or gone underground.

Women have been active at every stage of this history. The opposition to Chávez often points out that women have not taken to the streets and to the courts as often as they did in 2002–3, the year of the greatest confrontation. They are correct: never before or after have women (or men) taken to the streets as passionately as they did then. The marchers numbered in the millions from all across the political spectrum, many more than the hundreds of thousands of student demonstrators who had marched in the past.

After the referendum of August 2004, the street "froze" again, and it stayed cold through the legislative elections of December 2005 and during the 2006 presidential campaign. The opposition was divided into two groups. One, led by Henry Ramos Allup, the ex-deputy and secretary-general of the Democratic Action (AD) Party, claimed that Chávez had won the referendum by fraud and blamed the National Electoral Council (CNE). A more moderate sector of the group did not claim fraud or fault the CNE, but put up candidates who ran against the *chavistas* and won three out of five mayoral races in greater Caracas (in Baruta, Chacao, and El Hatillo) and governorships in the states of Zulia and Nueva Esparta. Until they withdrew from elections in December 2005, the opposition held 53 seats (counting elected substitutes) in the National Assembly, in which pro-Chávez candidates from several parties held 167.

It is understandable that an opposition that lost in April 2002, February 2003, and August 2004, and then withdrew just before the December 2005 elections, would not easily agree on an opposition candidate for the 2006 presidential race. However, Teodoro Petkoff, an ex-communist, the founder and twice presidential candidate of the MAS (Movement toward Socialism) Party (which he left in 1998 when the majority of its members decided to support Chávez), and the editor of the evening newspaper *Tal cual*, brokered negotiations that led to a single opposition candidate: Manuel Rosales, a former mayor and twice governor of the state of Zulia.

When the press published the final list of candidates on August 28, it included, besides Chávez and Rosales, Benjamin Rausseo, a radio, TV, and cabaret personality who declared that it was time to stir up the "hornet's nest," which he felt no one else had the courage to do. From the beginning he made a pact with Rosales that whoever trailed in the polls by mid-November would concede his place to the other, which he soon did. But along the way,

"Count" Rausseo was able to say "in jest" many things that could not be said by supposedly serious people without facing a barrage of criticism from Chávez and his supporters through all media outlets.[3] Among the twenty additional candidates, all totally ignored by the media, were six women who campaigned on platforms emphasizing women's issues, a record number, and a seventh would have registered, but she was too young and lacked the necessary seventy-five thousand signatures.[4]

### Support for Chávez: The Role of the *Misiones* ⸙

Women who support Chávez belong to what is called the Bolivarian Force of Women (Fuerza Bolivariana), which has thirty, forty, or fifty thousand women members, depending on the source. They are organized in so-called meeting points, each comprising five or six women. Most of these women, even those who are well organized, like the members of Inamujer,[5] are not committed to—or even aware of—what feminists in Latin America and the Caribbean would consider a minimal women's agenda. They are committed to the defense of the "maximum leader" and the process he is leading, and above all to those programs that directly benefit them. These programs are not directed solely at women; they are intended by Chávez to reach the poor who have long been economically and politically marginalized. The government has declared the women of the Fuerza Bolivariana the "leaders of their communities and administrators of their homes."

The Chávez government has established twenty-five social programs, or *misiones*, and several more are planned, including one called Families without Violence. They include the Mercal program, which provides poor communities with food and other essentials at low prices, offering three meals a day in communal kitchens in the poorest communities. There are programs for medical and dental care, staffed by Cuban doctors and dentists (Barrio Adentro I, II, and III); for literacy training (Robinson I and II); for worker training (Vuelvan Caras); for high school (Ribas) and university degrees (Sucre); for cataract and other operations (Milagro); for loans to single women who have more than three children (Madres de Barrio); and for the financing, promotion, and distribution of various expressions of popular culture (Cultura). Women have benefited from redistributional programs timed to coincide with elections, such as the Christmas bonus for the Madres de Barrio, distributed a month before the December 2006 election date.

Chávez explained the origins of the *misiones* in a talk he gave at the Military Academy in November 2004. The inspiration came came when his poll numbers were sagging prior to the 2003 referendum and some polls were predicting he might lose. He decided to "go on the attack," to mobilize support "from below" against his (upper- and middle-class) opposition. An action and investigation team from the Central University of Venezuela (UVC) turned the concept of an "attack from below" into an immediate and massive flow of assistance to the most dispossessed sectors. In his speech, Chávez added that he had consulted with Fidel Castro, and that Castro had faith in the plan, "because if there is one thing I know how to do it is 'attack from below.'"[6] The early missions were obviously motivated by Chávez's desire to win the referendum, which he succeeded in doing. They have in fact improved the quality of life for the poorest Venezuelans in the large and medium-size cities, although this level of social spending based on the high price of oil may not be economically sustainable in the long run.

Women Activists and Women's Issues ⚜

In all the *misiones*, women take leading roles and are the primary beneficiaries. However, like the women of the opposition (who went back to the streets half a dozen times to support the opposition candidate, Rosales), the "mission" women have not mobilized for women's issues. Sexual and reproductive rights and discrimination should concern both the women who support Chávez and those who oppose him. But neither group supports the decriminalization of the voluntary interruption of a pregnancy or protests job discrimination against gays and lesbians. Neither is likely to know that AIDS is a disease not limited to homosexuals or that their partners could have infected them with one of the HIV viruses.

On November 25, 2006, the International Day against Violence against Women, the Venezuelan National Assembly approved the Organic Law on the Right of Women to a Life Free from Violence,[7] replacing a 1998 law that had run into legal objections from the government. The 1998 law had prescribed actions to separate an abuser from his victims, and even remove an abuser from the household where the crime was committed, but the Supreme Court (Tribunal Supremo de Justicia) annulled these measures at the beginning of 2006 on the grounds of their unconstitutionality. From the moment the government brought a petition to annul these provisions in 2003, women inside and outside the government began working together to draft a new law that would allow these protections without violating the 1999 Constitution. Women working in NGOs and women deputies of the National Assembly's Commission on the Family, Women, and Youth agreed on a new law,[8] which was approved in November 2006 and implemented by the president in March 2007.

Most women on both sides of Venezuela's polarized debate over Chávez and his policies remain unaware of the existence of the Organic Law on Social Security, which provides social security for housewives as called for by the 1999 Constitution and which was approved in December 2002, when the streets were still filled with demonstrators. They are even less likely to know about the Social Service Law, approved in 2005, giving housewives of retirement age who are "in need" a payment equal to 60–80 percent of the urban minimum salary.

The Organic Law of Suffrage and Political Participation stipulates that women must make up 30 percent of the nominees on party electoral lists, but women are not pushing for the law's implementation, and it has largely been ignored by male party leaders. The president of Inamujer has asked that this article be replaced by one calling for "parity" — that 50 percent of all those nominated for political office must be women, and that women's and men's names must alternate on the ballot to ensure that women make up 50 percent of those elected. These proposals have received some publicity because it is in the interests of politically active women on both sides of the political divide, whose political aspirations have been on hold since 2000, to support them. Three of the five principal members of the electoral commission (CNE) issued a statement supporting parity. But only the National Assembly has the authority to change the law, and in the end women gained fewer than 30 percent of the positions on the lists for the National Assembly elections in 2005.

On election day, the abstention rate was 75.5 percent, only slightly higher than is the habitual rate in Venezuela for nonpresidential elections (because most Venezuelans consider only the head of state important). Undoubtedly voters were confused by the fact that most of the opposition groups had withdrawn forty-eight hours before the close of the campaign — after the ballots had been printed and after the candidates had spent their savings to fund their campaigns. Yet even women from the diverse parties and groups that supported Chávez received only 20 percent of the seats, counting both delegates and alternates.

Despite these results, which violated the quota, women party activists from across the political spectrum did not object. Instead, they agreed that counting the women who had been nominated as alternates and allowing two men to be nominated if there were only two positions on a given list for a particular district would meet the quota. Chávez himself chose the candidates of his coalition from names provided by his supporters in each state. The women elected (in the end, 27 percent of the National Assembly) got their positions the same way the male delegates did: because they were on lists of groups loyal to Chávez and not for their commitment to women's issues.

This is not to say that *chavista* candidates ran against women's issues. On the contrary, the Law against Violence of November 2006, brought to the National Assembly by its Commission on the Family, Women, and Youth was approved unanimously and with support from both male and female deputies. It is striking, however, that women party activists, both loyalists and those from the opposition, did not oppose male control of the candidate lists. This suggests that women themselves think that women are less suited to politics, in spite of what the law says and the CNE advises. Yet these were the same women who went on radio and TV to educate women on their political rights. Machismo triumphed over a clear and explicit law.

The majority of women in the opposition National Front of Women (which has virtually disappeared since the opposition withdrew in 2005) and the majority of women from groups within the pro-Chávez Bolivarian Women's Force (which is working to be named the Venezuelan affiliate of the International Democratic Federation of Women, headquartered in Cuba) are unaware of the events just summarized, not because they are shut up in their houses but because they are mobilized to support causes that do not include any women's demands, that is, to support or bring down the president. For this reason some feminists have suggested that Venezuelan feminists need to return to the consciousness-raising groups of the 1970s to regain the understanding we had then of how discrimination works and of how women let it happen.

The women of the political parties in power from 1958 to 1998 were able to meet and work out common positions despite their differences because they listened to each other. They included many who are now inside or support the Chávez government. This mutual trust across party lines survived many difficult tests and allowed women to cooperate on specific issues (like violence against women and the 50–50 rule for women's representation) although not on all (such as abortion and sexual choice). They were able to talk to one another openly yet to maintain their principles. In the fight to preserve the controversial measures of the 1998 law on violence against women and in support of the new law in 2006, for example, women party members were as active as the women who had been elected to the National Assembly and the feminists in universities.[9]

But the will of the core activists to act as a group is weakened each time it becomes clearer that Venezuelan women appear to be resigned to their inequality, fighting for or against Chávez rather than for the democratic goal that had united them since Venezuela returned to democracy in 1958.

The Core Today: New Challenges for Feminist Activists ✦

I have been an active member of the small group that constitutes the activist core. Our work has been made more difficult by the need to mediate between new groups that are closer to the Chávez government (including Clase Media Revolucionaria, Revista Feminista "Matea," Movimiento de Mujeres "Manuelita Sáenz," Colectivo "Mujer tenía que ser") and those from opposition parties (including Acción Democrática, COPEI, Movimiento al Socialismo, Proyecto Venezuela, Bandera Roja) and from other opposition organizations, including the National Women's Front, of which Women Democrats United (Democráticas Unidas) and Women for Freedom (Mujeres por la Libertad), among others, are members.

The core has always been able to mobilize more groups for some issues than others. But since 1998, and particularly since 2004, it has been almost impossible to find opportunities to build agreement on a face-to-face basis, although like-minded people can connect using e-mail to support a particular issue, as was the case with the law on violence against women. Not all groups agree on the steps to be taken. For example, there is no consensus on decriminalizing abortion, so that the document submitted in favor of this change in 2004 required signatures to indicate who within each group supported it and who did not. Many opportunities have been lost when fewer than a dozen women show up at meetings; instead, we organizers return to our offices to find three dozen e-mail excuses. On other occasions, we have succeeded in getting signatures from fifty organizations by e-mail, but they were the signatures of the heads of the organizations only, not from the members, making it difficult to claim broad support. There was an e-mail consensus on the draft documents on penal reform that we presented to the National Assembly in January 2004, and on the agenda submitted to candidates running for the National Assembly in November 2005. However, statements produced by e-mail "consensus" are less representative and politically effective than positions arrived at by a face-to-face process.

With few exceptions, the bulk of the activist core today is made up of university professors, particularly by those at UCV in Caracas and at other universities, including the University of Zulia, the University of Carabobo, the University of the Andes, and public universities in Maracay (La Morita), Maracaibo, and Mérida. In 1985 a coordinating group of NGOs (the CONG) was created at UCV. Seven years later, when the CONG no longer existed, a group of professors who had been part of it and women from other organizations proposed the Center for the Study of Women (CEM at UCV), finally established in May 1992 (between the two coups attempted by Chávez in February and November of that year). In 2002 a master's program in women's studies was added to the Faculty of Economic and Social Sciences at UCV.

Old patterns of communication between civil society and the state are now under stress. The CONG as it was created in 1985 did not include women representatives from the government. In 2003 some "femocrats" in legislative and executive positions tried to create a similar group of women's organizations that would also include government representatives. This proposal did not get off the ground, but there has been a long tradition of formal and informal agreements between government "insiders" and women activist "outsiders" in Venezuela, and feminists have found diverse ways to influence the political agenda.

Today, however, there is no point of connection between femocrats and women's NGOs. When women in the core connect with women in government, it is usually to make specific requests to Inamujer and to the National Assembly's Commission on the Family, Women, and Youth. In Venezuela's highly polarized environment, public universities have provided the best setting for women in government to exchange opinions with women in opposition NGOs and to connect with various organizations that assist women but have no political affiliation. These meetings have allowed women in government to plan programs that, if not fully consensual, are at least not contradictory or exclusionary.

As a group, we are now proceeding cautiously. The cross-party confidence that sustained the core activists does not extend to male political leaders or to the men who control the unions and other political groups in the Venezuelan political system. Today, it would be dangerous to project an image of women united to support the 50–50 rule or to decriminalize abortion. It is necessary for us to work silently, at the base, where no one takes media photos or invites us to talk on TV, to become consultants to international organizations, or to advise those who must make decisions on legislation affecting women.

New Alliances? ⚜

Although they share a commitment to the academic programs and to equality and equity between the sexes, the academics who proposed and worked toward the legislative changes outlined above have had differing responses to the political events shaping Venezuelan politics today. The Central University of Venezuela became a meeting place for organization women from both poles, women from autonomous groups (without connections to political parties), and new and old feminist militants.

Between 2004 and 2006 there were about twelve meetings of what has come to be called the Women's Assembly at UCV and at Los Chaguaramos in Caracas. Among the Women's Assembly's accomplishments was a statement on the underrepresentation of women on the lists for the December 2005 National Assembly elections. Titled "The Story That Does Not End," the document concluded:

> We are sure that we will be accused, by the government and by the opposition, of giving support to "the enemy" by our support of the Constitution, of Article 144, and the CNE declaration [in support for the 50–50 rule], but we will run that risk. We are the women who do the dirty work of campaigns, and we are half the votes. We don't excuse ourselves from the responsibility we bear for the lack of women on party lists, from our failure to fight for our rights in our organizations, allowing the male elites to put together the lists. In fact, we believe that we have to win the battle inside ourselves to recognize ourselves as worthy, and not to concede, as we are

accustomed to doing, the places we deserve on our merit to the males in our lives who may be less qualified than we—the boyfriend, husband, father, and the leader. We should not just be good *compañeras*. No one gives up power without a fight. This is as true for political militants as for any other group. No one is going to simply hand power over to women. This has been clear since 1945, and nothing has changed in this regard. Therefore we have to take power bit by bit inside the organizations we belong to, rather than complain about our exclusion, as we are now doing, after the fact.[10]

Not all organizations that participated in our meetings signed this declaration. Other organizations, like the Venezuelan Federation of Women Lawyers (FEVA), AMBAR (the organization of sex workers that has been involved in AIDS prevention among women of the barrios of Central Caracas), and the Affirmative Union (an organization of Venezuelan gays, lesbians, transvestites, transsexuals, and bisexuals) may attend our meetings, but they have not brought their own demands to the table.

The activist core describes itself as committed to equality and equity, but it has left the resolution of disagreements between those who favor legal, political, social, and economic equality and those who emphasize the differences among women (by sexual orientation, class, ethnicity, age, and so forth) to some future point, after the goals we agree on have been reached. The core group did not take up the cause of lesbians, gays, and others, or of sex workers, or of any other group making specific demands except once, in the mid-1980s, when the group supported the demands of the Union of Black Women in its preparations for the UN Conference on Women in Nairobi. When someone from the Affirmative Union or from AMBAR attended a meeting of the Women's Assembly, they came to listen or to speak for a particular initiative. They never asked for the floor to begin a discussion of sexual or other forms of difference, much less to ask support for a cause of theirs except for a signature or to back a candidate for the National Assembly (as when, in the most recent election, two militant gays were on the ballot). These groups acted on their own, and they signed only their own petitions.

Whatever the future of feminist issues in Venezuela, the future for groups defending sexual orientation is even less promising. They face widespread prejudice. When a journalist on the state TV channel asked a group of deputies from government and opposition parties whether they would support a bill recognizing gay marriage, for example, both groups laughed out loud in unison. A collective letter protested that a state TV channel had been used to denigrate a marginalized group, but there was no overlap between the groups that signed that letter and the core signatories of the six-point women's agenda, discussed earlier.

At the end of 2006, aware of the changes taking place among feminists in the region, many of us in the core group began to think that perhaps the UCV could become a bridge between egalitarian feminists and those who support the recognition of sexual difference. A new organization, Against-Nature (ContraNatura), was active on the UCV campus, but its members had not responded to invitations they knew were intended to gain their support for our feminist egalitarian agenda rather than to provide a real opening for their concerns. A first step toward this opening occurred when differences of all types were discussed at the World Social Forum, held in Caracas in January 2007.

The National Assembly's passage of the Enabling Law in January 2007 (giving Chávez decree powers for eighteen months) provided the impulse for closer cooperation. On February 2, 2007, a new group was created, grupo ese. Heterosexual feminists and men and women LGTB activists have met weekly to understand each other's goals and have united around a common agenda to address the ongoing process of constitutional reform and to respond to the Enabling Law. It is very early to draw conclusions about what will result from these meetings, but grupo ese constitutes an important beginning. Yet from my experience as a women's movement activist at least since 1978, I would say that there are few reasons to think that grupo ese will survive. It was created to propose an agenda to the Constitutional Reform Commission, but the agenda was completely ignored by the commission and the National Assembly. The group itself is politically divided, with just under 50 percent of those voting in favor of both sets of reforms proposed by the Chávez government, and just over 50 percent opposed, yet nearly 45 percent of those who could vote abstained.

In the early hours of December 3, 2007, Chávez gave a press conference conceding that he had lost the vote and observing that more than 3 million Venezuelans who had voted for him in 2006 had abstained from voting in favor of the constitutional reforms. This seemed to us a strong and clear message that Venezuelans recognized the difference between the democratic choice of electing a president from a list of alternatives and giving this president all the powers he was asking for to carry out his vision of twenty-first-century socialism, which included extending the presidential term from six to seven years, with no limit on reelection. The vote offered some hope that Venezuela could remain politically open and pluralist, and that it would be able to maintain the feminist core and find new spaces in a democratic, if polarized, environment.

Notes ⚜

1   Those who have been heads of households for more than twenty-five years, who are not covered by any of the social security programs (of which there are some four hundred, both public and private) either on their own or as dependents, and who are duly registered with the Institute of Social Services. These criteria were developed by the Commission on Family, Women, and Youth of the National Assembly.

2   Women from both ends of the spectrum and those in between campaigned in 2005 against beer ads (by the brands Draft and Regional) that appeared on walls and in the media; in September 2006, we returned to the issue of newspaper ads for the Luvebras supermarkets. In all cases, the ads showed women without heads, offering parts of their bodies as a bonus to consumers of the product advertised. The new law against all forms of violence against women provides sanctions against media outlets that permit the use or abuse of stereotyped images of young or adolescent girls and women to sell any good or service. Since March 2007 Inamujer has pressed the matter and Chávez has referred to it on his Sunday TV program, saying that some billboards seem to be taken from the pages of *Playboy*. This kind of representation constitutes one of the types of violence against women under the law, and Chávez's advisors have made him understand that violence is not only physical but also symbolic.

3   Another candidate who withdrew at the last minute to support Rosales was Jesús Cabrera Infante, an evangelical who had headed the Fund to Guarantee Deposits and Protect Banks (FOGADE) under the Chávez administration and was accused of corruption in the National Assembly.

4   The 1988 election had a record-breaking twenty-three candidates. The six unknown women who nominated themselves or were nominated by electoral groups not known to the major women's organizations or to the media were: Brigida García, Carolina Contreras, Lourdes Santander, Venezuela Da Silva, Yudith Salazar, and Isbelia León. The young woman who did not succeed in registering herself was Belkis Ortiz. Before the opposition had decided on a single candidate, two other women had also put themselves forward: Cecilia Sosa, the former president of the Supreme Court, and Rhona Ottolina, the daughter of

a well-known Venezuelan television producer. Lourdes Santander, along with Angel Blanco, Enoés Sánchez, José Chávez, and Abaddes Vásquez, decided not to run but to support Chávez.

5 Inamujer has been made part of the new Ministry of Popular Participation and Social Development, which is led by a young communist, David Velásquez, the only communist in the cabinet.

6 From a transcription of the speech, read on Globovision's program *Grado 33*, August 8, 2006.

7 The term *organic* means a law that supersedes all others on the same subject.

8 Principally Gabriela del Mar Ramírez, an activist in the Middle-Class Revolutionary Movement; Flor Ríos from Chávez's party, the Fifth Republic Movement; and Lelis Páez from Patria para Todos.

9 Primarily Elida Aponte and Gloria Comesaña, of the University of Zulia; Carmen Teresa García, of the University of the Andes; Magdalena Valdivieso, Ofelia Alvarez, and Adicea Castillo, of the Central University of Venezuela (UCV); and Marbella Camacaro, of the University of Carabobo.

10 This document was signed by the Manuela Sáenz Women's Movement, Miranda; the Josefa Joaquina Sánchez Collective, Vargas; the Women's National Front; the Venezuelan Association for Sexual Choice (AVESA); the Woman Has to Be Collective; the Center for the Study of Women, UCV; the Women's Studies Program, UCV; the Women's Center Juana Ramirez la Avanzadora, Maracay; CEFORMAN (the Center for Training and Study of Women), Mérida; the Gender and Sexuality Studies Group (Gigesex), ULA (Universidad de los Andes), Mérida.

II

## ✢ LEGAL STRATEGIES AND
## DEMOCRATIC INSTITUTIONS ✢

# 4

# The Effectiveness of Legal Strategies in Argentina ✦

*Beatríz Kohen*

The restoration of democracy in 1983 and the constitutional reform of 1994 constituted milestones in the expansion of women's rights in Argentina and in the use of legal means to demand their enforcement. They also created new opportunities for citizen participation. In this essay I review key legislative changes related to women's rights and the legal instruments introduced to guarantee their defense, explore the ways in which Argentine women's organizations have used litigation strategies, and examine the barriers that continue to limit their use. I also suggest how women's groups might make more effective use of legal advocacy in the future.[1]

## Background: Democracy, Citizenship, and the Judicialization of Conflict ✦

The broad social, historic, and economic changes that Argentina has undergone since the return to democracy in 1983 have been marked by the coexistence of opposing tendencies (Sanchís 2006). A progressive expansion of citizenship rights to the general public and particularly to women went hand in hand with increasing social polarization, and unprecedented levels of social inequality, and a loss of social and economic rights (Abregú 2007). Democracy was reinstated in the context of endemic economic crisis, wild privatization, and exclusionary social policies. The state, frequently charged with corruption, was weakened, undermining the ability of the institutions of representative democracy to mediate among conflicting interests and to channel popular demands, as they had in the past.

This institutional crisis produced a vacuum partly compensated by the judicialization of social conflict, which transferred public demands from the executive to the judiciary. Democratic rule created a new role for the legal system, including providing a means to confront those in the military who had been responsible for the repression during the junta's rule from 1976 to 1983 (Smulowitz 1997). Despite economic and institutional crises, Argentina has had a stable democracy, with elected governments succeeding each other peacefully. However, political participation has remained very weak except during periods of social emergency, especially the economic crisis of 2001–2. There has been a dramatic loss of confidence in political institutions and political parties. At the same time, there has been an unprecedented growth of civil-society organizations, some of them devoted to making democratic institutions more robust by increasing transparency and government accountability and by fostering citizen participation.

While many described the form of democracy emerging in Argentina since the transition as "delegative" and "plebiscitarian," a process of constitutional reform introduced, seemingly paradoxically, profound changes in concepts and laws about gender equality. The recognition of the right of nondiscrimination and the creation of special legal guarantees enabling citizens to go to court to enforce their constitutional rights opened the way for new strategies of citizen participation based on litigation, and these have been used by groups seeking to reinforce women's rights.

A New Legal Context for Claiming Women's Rights ⁕

During the past several decades there have been very important advances and a gradual modernization of Argentine law regarding women and the family. Argentina signed the International Convention on the Elimination of All Forms of Discrimination against Women (CEDAW) in 1980, and it gained legal standing in 1985, although the Optional Protocol was not ratified until 2006. The process of ratifying the CEDAW in Argentina encountered strong conservative resistance, as some feared that ratification would open the door to other sensitive issues such as abortion.

When it signed onto the convention and through its participation in the

United Nations conferences that established new international norms with regard to gender, Argentina committed itself to a series of steps to achieve gender equality. Like other signatories, Argentina must present periodic reports on its progress in meeting its commitments to the CEDAW Committee. On the basis of these reports the committee can make recommendations and/or initiate special investigations, gathering evidence and drawing international and domestic attention to persistent problems. During the 1990s Argentina was often late in producing the required reports and, because these tended to emphasize the government's accomplishments and understate its shortcomings, a variety of civil-society organizations began to write so-called shadow reports to communicate relevant information to the CEDAW Committee.[2] As a result, UN and OAS (Organization of American States) agencies sent special reporters to investigate issues related to women's human rights, such as the traffic in persons, prostitution, pornography, and health (Bergallo and Motta 2005), which further provided a means to gauge the success of Argentina's legal reforms.

FAMILY LAW AND VIOLENCE AGAINST WOMEN

The transition to democracy precipitated a process of legislative reform aimed at eliminating gender discrimination, especially in family law. In 1985 two important laws were passed: the so-called law of filiation, which concerned the rights of "illegitimate" children, and the law of *patria potestad* (parental authority) on the rights and responsibilities of fathers and mothers. The law of filiation makes children born out of wedlock legally equal to so-called legitimate children. Under this law, a mother, as the representative of her child, can ask that the father legally recognize a child born outside marriage. If paternity is contested, the issue can be decided by a judge, aided by the law of *patria potestad*, which gives the mother the option to ask for DNA tests to prove paternity. The civil registrar can no longer distinguish between matrimonial and extramatrimonial children on birth certificates; the new status given to children born out of wedlock constituted the first legal challenge to the norm of the traditional matrimonial family (Birgin 2000; Torrado 2003).

A new law of civil marriage was enacted in 1987, making both spouses legally equal in divorce. When a marriage ends, the couple has two options: legal separation or divorce. Separation does not end the legal bond and therefore does not allow the spouses to remarry. Couples who have been married for at least three years can apply for a divorce by mutual consent. Adultery, attack on the life of the spouse or children, criminal offenses, desertion, and separation for a period of three years are also recognized as legal grounds for divorce.

The law of *patria potestad* gives both fathers and mothers the same rights and duties with regard to their children. In case of divorce, *patria potestad* is exercised by the parent who has custody of the child. Whether divorced or legally separated, both parents are responsible for child support, regardless of who has legal custody. Under the new law, both spouses share certain decisions that the husband previously had the sole legal right to make, including the establishment of the family residence. In marriage both spouses are bound by identical and mutual obligations, such as faithfulness, mutual assistance, and the provision of food for each other and the children. In the event of divorce both spouses are obliged to provide maintenance, although this obligation ceases when one of the spouses is living with a third party (Birgin 2000; Torrado 2003).

The 1987 law also affected the treatment of marital assets, which are now defined as an estate made up of each spouse's properties at the time of marriage along with any new properties acquired during marriage. Property gained by inheritance, donation, or legacy is not included. Each spouse has the right to manage his or her own property and the commonly owned goods obtained through their labor. Spousal consent is required to sell, encumber, or transfer jointly owned real estate, including the house where the children live, even if only one spouse owns it. The 1987 law is a milestone in granting women property rights, the latest advance in a process that began in 1926. An additional law gives a woman the right to decide whether she wishes to add her husband's surname to her own. Previously wives were required to use their husband's surname, preceded by the preposition *de* (of), implying that the wife "belongs" to her husband.

These family law reforms have proven quite effective in terms of achieving a more egalitarian treatment for men and women. However, there are still important issues that have not been addressed, including the rights of concubines (or second families, which are not uncommon in Latin America); partners in homosexual unions; and the issues raised by the use of artificial reproductive techniques (Harari 2005). In addition, women still face serious discrimination, particularly with regard to work. They must juggle family and work responsibilities with little help from men and without a public child-care system, and they must deal with employers who do not offer flexible work schedules to accommodate women's (or men's) family responsibilities. Whether or not women participate in the waged labor market, they perform a disproportionate share of domestic work. And although spouses are required to pay maintenance after separation or divorce, the law is not well enforced. This puts a double burden on women whose children usually live with them after a divorce and who must get jobs but are also responsible for all the unpaid labor of household and child care.

Women's groups engaged in several campaigns during the mid-1980s, when these laws were passed, to give women equal standing in family law. But Haydée Birgin (2000:156) and others have argued that, with the exception of the law revising *patria potestad*, family-law reform resulted more from the overall process of democratization than from pressures exerted by the women's movement. Nonetheless, the process has opened up new ways of defining women's interests and has established new channels for women's activism. Many women's organizations have emerged since the transition, and they have the potential to influence the media, universities, and public institutions, as well as to affect the legislative process. The National Law of Domestic Violence, passed in 1994, constituted a major victory for the feminist movement, which had campaigned for this legal tool for several years. Most provinces also changed their laws to address the crime of domestic violence during the 1990s, and in 1996 Argentina signed the Inter-American Convention on the Prevention, Punishment, and Eradication of Violence against Women (the Convention of Belém do Pará).

The law recognizes that domestic abuse is not a private problem but a public issue. It is enforced mainly by family-law judges with the support of public and private agencies such as public hospitals, the police, social services, schools, and other community associations. The law enables the victims of physical or psychological abuse by a family member to resort to the family-law courts, where the judge receiving the complaint may request an expert diagnosis of the family, remove the perpetrator of violence from the conjugal home, and forbid the latter's access to the victims' home, school, or workplace. If victims had to leave their homes for security reasons, the judge can order their return under safe conditions and can establish provisional regimes of alimony, custody, and visits.

Since 1983 official institutions for the promotion of women have been set up by democratic administrations in Argentina, including the National

Women's Council (Consejo Nacional de la Mujer) in 1992 and similar units at the provincial level. In general, however, they lack funding and receive little support from the women's movement. Yet they deserve credit for working alongside women's NGOs to get the 1994 domestic-violence law passed. A relatively new organization, ELA (Equipo Latinoamericano de Justicia y Género [The Latin American Group on Justice and Gender]) was established to promote the enforcement of women's rights through law and public policy, analyzing laws and public policies from a gender perspective and proposing institutional reforms to improve women's access to justice.

One way in which ELA has made a difference is by assessing how the changes in the Argentine political economy, culture, and law have affected women's lives. A 2006 survey of women living in Argentina's three largest cities (Buenos Aires, Córdoba, and Rosales), for example, shows that although men now more actively participate in taking out children (25 percent), taking them to the doctor (28 percent), and shopping (30 percent), women still do most of the domestic work. Women who do not participate in paid employment work thirty-seven hours a week on domestic chores, and women who work outside the home spend twenty-three hours on them. Hired domestic help does not have a significant impact and is mainly employed for cleaning the house in 11 percent of the cases and for washing and ironing in 7 percent of the cases (ELA 2007).

It is impossible to know the extent of domestic violence in Argentina as the government does not collect the necessary data. Yet violence against women continues to be the most significant violation of women's human rights. The ELA survey showed that a majority of interviewees saw family violence as a very serious problem for Argentine women. The government's failure to provide relevant information violates both its commitments under the CEDAW and a finding and recommendation by the CEDAW Committee. There are isolated local efforts but no national program to address violence against women, and extant legislation is not effectively enforced (Birgin and Pastorino 2005).

Domestic-violence laws have been successful in one sense: women now have the right to go to court and may receive justice when the family law judiciary responds in an effective and timely way. In 1995, according to the statistics provided by the Civil Upper Court, women brought 1,009 family-violence claims. By 2004 the number had risen to 3,000, which overwhelmed the system (Birgin and Pastorino 2005). However, many more women are barred from seeking legal redress by the lack of subsidized legal aid (Birgin 2006; Kohen 2006; Gherardi 2006).

POLITICAL REPRESENTATION

Women's political representation provides another example of legal progress for women, although a litigation strategy was critical to ensure the enforcement of Argentina's pioneering gender quota law. In 1991, under pressure from women politicians and with the strong support of President Carlos Menem, a gender-quota law (Ley de Cupo) was adopted; it required that all political parties nominate women to at least 30 percent of positions on their party lists during parliamentary elections. In 2002, following the precedent set by the Ley de Cupo, a proportional quota was set for women's participation in union leadership, from which women have been largely excluded. Quota laws were also passed for elective positions in most provincial electoral districts, but they have not yet been applied to appointments to executive and regulatory positions at the national or provincial level. As a result of the Ley de Cupo, Argentina ranks among the top countries in the world in terms of women's political representation, with levels between 30 and 40 percent.

Until recently the quota law had the effect of making the 30 percent quota a ceiling rather than a floor (Gherardi and Kohen 2005). By 2007, however, women's participation in Congress had risen considerably, to 42 percent in the Upper Chamber and to 36 percent in the Lower Chamber. The implementation of gender-quota laws did not proceed without difficulties. In several cases, parties placed women so low on their electoral lists that their election remained unlikely. Complaints were filed in local courts, and one reached the Inter-American Commission on Human Rights (IACHR), which led to a modification in the regulatory decree to ensure that parties would have to place women in winnable positions on their lists.

Beyond the numbers it is difficult to assess the effect of the quota law. Despite thirteen years of experience and the recognition of the need for affirmative action to ensure equal opportunity in political parties, women's participation in party decision making still falls short. Nor has the government taken an active role in promoting women's political participation or in monitoring the enforcement of the existing laws, although parties that do not comply face sanctions. The political parties treat women's equal representation as a marginal concern, as their platforms show.

Women have largely remained absent from decision-making roles in the executive branch as well, both at the national and local levels. The Néstor Kirchner (2003–7) administration increased the number of women in the cabinet, appointing women to head three of the ten ministries. (Kirchner's wife, Cristina Fernández de Kirchner, was elected president in October 2007.) Prior to Néstor Kirchner's presidency women had headed the ministries of Health and Social Development, but they had not been able to break into areas such as the economy, foreign affairs, planning and public investment, or security. Kirchner appointed women to head the ministries of Economics and Production, of Defense, and of Social Development. There were no women governors at the provincial level, however, and women served as vice governors in only four of twenty-four provinces. In 2005 women headed 8.5 percent of Argentina's twenty-one hundred municipal governments, but that number dropped to 7 percent in 2007.

Women's participation in the judiciary remains limited. No woman served on the national Supreme Court until 2004 when, in response to an institutional crisis, a new process of choosing Supreme Court magistrates was adopted that included gender representation and public participation in the nomination process, and two women were nominated under this system. In 2007, however, eight of twenty-five provincial supreme courts had no female members, and there were only 24 women (18.7 percent) among the country's 128 magistrates or high-level judges. Women experience both vertical and horizontal segregation in the judiciary. They occupy the lowest levels and are found in the less prestigious jurisdictions, such as the lower levels of the family and labor courts (Gherardi and Kohen 2005). Further, women constitute only 8 percent of Argentina's ambassadors and 6 percent of its consuls, and there are no women assigned to the multilateral organizations in which Argentina has permanent representation (Gherardi and Kohen 2005).

Although the effectiveness of the Ley de Cupo can be seen in the composition of the legislature and in the growing number of women cabinet ministers, few women occupy top positions in other areas of government. Governments could do more to make gender quotas part of a more integrated plan to incorporate women into public life by appointing them in all areas of government and including them among Argentina's representatives to international institutions.

Quotas have brought measurable progress in women's democratic representation, but equality seems more difficult to achieve in other areas. Argentina ratified the International Labor Organization (ILO) Conventions in 1987, and a clause establishing equal pay for equal work was incorporated into the Labor Employment Law. Housewives were integrated into the social security system along with domestic workers. Dismissal based on race, sex, or religion was made illegal, and legislators passed a law ensuring equality of opportunity in the workplace. Efforts have been made to give women job stability, including pregnancy leaves, but because these developments involve changing the behavior of the private sector, they have proven difficult to enforce (Bergallo and Motta 2005).

In statistical terms, the gender gap in economic participation has narrowed, yet working women's social rights have suffered important setbacks. During the past decade, unemployment and underemployment increased drastically, affecting both men and women (Pautassi 2005; Faur and Gherardi 2005a). Labor legislation has made work more precarious, reducing protections for both men and women workers. At present, women are more likely than men to be working in the informal sector, and there are persistent gender gaps in both income and positions attained. More than half of the Argentine female working population receives no labor benefits (Pautassi 2005).

The survey conducted in 2006 by ELA shows that in the three largest Argentine cities, only 50 percent of the female working population receive all the benefits established by law, while 19 percent receive some benefits and 31 percent none. Domestic workers, who constitute 14 percent of the female workforce in these cities, suffer the worst situation (ELA 2007). Women's massive incorporation into the labor force has not changed the fact that domestic and child-care activities remain their responsibility. The ELA survey shows how vulnerable working women are, and the difficulties they face in combining productive and reproductive work. In some cases, the women we interviewed said they must leave their children alone (4 percent) or take them to work (3 percent) because too few child-care centers, either private or public, exist. In Buenos Aires public nurseries account for only 1 percent of child-care facilities.

The CEDAW Committee and the Inter-American Committee of Economic, Social, and Cultural Rights have urgently requested the government to implement measures to protect informal workers, count domestic activities such as care work within national statistics, and address pay discrimination. One success in this area, achieved thanks to the implementation of affirmative-action measures, has been the increased presence of women in leadership roles in unions, an important innovation highlighted by the Inter-American Committee.

WOMEN'S HEALTH

Traditionally healthcare has been linked to employment, so Argentina's economic crisis, which produced more precarious and unstable employment conditions, led to a marked decline in healthcare for the general population. Many people who used to be treated in the private health sector have turned to the health services provided by the state. Statistics show noticeable increases in breast cancer, cervical cancer, and AIDS (Pautassi 2005). The ELA survey indicates that although 71 percent of the women with private health coverage had had all the appropriate gynecological health tests over the previous year, only 51 percent of women without private health coverage had done so. The public health system does not produce reliable data disaggregated by sex.

Feminist legal innovations in the health field have been concentrated in the area of reproductive health. Sexual and reproductive rights have been incorporated into Argentine law by fits and starts. When democracy was restored in 1983, highly restrictive laws, imposed first by the government of Isabel Perón in 1974 and then continued by the military dictatorship, prohibited all forms of contraception. The ratification of the CEDAW in 1985 opened the path to dramatic change. The restrictions were dropped, but it took some time for the national government to improve women's access to these rights (CEDES 2005). In 1988 the municipal council of the city of Buenos Aires initiated a program called Responsible Procreation that provided access to information on reproductive health and contraceptive assistance, and most provinces created similar programs between 1991 and 2003. But these programs varied greatly in terms of the kinds and the quality of services provided, and they did not coordinate with other social service agencies (CEDES 2005).

In October 2002 Congress approved a law creating the National Program of Sexual Health and Responsible Procreation, and the Ministry of Health began its implementation in May 2003. The purposes of the program, whose creators wanted people to make choices free from discrimination, pressure, or violence, were to enhance maternal and child health, to reduce infant and maternal mortality, to prevent undesired pregnancies, to promote adolescents' sexual health, and to detect and prevent sexually transmitted diseases, including AIDS. The program diagnosed and treated genital and breast pathologies and guaranteed universal access to information to foster women's agency when making decisions on their sexual health and procreation (Defensoría del Pueblo de la Ciudad de Buenos Aires, CEDES 2005).

The program has proven quite successful in promulgating knowledge about contraception and distributing contraceptive methods. Yet some problems persist. The statistics from the Ministry show that AIDS is increasing rapidly in the female population: in 1998 the ratio of men to women with HIV/AIDS was just over 14 to 1; by 2002 it was only 2.6 to 1. The increase in women's rates of infection is higher among younger women (between the ages of thirteen and twenty-four), where women are now becoming infected at a rate slightly higher than that of men (Faur and Gherardi 2005).

The average rate of maternal mortality in Argentina is 46 for every 100,000 births, with large regional variations (e.g., 197 per 100,000 births in the province of Formosa, and 9 per 100,000 in the province of Buenos Aires). Abortion complications account for 31 percent of maternal mortality. It is estimated that between five hundred thousand and seven hundred thousand abortions are performed in Argentina each year (Faur and Gherardi 2005), although induced abortion remains illegal in the country except when the life or health of the pregnant woman is at stake or when pregnancy has resulted from the rape of a mentally challenged woman. Emergency contraception (the so-called morning-after pill) is available in a few provinces, but little information has been made available about its benefits.

In its review of Argentina's progress, the CEDAW Committee highlighted the high percentage of pregnancies among adolescents in Argentina and emphasized the role of illegal clandestine abortions in maternal mortality (Birgin 2006). Yet the government has not taken any steps to modify the law criminalizing abortion, and there have been several cases in which women have had to go to court to receive even abortions permitted under the law. In a few cases the courts have been asked to authorize abortions clearly permitted under Article 86 of the Criminal Code but not required because of an extreme threat to the mother's health. So-called pro-life conservatives have used legal strategies to contest those requests and prevent abortions in such cases.

The Federal Education Law was written based on nondiscriminatory principles, including equality between men and women. Today women are statistically equal to men at all levels of educational attainment, and there are more women than men in higher education. Some additional gender issues have been taken into account in planning curicula, including the introduction of sex education (García Frinchaboy 2005). The issue of whether pregnant girls should be allowed to attend school provoked a national discussion that resulted in the passing of two very important laws in 2000 and 2002. The first extended the number of permitted absences from school for pregnant girls and allowed time off from school for breast-feeding mothers during the first six months after a child's birth. The second forbids school authorities to hinder the normal educational progress of any pregnant girl. Complaints with respect to other types of discrimination, such as sexual harassment or abuse, rarely occur (García Frinchaboy 2005). Although there is a law against sexual harassment in public employment and a bill to extend it to the private sector, feminists have not made this issue a priority.

Most women teachers work in primary and secondary education, with the percentage of women decreasing the more one advances in the hierarchy. Hidden curricula and unequal treatment in the daily life of educational institutions that lead to gender discrimination and diminished self-esteem for girls are not easy to identify and even harder to eradicate (García Frinchaboy 2005). The Inter-American Committee has urged the Argentine government to address these issues in educational programs, curricular content, and in the training of teachers (Birgin 2006), but, very few cases have been brought to the courts relating to discrimination in education.

International Conventions and Constitutional Reforms ⚜

The Argentine Constitution of 1853 established the principle of equality before the law, but the 1994 constitutional reform, inspired by a participatory democratic ideal, expressly incorporates the principle of equal opportunity for men and women and the right to nondiscrimination. It calls on the Congress to legislate and promote affirmative action ensuring the law's full enforcement. The 1994 constitutional reform marked a turning point in that it explicitly extended rights and guarantees to women and introduced the legal tools and mechanisms for the enforcement of all rights recognized by the Constitution and international human rights conventions.

With respect to family law in particular, the incorporation of human rights conventions into Argentine national law reinforces the family-law reforms analyzed above. Eleven international human rights conventions—including the UN Declaration of Human Rights, the International Civil and Political Rights Convention, the International Social and Economic Rights Convention, the Rights of the Child Convention, and the CEDAW—were incorporated into the national Constitution and made directly applicable in Argentina, and in 1996 Argentina signed the Belém do Pará convention on violence against women (Birgin 2000). Because the CEDAW is an international convention, its ratification by Argentina means that its articles can be applied directly. This has opened the way for women and women's organizations to use the courts to gain the enforcement of women's rights nationally, in the inter-American system, and through international courts.

During the 1990s many Argentine provinces also voted for new constitutions that incorporated the principles of gender equality and equal opportunity for men and women. The most recent (and most egalitarian) is the constitution approved for the City of Buenos Aires, which gained its autonomy in 1996. The Buenos Aires constitution sets out an ambitious egalitarian agenda. It bans any kind of discrimination that could lead to segregation in terms of race, ethnicity, gender, or sexual orientation; and it grants the right to be different. There is an entire chapter on sex equality. The document favors positive actions by the state to encourage equality in both the public and private spheres (chapter 9, Articles 36, 37, and 38), including access to public posts and the management of fiscal resources. It forbids political parties to have more than 70 percent of persons of one sex on party lists and, in an effort to avoid the problems encountered with the national quota law, requires that no more than three persons of the same sex be listed consecutively.

The constitution calls on the legislature of Buenos Aires to act to ensure equality between women and men and to carry out educational programs with a gender perspective, especially in the areas of human rights and sexual education. In the area of reproductive rights, the city's constitution gives couples the right to make reproductive decisions and mandates the provision of legal contraceptives; the state is obliged to provide comprehensive pregnancy, delivery, and postpartum care. The city's legislature passed laws on the "equality of opportunities and treatment" of women on reproductive rights in part because of efforts by women's groups. Yet to date the enforcement of these laws has remained uneven. There are budgetary provisions to finance the requirements of the Law of Reproductive Rights, which seems to be running quite smoothly. By contrast, there has been very little effort to ensure that women have equal opportunities, which requires a profound reorientation at all levels of the city's administration. There is no agency to monitor enforcement and no budget line. Thus far the main criticism leveled against the Buenos Aires government is that it has made no new professional appointments to address the new constitutional requirements.

Litigation as a Feminist Strategy ✦

The legal reforms that accompanied the return to democratic government in Argentina brought the issue of equality between the sexes into public view, giving rise to a critical awareness of the way social institutions work and of the gap between laws and enforcement. Although few laws now discriminate, a wide gap exists between rights granted and rights effectively protected (Birgin 2000). Recognizing citizen participation as necessary to an egalitarian democracy, the Constitution includes collective rights and guarantees for their full enforcement (Article 43). As a part of that process, citizens may make claims before a court of law when their rights are either under threat or violated by the state or by a private individual. This guarantee, called *acción de amparo* (literally, a "claim for protection"), constitutes a summary proceeding that allows citizens, either individually or collectively, to take legal action to demand the restoration of a constitutional right that is threatened or violated. This fulfils democratic and participatory ideals and grants citizens an important role in determining the impact of governmental actions.

The 1994 constitutional reform and the constitution of the City of Buenos Aires introduced a vast new menu of possibilities for citizen participation in government decision making, including institutional tools such as popular initiatives, referendums, and public hearings. There is a constitutional recognition of the right to free access to public information, and the individual and collective *amparo* gives citizens the right to access national and international jurisdictions, while ombudspersons are charged with the responsibility to ensure that the state respects citizens' human rights.

The explicit intent of these reforms was to move beyond a concept of democracy limited to the sporadic act of voting. As Daniel Sabsay (2000) maintains, the Argentine constitution aims to create a governance model that can compensate for the shortcomings of representative democracy, increase transparency, and render the administration accountable. It is designed to improve the relationship between citizens and their representatives and to complement other participatory strategies such as citizen lobbies, which were adopted by local human rights organizations even before the return to democratic rule. Ideally, citizens can use these mechanisms to make authorities accountable, challenge the legality of government actions, and demand that public institutions fulfill their obligations. Citizens can bring cases that create new precedents, introduce themes in the public agenda, and promote respect for human rights. When citizens challenge the laws or seek to change the ways they are interpreted, both civil society and democratic institutions are strengthened and citizens gain a sense of their own agency (Varas 2000:21–34; Saba and Böhmer 2000a:15–36; Böhmer and Matus 2000:489–520).

The neoliberal economic policies adopted by Argentina in the 1990s shifted decision making to the private corporate sphere and limited the role of the state, dramatically reducing the capacity of traditional political institutions to address social conflicts and shifting power to the courts. Judges are now called on to solve matters formerly addressed by stronger and more representative political institutions, such as unions, political parties, or social movements. In Argentina judges have the power to decide the constitutionality of substantive law, including any law that violates the right to equality, and they can penalize human rights violations.

In the mid-1990s, inspired by the work of the American Civil Liberties Union (ACLU) and the success of litigation strategies in the United States, the United Kingdom, Canada, and the European Union (Bergallo 2007), several young lawyers joined in a movement to use the courts to promote the public interest. Often educated at U.S. universities and with strong ties to human rights NGOs, they saw an opportunity to bring together various personal, political, and professional interests using litigation to promote fundamental rights and to change the legal culture. In their view, virtuous strategic alliances between human rights organizations, groups of committed lawyers, and the media would give victims of discrimination the opportunity to demand the enforcement of their rights.

Argentina's civil legal system differs quite markedly from the common law system in place in the United States and Britain. Under common law, a decision becomes a precedent for all similar cases brought under a law. In Argentina, actions to challenge a law must be brought by individuals or groups of citizens, and in general the effects of the ruling apply only to that particular case. Citizens can use the broad powers of judges to claim their rights and defend the public interest, but legally judges can only declare a law unconstitutional in a specific case. This means that individuals and organizations must continue to bring cases before the courts, which requires active citizens who are knowledgeable about their rights, willing to exercise them, and able to give their time, energy, and often their financial resources to do so. Despite the hurdles, however, litigation strategies can have a real impact. Although the weight of precedent is less in Argentina, particular decisions often become incorporated into legal discourse and may be used as doctrine in legal arguments. Litigation can bring issues onto the public agenda and, even when cases are lost, they can raise public awareness and orient legislatures, public officials, and the media toward themes they need to address.

Initially, the human rights–oriented litigators did not recognize women's groups as important potential clients, and women's organizations did not demand otherwise. Because Argentine women in general tend not think about their daily problems in terms of the language of rights, few saw how the new laws could help them put forward their collective demands. The necessary connections between activist lawyers and women's groups have only just begun to form. The government has provided an opening for women through its ratification of international human rights conventions. The litigation strategy has the potential to strengthen both the women's movement and the judiciary, promoting the public interest and the rule of law and thereby reinforcing democratic legitimacy (Böhmer and Matus 2000:489–520).

To date, however, Argentine women have made relatively little use of litigation. This is not because they have nothing to contest. Legal barriers to women's equality have been removed, but women still face invisible barriers, endemic discrimination, and the weak enforcement of laws that do exist. The proverbial glass ceiling remains unchanged in both the public and private sectors and, although Argentina now has a female president, women are generally marginalized from decision-making roles in both government and business (CELS et al. 2002; ELA 2005). Women are the main victims of violence and sexual assaults, and they suffer sexual harassment, which has remained a largely invisible issue. Women are the most affected by the conditions of informal work, and they constitute the majority of domestic workers.

They lack full sexual and reproductive rights and suffer the ill consequences of illegal abortions performed under conditions that risk their health. These inequities can become cumulative when women are further marginalized by class, ethnicity, sexual orientation, and disability.

Although there are many gender units in different government departments that are charged with promoting and monitoring policies for women, they vary in quality and effectiveness. Their budgets are small and their infrastructures weak, and there is almost no coordination among them or with other governmental agencies. They have not had consistent support from presidents or political parties. As a consequence, they have proven quite ineffective in producing relevant and reliable data or in promoting policies that would make significant changes in the lives of women. In 2004, for example, the CEDAW Committee was critical of the limited role played by the National Women's Council, which lacks cabinet status, and noted the lack of any gender perspective in the government's policies to reduce poverty, which were introduced after the economic crisis of 2002, when the number of Argentines living in poverty jumped from under 20 percent to well over 40 percent. The committee also noted that Argentina addresses women mainly as beneficiaries rather than as social actors who should be participating in the design, implementation, and evaluation of programs. It pressed the Argentine government to take a much more active role in supporting women's political and economic empowerment and called for a halt to actions that perpetuated stereotyped and sexist views concerning men's and women's roles (Birgin 2006).

More than a decade has passed since the national constitutional reform, but women's groups have taken little advantage of the legal mechanisms it offers, and they have rarely used the new instruments for citizen participation the constitution makes available to address their issues. At one point, the Public Defender's Office (*defensoría del pueblo*) of the City of Buenos Aires was very active in promoting and defending women's rights, but women's issues virtually disappeared from its agenda when the government changed in 2004. In Argentina as elsewhere in the region, women's agendas often depend on the personal priorities of political leaders and appointees. When the women's movement failed to respond to the change, they lost an important institution that had proved it could be instrumental in promoting women's rights.

The human rights section of the Public Defender's Office of the City of

Buenos Aires was particularly vigorous in working toward the resolution of various issues related to sexual and reproductive rights such as sterilizations, anencephalic pregnancies, and adolescents' access to information about sexuality and contraception. It filed complaints against hospitals that denied patients procedures granted by law, and the health secretary passed several important decrees, for example, ordering doctors in the city's public hospitals to perform fallopian tube occlusions when the health of the mother was at risk and to provide information about contraception to young men and women, even if they arrived unaccompanied by parents.

The Public Defender's Office has legal standing to take cases to court for citizens whose rights have been violated and to force public institutions to comply with the courts' rulings. Even the implicit threat that a legal action might be initiated has had the effect of promoting normative changes. But when compared to the litigation activities undertaken by environmental or consumer organizations, the complaints filed by women's groups have remained relatively few. More disturbingly, conservative and so-called pro-life groups quickly saw the usefulness of these participatory options and have used the courts to resist the expansion of women's reproductive rights and to deny women equal access to education. Women's groups have focused on lobbying to change the laws rather than using the courts to demand the enforcement of laws already on the books, apparently more interested in the symbolic aspects of legal change than in using litigation to advance women's rights in practice. Lack of information about the law, the barriers confronting those who try to gain access to the justice system, especially poor women, and a widespread lack of confidence in the justice system present additional reasons why litigation strategies have remained relatively unused, despite their immense potential.

How well has the litigation strategy worked? It is easier to document changes in judicial discourse than in legal practice. Paola Bergallo (2007) argues that Argentine courts have not contributed as much to a more progressive discourse of gender equality as their counterparts have done in other countries. My research takes a different approach, documenting women's initiatives and tracing several specific cases in which women have used the legal system to further their rights. A fully inclusive list would require systematic research across jurisdictions and would be very difficult to carry out because Argentina has a federal system and there is no registry that documents the cases brought before the courts. I have based this account on information I gathered through interviews with human rights and women's organizations and from researching Web pages and the press.

The cases can be divided into two major types: cases decided by international courts after the exhaustion of domestic resources, and cases decided by domestic courts. Among the latter I have found examples in a range of areas: political and economic discrimination, family law and domestic violence, education, sexuality, and reproductive rights.

International Cases ⚶

Perhaps the most important international case was brought by María Merciadari de Moroni Morini (see also Marx, Borner, and Caminotti this volume), who filed a petition in 1994 before the Inter-American Commission on Human Rights (IACHR) to enforce the provision in the gender-quota law that women should occupy winnable positions on party lists. She argued that the Argentine Republic had violated her rights to due process, to participate in government, and to judicial protection set forth in the American Convention on Human Rights because, on the list of six candidates running on the Radical Civic Union (UCR) party ticket for election as national deputies from the province of Córdoba, one woman was placed fourth on the list and a second woman sixth, a violation of the quota law and its governing decree, which required that two women be listed among the first five positions. When the Supreme Court denied her appeal, the IACHR declared the case admissible and placed itself at the disposal of the parties for the purpose of reaching a settlement. On March 8, 2001, the parties signed an agreement in Buenos Aires, based on a 2001 presidential decree (#1246), that ensured women would be placed in winnable positions and provided effective sanctions in cases of noncompliance. This ruling has proven critical in making Argentina's electoral quota law the most successful in the region.

Two other cases have been brought to the IACHR. The first was brought by a woman and her daughter who were subjected to intrusive search procedures, including vaginal inspections, when they visited the husband/father in prison. Argentine lawyers and Human Rights Watch took their case before the IACHR in 1990, after an Argentine judge had declared that the inspections were appropriate to maintain the security of the prison. The petitioners argued that the inspections violated several provisions of the Inter-American Convention on Human Rights, including Article 24 against the discrimination of women. After a very long process, in October 1996, the commission concluded that by imposing an unlawful condition for the fulfillment of their prison visits, the State of Argentina had violated several rights guaranteed in the convention, including personal integrity, protection against attacks on personal honor and dignity, protection of the family, and the right of a child to be protected by the state. The commission recommended that the laws and regulations be changed and that the women receive adequate compensation.

A second case, *Rosales v. Argentina*, involved domestic violence and was originally tried in a provincial court that allowed the sexual history of the wife to be considered as attenuating evidence in deciding how to punish a husband who strangled and nearly killed her. The petitioners claimed that the prosecution had violated the wife's right to equality and nondiscrimination, as well as her right to privacy, noting that she was not allowed to defend herself or contest the accusations made regarding her honor and private life. In November 2005, lawyers from the Center for Legal and Social Studies (CELS), a legal and human rights NGO, filed a petition for her, alleging that Argentina had violated rights recognized in several articles of the American Human Rights Convention, the American Declaration of the Rights and Duties of Man, and Articles 4 and 7 of the Convention of Belém do Pará. In February 2006 the IACHR announced it had received the case, a first step toward having the case considered by the commission.

Cases Brought before Domestic Courts ⸙

GENDER DISCRIMINATION

Various studies (Bergallo 2007; Lázaro and Fraquelli 2003; Minyersky 2001; Tula 2002) have found that as many as 116 complaints of political discrimination were brought under the quota laws in Argentine provincial jurisdictions from 1993 to 2003, with the largest number filed in the City of Buenos Aires. The number of cases fell sharply in 2000, after the regulatory decree was reformed as a result of the IACHR ruling. Most involved the placement of women's names on party candidate lists. Other cases included *Barcena v. IOMA* (1996) on the grounds that women in association of public employees (IOMA) were denied the right to free health benefits for spouses that male members of the association enjoyed. The Supreme Court agreed with the plaintiff. In a very different case, Elvira Bella sued the Argentine Shooting Federation for denying her the title of national champion in 1997, when she had the best score, on the grounds that shooting was a "male category." Bella was legally represented by the lawyers of the Association for Civil Rights (ADC) after the case was brought to them by a women's group, the Women's Social and Political Institute (ISPM), and she won her case in both the lower and the higher courts.

An employment discrimination case was filed by a women's organization, Mujeres en Igualdad (Women in Equality, MEI), and litigated by the legal clinic of the Law School of Palermo against Freddo, S.A., a traditional chain of ice cream stores that employed only men on the grounds that all employees had to perform tasks involving challenging physical labor and had to have knowledge of motorcycle mechanics in addition to serving ice cream. Therefore they were "protecting" women, not discriminating against them. The judge disagreed and ordered the company to hire only women until women constituted half of their workforce. When a progress report showed that the firm had hired 107 men and only 26 women, the company was ordered to pay fines that would increase each day the company was out of compliance. In another case, in 2004, a young mother of a four-year-old girl was barred from joining the army under a regulatory decree that those entering the army must not have children or other dependents under their charge. The case became moot after the Congress changed the law.

Several cases were brought involving educational discrimination. The legal clinic of the University of Palermo Law School and MEI filed a suit alleging that a city institution that trained physical education teachers offered more vacancies to men than to women candidates, and won their case. New laws guaranteeing that pregnant girls can continue to attend school were tested in several cases. In one case, in Formosa Province, a judge decided in favor of a family whose daughter was denied access to a Catholic school, producing an intense debate involving the provincial church authorities. But the case of *Parents' Association v. University of Córdoba* was brought with the opposite intent. In 2000 a group of parents of students of the Monserrat Secondary School, part of the National University of Córdoba, challenged admitting girls to a school that had in the past only admitted boys. The national Supreme Court decided in favor of the university, invoking the obligation of the government to provide equal public education for men and women, constitutional antidiscrimination principles, and the CEDAW as well as other international human rights treaties.

Sexual identity was the issue behind other cases of alleged discrimination. In one case, the petition of ALITA (the Association for the Struggle for Transvestite and Transsexual Identity) asking to be granted legal standing as a civil association was denied on the grounds that the association's objectives were against the common good. The case eventually went to the Supreme Court, which granted legal standing to ALITA after a two-year silence. In 2007 two leaders of the Argentine Lesbian Federation requested an appointment with the civil registrar of the City of Buenos Aires to get married. The civil registrar denied their request, arguing that under the Argentine Civil Code marriage applied to a man and a woman acting by mutual consent and not to two persons of the same sex, offering instead the possibility of civil union.

The petitioners rejected this on the grounds that the conditions of civil union in Buenos Aires are very restrictive. The Gay, Bisexual, and Transsexual Federation of Buenos Aires presented a fifty-page file, carefully prepared by a team of activist lawyers, summarizing the international cases that had led to the recognition of homosexual marriage in other jurisdictions, such as Spain and South Africa, to demonstrate that denying homosexuals the right to marriage was unconstitutional and violated human rights treaties. The case has received extensive coverage in the local press, and the petitioners have stated that if there is no reform of the marriage law, they will take the case to the Supreme Court and to the IACHR. The National Civil Court has yet to decide on the matter.

### REPRODUCTIVE RIGHTS AND ABORTION

Several cases involved reproductive rights, where the courts have become an arena of conflict between so-called pro-life and pro-choice groups. Over the past decade, the Argentine judiciary has taken many decisions as a result of actions filed by attorneys general and by antiabortion groups and individuals, although the latter have no clear standing to stop abortion procedures. Injunctions and detentions are often based on incorrect interpretations of the law, encroach on the legislative power, and are sometimes decided in clear contradiction to the existing law and in violation of Argentina's obligations under international conventions. This has created serious ambiguity about the scope of exemptions from criminal liability in abortion cases under the Argentine Civil Code. The situation has made doctors very cautious, and women are often denied abortions to which they are legally entitled. Doctors, fearing the possibility of criminal prosecution, often fail to seek judicial authorization to perform abortions (Gherardi and Kabusacki 2006).

Abortion is illegal in Argentina, as noted earlier, except under certain limited conditions, yet it is estimated that half a million abortions are performed in Argentina each year, and postabortion complications are one of the country's leading public health problems. Middle- and upper-class women can pay private physicians to perform relatively safe abortions, but poor women resort to dangerous procedures. Fifty-five thousand women each year end up in public hospitals due to complications arising from clandestine abortions. The distribution of power between the opponents in this battle is very unequal due to the association of pro-life groups with the Catholic Church, large legal firms, and other traditional power centers in Argentine society.

According to the 2006 ELA survey, 47 percent of the women interviewed support the decriminalization of abortion under certain restrictions, while 31 percent believe it should not be considered a crime, and only 19 percent believe it should remain illegal. Many of those who favor some kind of decriminalization are Catholic: 49 percent of less committed, and 22 percent of more committed Catholics agree with some form of decriminalization. Most consider abortion legitimate when a woman is pregnant because of sexual assault, when there are malformations of the fetus, or when a pregnant woman feels she will be unable to care for the baby properly because she is a minor, already has many children, or because of other economic reasons. Although women's groups have been militant in demanding the decriminalization of abortion under specific circumstances, the Catholic Church remains strong in opposition. Various bills decriminalizing abortion have been prepared by members of congressional commissions, but they have never made it to floor debate.

Other legal cases address whether contraception or abortion should be legally allowed to mentally challenged women, as called for under Article 86 of the Criminal Code. In 2001 the national Supreme Court reversed a first-instance decision denying an IUD (intrauterine device) to a young girl who had been raped, invoking international human rights norms and the Beijing Conference Platform. That same year, in response to the appeal interposed in representation of the unborn baby, the Supreme Court, using medical arguments, confirmed a decision of the Superior Court of the City of Buenos Aires to authorize an induced delivery of an anencephalic fetus, but it insisted that it had not granted permission to perform an abortion.

Another case in Bahia Blanca in 2003 involved a young girl who had been raped by her father and was three months pregnant but who had been denied an abortion by a judge, although Article 86 of the Criminal Code allows a "therapeutic abortion" if a pregnancy endangers the woman's life or her health. The girl stopped going to school and threatened to commit suicide, refusing to eat or get medical checkups. Psychologists confirmed that suicide was a real danger, and the official public defender recommended that the abortion be allowed because the girl had been raped and because the pregnancy might endanger her life. The Ethics Committee of the hospital and the Juvenile Court supported the request, but the judge who had originally denied the abortion rejected it and ordered the Juvenile Court to monitor the case closely. At her meeting with the judge, "Miriam" fell to her knees, imploring: "Please help me, otherwise I will not live. You are all grown-ups, you must help me." But instead of granting the girl the right to terminate the pregnancy, the judge decided that she should undergo psychological treatment and that social support be provided for the girl and her family. In this case, both the judge and the physician (by refusing to act without the judge's authorization) disregarded the law, making it impossible for the girl to terminate a pregnancy within the time limit allowed for therapeutic abortions.

Other recent cases in this area involve a mentally disabled girl who was granted the right to have an abortion but denied one by the physician at the hospital, saying a pro-life group had obtained a judicial order against it. The mother then initiated a new action before the supreme court of Mendoza province, which authorized the abortion and ordered it to be carried out in a public hospital without disclosing the name of the hospital or of the physicians involved. In 2006 a physician refused to perform an abortion on a mentally handicapped girl who was two months pregnant. The mother, represented by the public defendant, petitioned for authorization under Article 86 on the grounds that the pregnancy seriously endangered the girl's life and that the fetus was likely to be physically impaired as a consequence of the medication the girl was taking to control her mental illness. Under the strain, the girl eventually had a spontaneous abortion. Ginés González García, the minister of health, has used the case to argue that the law allowing an abortion to a mentally handicapped woman should be enforced.

In a third case that year, a mother's request that an abortion be approved for her mildly mentally handicapped daughter who had been raped and was two and a half months pregnant was denied by a lower Buenos Aires court and by the civil court, which invoked Article 4 of the Pact of San Juan Costa Rica, which declares that human life should be protected from the moment of conception. However, the Buenos Aires Provincial Court ruled that the exceptions to the abortion ban do not violate the constitutional provision protecting children's rights, and the supreme court of Buenos Aires Province ruled that a mentally impaired rape survivor could undergo an abortion under the exceptions to the Argentine law banning abortion. The Corporation of Catholic Lawyers is considering an appeal of the ruling to Argentina's Supreme Court on the grounds that the provincial supreme court had decided to kill an "innocent person." A coalition of several women's organizations has also participated in the controversy, presenting an amicus curiae brief before the supreme court of the province of Buenos Aires.

In February 2007 a judge authorized an abortion for a fourteen-year-old girl who had been raped by her father, a decision unanimously confirmed by the Civil Criminal Court of Appeal, but in March the girl had a spontaneous abortion as a result of nervous stress.

These cases pit the human rights of the unborn child against the sexual and reproductive rights of women, both of which are protected by international human rights conventions. Argentine law allows therapeutic abortions and sterilizations when the pregnancy constitutes a serious threat to a woman's health. In 2004 a thirty-seven-year-old woman who had just given birth to her sixth child was allowed to have her fallopian tubes tied after the hospital refused to do so, in a case filed by the ADC. In 2005 a woman with a heart condition that threatened both her life and the health of her fetus was allowed to have a therapeutic abortion in a provincial hospital, although a local judge tried to stop it.

Pro-life groups have used the courts to attack the government's National Program of Sexual and Reproductive Health and Responsible Procreation. An organization called Mujeres por la Vida (Women for Life) demanded that the law establishing the program be declared unconstitutional. An acting judge granted their petition, but in March 2003, the Federal Upper Court of

Córdoba granted an appeal by the Health Ministry on procedural grounds. Mujeres por la Vida appealed the decision to the Supreme Court to stop the national program.

In 2001 the League of Housewives, Consumers, and Users, a pro-family association, contested two articles of the Law on the Sexual and Reproductive Health of the City of Buenos Aires on the grounds that these articles violated international human rights treaties and the law of *patria potestad*. The petition was rejected by the Higher Tribunal of the City, and the Supreme Court refused to take it up, leaving the more progressive Buenos Aires city legislation intact. Pro-life forces gained a victory, however, in a case involving the emergency contraceptive pill. The group Portal de Belén (Bethlehem Gate) petitioned to prevent the production, distribution, and advertising of the Immediat pill on the grounds that it is abortive, and the national Supreme Court approved the petition.

The Prospects for Litigation Strategies: Practical and Philosophical Issues ⸙

One reason Argentine women have brought so few cases before international courts is because few women's organizations have the credentials to present reports or file complaints before these courts, which makes it less likely that cases will be taken to the international level. However, the approval of the CEDAW Optional Protocol in 2006, which promotes such actions, should increase the number of cases. In my view, Argentine women have made little use of legal strategies because they lack confidence in the legal system, are unaware of their rights, and face serious hurdles in accessing the justice system. In addition, the connections between women's groups and human rights organizations are weaker than they should be.

Argentines in general do not trust the judicial system. Opinion polls show that confidence has been declining since the country returned to democracy, ranging from 30 percent at its highest to 18 percent (TNS-Gallup Argentina 2006; FORES 2005–2006). The lack of legal aid and the gap between the legal system and the realities of women's lives makes the situation worse for women. This gap could be mitigated, as it has been elsewhere, by training and support for those who provide legal aid. Legal training in Argentina does not incorporate the study of gender, and there is no program to make the judiciary more sensitive to women's issues.

Catalina Smulowitz (2001) has argued that social factors strongly determine the kinds and levels of citizen participation. Using the mechanisms of participatory democracy—including going to court to defend one's constitutional rights—requires knowledge, money, and personal effort, all scarce resources. Feminist political scientists have written much about the difficulties women face in the exercise of their citizenship rights (León 1994; Lister 1997; Jelin 1987, 1996; Phillips 1993, 1996; Fraser 2000; Moreno 2003). They have emphasized that conceptions of political participation in the West, which appear gender-neutral, in fact make the male citizen the norm and thus block, obscure, and trivialize women's ways of participating. Classical and Enlightenment conceptions of citizenship emphasize the distinction between the public and private spheres, assigning women to the household and excluding them from the political domain. It is not enough, however, to just "add women," as women differ from one another. A concept of citizenship that effectively includes women will have to transcend the limits imposed by representative democracy as conventionally understood.

Feminists have been drawn to notions of participatory democracy, in part because of its implied promise to democratize spheres previously defined as private. But any such model must take into consideration how gender impinges on the possibilities for political activism. Giving women primary responsibilities in the domestic realm limits the time they can devote to public participation, while their economic dependency deprives them of the autonomy, self-esteem, and resources necessary to full participation. Therefore feminist scholars have advocated for the inclusion of difference within conceptions of equality, and for multiplicity within the category "woman." Some have argued that women's political participation and the use of legal strategies simply play into patriarchal oppression. But women's organizations advocate women's formal and informal participation and think that, on balance, such participation strengthens women's ability to shape policies and increases women's self-esteem (Moreno 2003).

The 2006 ELA survey found that the level of Argentine women's social participation is very low: 72 percent of the women from the largest Argentine cities do not participate and have not in the past participated in any public institutions outside the home. Rather, women are active in religious organizations (46 percent), voluntary charitable organizations (15 percent), community or hospital community associations (11 percent), neighborhood associations (8 percent), political parties (8 percent), professional associations

(5 percent), and unions (4 percent). Only 3 percent are active in women's groups.

Many Argentines reject contemporary feminism as anathema, which means that many women strongly committed to women's progress are reluctant to call themselves feminists. Most of the women interviewed in the survey think that poverty, unemployment, public education, and public health are far more important issues for women than women's subordination. Since the 2002 economic crisis that shook Argentina to its core, women have taken leading roles in *piquetero* (street protest) and other popular movements (Moreno 2003; *Contrainforme 2002*; Auyero 2003), although their numbers are small and the importance of these mobilizations has tended to diminish over time.

The ELA data show that women have a little knowledge of their own rights. For instance, only 32 percent know of the existence of the quota law, and only 40 percent are aware that there is a law protecting them from family violence. Women are more aware of their reproductive rights: seventy-two percent know that the state has the obligation to provide information about contraception and actual contraceptive methods, and 66 percent are aware that the state has the obligation to provide clinical tests, such as Pap smears and mammograms, at no cost to them. Women are more aware of these rights because they have been the subject of a series of public campaigns. This suggests that public campaigns can be effective in informing women about their constitutional rights, clarifying the obligations of the state, and making the public aware of women's legal capacity to demand the effective enforcement of laws.

Many Argentine women are not aware of gender discrimination, and those who are do not know how to counteract it. Sixty-two percent of the women interviewed believe that women have fewer opportunities to access top public positions, and 51 percent think they have fewer opportunities to reach the higher echelons of private firms. Fifty-one percent know that women are paid less than men for the same work, and 41 percent think that women have less of a chance to find a job than men. When asked whether women were ready to engage in political participation, only 5 percent declared that they were not; 27 percent said that they were prepared to participate in demonstrations; 34 percent were ready to attend public meetings to obtain a better picture of the conditions affecting women's lives, while 74 percent said they wanted to engage in dialogue and exchange information with friends and acquaintances to learn more about gender discrimination. Seventy-seven percent said they were ready to initiate complaints about concrete situations of discrimination before the relevant bodies, and 78 percent wanted to have more information about all areas of women's subordination.

Women's claims can easily be translated into a language of rights, and under democratic governments women's groups have learned to lobby. But the women's movement in Argentina has not made seeking justice through litigation one of its preferred strategies. Innumerable small organizations have appeared that use rights language and work on women's issues on topics such as violence or sexual and reproductive rights. There has been little co-ordination among them, however. Instead they compete for scarce resources and have few ties to human rights organizations or to the state. On reflection, given the fragility of women's groups, perhaps it is not surprising that they have not made extensive use of the litigation strategy; instead, it is remarkable that they have succeeded as well as they have.

## Conclusions ⚜

Despite the obvious advances in women's rights in Argentina during the past quarter century, many inequalities and forms of gender discrimination persist. Yet women have not made intensive use of a litigation strategy despite its successes, as can be seen from the cases brought before the courts under the new federal and provincial constitutions.

In the 1990s rights organizations did not pay much attention to women's demands. But over the past fifteen years these have progressively gained legitimacy, and connections between human rights organizations and women's groups have improved. Some organizations, such as the Center for Legal and Social Studies, the ADC, and the legal clinic of the University of Palermo Law School, have taken important steps to establish strategic alliances with women's organizations, which should improve the possibilities of using the courts to defend and enhance the enforcement of women's rights in the future.

Although they remain too few, several of the cases that have been brought have been quite successful, triggering press coverage and generating changes in laws and public policies. They show the potential for more sustained cooperation between women's groups and human rights organizations. There is increasing awareness of the need for protocols at the national level to avoid having decisions about abortion and emergency contraception repeatedly taken to the courts, itself a measure of the impact litigation has had in activating public debate. These examples should encourage women's groups to give more thought to legislative advocacy and the benefits of putting pressure on the government to implement its laws and policies, rather than leaving enforcement to the discretion of the executive branch. Feminists and women's groups must be prepared to pursue these opportunities and to improve the understanding of gender issues among human rights militants (Vázquez Sotelo n.d.). Argentine women's groups have been responsive when called on, but they have not taken a proactive approach. They would find the use of litigation strategies an effective complement to the other political strategies they deploy.

Notes ∿

1 I would like to thank María Julia Pérez Tort and Denise Fridman for help with research on the cases.
2 Among the groups contributing shadow reports in 2002 were CELS, CLADEM, FEIM, and Instituto Social y Político de la Mujer; in 2004 the contributing groups included ADEUEM, ACDH, CELS, FEIM, Feministas en Acción, Instituto Social y Político de la Mujer, and Mujeres en Acción.

# 5

## Violence against Women in Brazil ⚜

### INTERNATIONAL LITIGATION AND LOCAL ADVANCES

*Flávia Piovesan*

Using an international litigation strategy developed by human rights networks to mobilize domestic forces for change, the women's movement in Brazil has succeeded in winning an important victory for women's human rights. This essay looks at the case of Maria da Penha, whose severe injuries combined with the inaction of the Brazilian state alerted the inter-American system to the problem of violence against women in Brazil. The guilty verdict by the Inter-American Commission on Human Rights (IACHR) against the Brazilian government paved the way for a new law that addresses violence against women, providing stronger penalties and establishing a new social infrastructure to treat the victims of domestic violence and educate the public on the seriousness of this crime.

To put the case in context, I show the scope of the problem of violence against women in Brazil, for which the Maria da Penha case provides dramatic evidence. I examine the role of the women's movement in Brazil's transition to democracy, as well as its impact on the rights-oriented Constitution of 1988. The women's movement's efforts to bring the issue of violence against women forward, change the law, and hold their government accountable were strongly reinforced by international litigation and the support of transnational human rights groups. The Maria da Penha case illustrates the success, but also the dilemmas and challenges, that have accompanied the use of legal strategies to promote women's human rights, and it provides a window through which to view the quality of democracy in Brazil.

## The Maria da Penha Case ⊰

*I Survived to Tell My Story*—this is the title of the autobiographical book by Maria da Penha, a victim of two attempted murders by her then husband in her own home in Fortaleza in 1983. The shots fired at her while she slept, the attempt to electrocute her, and the many assaults she suffered throughout her marriage made her a paraplegic at age thirty-eight. Her husband was found guilty by a local court, but fifteen years later he was still enjoying his freedom due to successive procedural appeals against his conviction in a jury trial. The case offered a dramatic example of impunity and the ineffectiveness of the Brazilian judicial system in the face of domestic violence against women. In response, in 1998 the Center for Justice and International Law (CEJIL-Brazil) and the Latin American and Caribbean Committee for the Defense of Women's Rights (CLADEM-Brasil) filed a petition to the IACHR under the Organization of American States (OAS). In 2001, eighteen years after the crime, the IACHR, in an unprecedented decision, found the Brazilian state guilty of negligence and failure to take action against domestic violence (Piovesan and Pimentel 2002a:A3).

The Maria da Penha case provides insights into a crime that primarily affects women: domestic violence. The case clearly illustrates two hallmarks of this form of violence: the perpetrator of the crime that caused her to suffer from irreversible paraplegia was no stranger, but her own husband; and the physical and psychological scars caused by this violence were aggravated by impunity (IACHR 2001).

## Domestic Violence in Brazil and the Convention
## of Belém do Pará ⊰

Studies have shown the epidemic proportions of domestic violence in Brazil. According to a report by Human Rights Watch (1991),[1] of every one hundred women murdered in Brazil, seventy of these deaths occur within the scope of domestic relations. A survey conducted by Brazil's National Human Rights Movement reveals that two-thirds of men accused of killing women are their partners (National Human Rights Movement 1998). In Brazil impunity further abets this form of violence (*Jornal da Redesaúúde* 1999). It is estimated that in 1990, in the state of Rio de Janeiro, not one of the two thousand cases of aggression against women reported to the police resulted in the punishment of the accused. In the state of Maranhão, of the four thousand reported incidents, perpetrators were punished in only two cases (Americas Watch 2000:171).

Domestic violence occurs not only in the socially less privileged classes and in developing countries like Brazil but in virtually all classes and cultures across the globe. The United Nations (UN) committee on the Elimination of All forms of Discrimination against Women (the CEDAW Committee) finds that "family violence is one of the most insidious forms of violence against women. It is prevalent in all societies. Within family relationships women of all ages are subjected to violence of all kinds, including battering, rape, other forms of sexual assault, mental and other forms of violence, which are perpetuated by traditional attitudes." Further, a lack of economic independence "forces many women to stay in violent relationships" that put "women's health at risk and impair their ability to participate in family life and public life on a basis of equality." According to the UN, domestic violence is the principal cause of injuries in women between fifteen and forty-four years of age (CEDAW Committee 1992).

An important consequence of domestic violence is its impact on women's ability to earn income. According to the Inter-American Development Bank, one in every five women who miss work do so as a result of having suffered physical aggression (*Folha de São Paulo*, 21 July 1998:1, 3). It is estimated that domestic violence costs Latin America 14.6 percent of its gross domestic product (GDP), or some US$170 billion. In Brazil, the price tag attached to domestic violence is 10.5 percent of the GDP (National Feminist Health and Reproductive Rights Network 1999:paragraphs 54, 55).

In 1994 several countries ratified the Inter-American Convention on the Prevention, Punishment, and Eradication of Violence against Women (the Convention of Belém do Pará), the first international human rights treaty to focus on violence against women as a generalized phenomenon that affects all women regardless of race, class, religion, age, or any other condition. It was ratified by Brazil in 1995. The convention asserts that violence against women constitutes a serious violation of women's human rights and impairs or nullifies the exercise of other fundamental rights. It describes violence against women as an offense against human dignity and a manifestation of the historically unequal power relations between women and men. Violence against women is defined as "any act or conduct, based on gender, which causes death or physical, sexual or psychological harm or suffering to women, whether in the public or the private sphere." In other words, gender-based violence consists of any violent act directed against a woman because she is a woman or any type of violent act that affects women disproportionately.

## The Women's Movement in Brazil ⚜

The Maria da Penha case provides an example of the relationship between the women's movement and the process of democratization in Brazil. The Brazilian women's movement has not evolved in a vacuum; it has been part of and has responded to larger transnational trends. The connection between the local and global arenas has proven particularly significant for the issue of violence against women. The Maria da Penha case, which strongly conditioned the Brazilian state's response to the issue, shows one impact of the women's movement in Brazil and how its strategy of international litigation secured local advances.

The collapse of Brazil's twenty-one-year military dictatorship, which lasted from 1964 to 1985, unleashed a process of democratization. During the period of authoritarian rule, the regime suppressed the most basic rights and freedoms, engaging in systematic torture, arbitrary detentions, forced disappearances and political and ideological persecution. The armed forces, acting as an institution, seized direct control of all government functions. The year 1985 marked the start of the gradual process of transition to democracy.[2] Although the transition process began as a result of the political liberalization introduced by the military regime largely in response to its internal problems (Hagopian 1992:245; Martins 1992:82–83), the opposition forces of civil society hastened its collapse. New social actors and movements began to emerge, and their demands and claims further strengthened the process of democratization in Brazil.

In contrast to the abrupt transition that occurred in Argentina in the wake of the military defeat in the Falklands/Malvinas War or to the military's control of the transition process in Chile, democratic transition in Brazil involved a negotiated process of return to civilian control. The return to democracy required the preparation of a new civil code to reshape the political and social charter. A national assembly was elected to develop the framework for a new constitutional order. The Federal Constitution of October 5, 1988, is a legal landmark in Brazil's democratic transition and its institutionalization of human rights.

The text of the 1988 Constitution reflects a new democratic consensus. After twenty-one years of authoritarian rule, it restored the rule of law, the separation of powers, and the principles of federalism. As the most wide-ranging and detailed document on human rights in the country's constitutional history, it marked an extraordinary advance in the consolidation of fundamental rights and guarantees in Brazil. Among Brazilian constitutions, the 1988 version relied most on the active participation of civil society in its preparation, and it enjoys great popular legitimacy.

From the standpoint of the women's movement, the period prior to 1988, when the Constitution was under debate, proved critical to advancing awareness of women's human rights. As various groups lobbied to have the new constitution reflect their concerns, and after extensive national discussion, women's groups prepared a "Letter from Brazilian Women to the Constitutional Convention" to address their primary claims. As Leila Linhares Barsted observes, the Brazilian feminist movement was a "key player in this process of legislative and social change, denouncing inequalities, proposing public policies, working together with the Legislative Branch, and . . . [interpreting] the law." Furthermore, since the mid-1970s, the Brazilian feminist movement "fought for the equal rights of men and women" and for the ideals of human rights, "defending the elimination of all forms of discrimination, both in the law and in social practices. Indeed, the organized action of the women's movement during the drafting of the Federal Constitution of 1988 was largely responsible for numerous new rights and corresponding obligations of the state." These include "equality in the family, condemnation of domestic violence, equality among sons and daughters, [and the] recognition of reproductive rights," among others (Barsted 2001:35).[3]

The extension of full citizenship to women in the Constitution of 1988 resulted from "an impressive political process of dialogue between society and the Executive and Legislative Branches." The fact that the Constitution addressed domestic violence "lent weight in the 1990s to the demands on state and municipal levels to create new services, such as shelters and legal aid services," which were provided by many states and municipalities (Barsted 2006:257).

As a result of the skillful maneuvering by the women's movement, a majority of its claims were incorporated into the constitutional text, including language that assures the equality of men and women both in the public and private spheres and the prohibition of discrimination.[4] There are also special protections for women in the labor market.[5] Family-planning decisions are to be made freely by a couple (with the government responsible for providing the educational and scientific resources needed for the exercise of this right). The government has a duty to restrain violence in the family.[6] In 1997 the issue of women's underrepresentation in Congress was addressed by a gender-quota law (see Marx, Borner, and Caminotti, this volume), and a law passed in 2001 deals with sexual harassment.

## The International Context ⋖

In Brazil's case, the demands of the women's movement were influenced by international advances, particularly the 1979 Convention on the Elimination of All Forms of Discrimination against Women (CEDAW), the Declaration and Program of Action of the 1993 World Conference on Human Rights in Vienna, the Action Plan of the 1994 World Conference on Population and Development in Cairo, and particularly the 1994 Inter-American Convention on the Prevention, Punishment, and Eradication of Violence against Women (Belém do Pará), as well as the Platform for Action of the 1995 World Conference on Women in Beijing. These international instruments enabled the women's movement in Brazil to demand the implementation of these norms. As Jacqueline Pitanguy describes the process: "As the new issues were incorporated into the human rights agenda, the women's movement also stepped up its campaigns directed toward national governments. The Conferences of Cairo (1994) and Beijing (1995), CEDAW and the Conventions like the one agreed to in Belém do Pará were fundamental for the institutionalization of women's citizenship and human rights in Brazil." She concludes that the women's human rights agenda "influenced the political discourse in Brazil and was responsible for the creation of new public policies, particularly in the fields of sexual and reproductive health, labor and welfare rights, political and civil rights, and gender violence" (Pitanguy 2006:29).

After 1988 Brazil adopted a comprehensive set of national rules on the protection of human rights and endorsed a number of international human rights treaties.[7] Since 1988 the legislature has passed more human rights laws than at any time in its history.[8] Brazil "not only signed all the documents relating to the recognition and protection of the human rights of women" but also created "a decidedly progressive legislative framework" on the equality of rights between men and women (Barsted 2001:34).

Despite the significant advances made at the constitutional and legislative levels, however, sexism and discrimination against women are still deeply ingrained in Brazilian culture, preventing women from exercising their most fundamental rights with full autonomy and dignity.[9] Among the most serious violations of women's human rights are discrimination, the denial of sexual and reproductive rights, and violence directed against them. After the adoption of the new Constitution, these issues became the main priorities of the Brazilian feminist agenda. Pitanguy describes the final decades of the twentieth century as "characterized by a process of consolidation of the new language of human rights, which began to take into consideration concerns with female citizenship and gender relations." But the emergence of a global institutional framework of human rights brought "new dimensions" to this agenda, including "topics such as reproduction, violence and sexuality." In Brazil "the debate around a modern concept of humanity, no longer modeled exclusively on the abstract figure of the man, prompted the adoption of public policies and laws in the field of sexual and reproductive health, labor, civil and political rights, and gender violence" (2006:16).

## Making Domestic Violence a Public Issue: The IACHR Decision ✢

The Maria da Penha case broke through the invisibility that shrouds the issue of domestic violence and became the symbol for a much needed campaign against impunity, a critical issue for the rule of law in Brazil. In 2001, the IACHR took an unprecedented step, finding the Brazilian state guilty of negligence and failure to take action against domestic violence, and recommended that Brazil "continue and expand the reform process" to "put an end to the State's tolerance and discriminatory treatment of domestic violence against women in Brazil." The commission noted that the tolerance of domestic violence in Brazil "is a tolerance by the entire system, which only serves to perpetuate the psychological, social and historical roots and factors that sustain and feed violence against women" (IACHR 2001:paragraphs 54, 55).[10]

The IACHR decision was based on the finding that Brazil violated the obligations it assumed when it ratified the Convention of Belém do Pará. The commission stressed that states that have ratified the convention are "obligated to investigate every situation involving a violation of the rights protected by the Convention. If the State apparatus acts in such a way that the violation goes unpunished and the victim's full enjoyment of such rights is not restored as soon as possible, then the State has failed to comply with its duty to ensure the free and full exercise of those rights to the persons within its jurisdiction. The same is true when the State allows private persons or groups of persons to act freely and with impunity to the detriment of the rights recognized by the Convention" (IACHR 2001:paragraphs 54, 55).

The second obligation that states assume when they ratify the convention is "to 'ensure' the free and full exercise of the rights recognized by the Convention to every person subject to its jurisdiction." This means that governments must create the necessary structures (laws, as well as monitoring and enforcement agencies) to "legally ensure" the "free and full enjoyment of human rights," and "prevent, investigate and punish any violation of the rights recognized by the Convention." Moreover, if possible, they must "attempt to restore the right violated and provide compensation as warranted for damages resulting from the violation" (IACHR 2001:paragraphs 42, 44).

The IACHR further recommended that the government (1) "rapidly and effectively" complete criminal proceedings against the person responsible for the assault; (2) conduct a serious and impartial investigation into the irregularities and unwarranted delays in the criminal proceedings; (3) pay the victim a symbolic compensation for the delay in delivering justice, without prejudice to the civil proceedings against the aggressor; and (4) promote the training of officials of the judiciary in human rights, particularly the rights contained in the Convention of Belém do Pará (IACHR 2001:Recommendations).

The Maria da Penha case marked the first time that a case of domestic violence resulted in a guilty verdict brought against a country within the inter-American system. The petitioning organizations (the Center for Justice and International Law and CLADEM-Brasil) hoped that international litigation would improve the protection of women's human rights in Brazil. On October 31, 2002, the offender was finally incarcerated in the state of Paraíba (*Folha de São Paulo*: 31 October 2002); the cycle of impunity had ended after nineteen years. The other measures recommended by the commission (such as reparatory measures, prevention campaigns, and programs to train and raise the awareness of officials of the judiciary, among others) were the subject of a commitment agreement signed between the petitioning organizations and the Brazilian government.[11] In November 2003 a law was enacted requiring both public and private health services throughout Brazil to notify the authorities of all cases of violence against women they treat.

Further progress was made when an Inter-ministerial Working Group was established in the Brazilian executive branch in March 2004, with members representing both civil society and government. Its purpose was to draft a law and set up additional instruments to tackle domestic violence against women. The group drew up a legislative proposal that was submitted by the president to the National Congress in late 2004. Those who argued for the law were able to point to the Maria da Penha case and cite the recommendations made by the IACHR. Nearly two years later, in August 2006, Law 11.340 (also known as the "Maria da Penha" law) was adopted, establishing measures for the prevention of domestic violence, as well as for assistance and protection for women suffering from violence.

The "Maria da Penha" Law ⚜

In contrast to seventeen other countries in Latin America, prior to 2006 Brazil had no specific legislation addressing violence against women; such cases were treated under a law (9099/95) that created Special Criminal Courts. These functioned like small claims courts to handle "criminal infractions of minor offensive potential," punishable by no more than one year of imprisonment.

By recognizing and punishing violent acts in the private domain, the state no longer supported the strict division between the public and private spheres, in which police had to "cross the private threshold" to arrest and prosecute those committing domestic violence. Returning the perpetrators to the very same domain and requiring only that offenders buy their victims a food basket or pay for half an oven or refrigerator, however, trivialized the crime and reinforced the widespread impression that cases of violence against women are merely "domestic quarrels." The law thus endorsed the erroneous notion that violence against women was a minor crime, not a serious human rights violation. Research has shown that, by failing to take violence against women seriously, the 1995 law legitimized domestic violence and reinforced gender hierarchy (Araujo 2005).[12] In some cases the courts had ruled that domestic violence was justified as a reaction to an act of "vengeance or antagonism by the victim" or found the victim at fault in some other way, employing the absurd logic that women can behave in ways that justify male abuse. The application of the law thus undermined the credibility of the Brazilian justice system (fragile in any case), an assessment further reinforced by the fact that only 2 percent of cases of violence against women ended in conviction.

Legally, however, the failure of the Brazilian state to take action in the Maria da Pena case was a breach of the Convention of Belém do Pará that obliged the Brazilian government to implement public policies to prevent, punish, and eradicate violence against women in accordance with international and constitutional standards. Its failure to act warranted the guilty verdict in the Penha case and led to the adoption of the "Maria da Penha" law (Law 11.340) in August 2006.

The new law incorporates seven remarkable innovations. The first changes the legal terminology for addressing violence against women. Violence against women, formerly treated as a *criminal infraction of minor offensive potential*, is now considered a *human rights violation*, and the new law expressly bans applying the earlier law to cases of domestic abuse. In a second innovation, the law incorporates a gender perspective by requiring that the specific conditions under which women suffer domestic and family violence must be taken into consideration. It provides for the creation of Courts for Domestic and Family Violence against Women, with both civil and criminal jurisdiction and specialized police stations that offer a variety of services to abused women. Third, the new law makes provisions for developing a preventive, integrated, and multidisciplinary approach to domestic violence, establishing integrated prevention measures that require coordination among the federal, state, and municipal governments and nongovernment organizations. It integrates the judiciary, the Public Prosecution Service, and the Public Defense Service with the areas of public safety, social assistance, health, education, labor, and housing. The law stresses the importance of running awareness campaigns promoting the prevention of domestic and family violence, as well as of the dissemination of the law and related legislation and the texts of international treaties that protect women's rights. It urges that issues such as human rights, gender and race equality, ethnicity, and the problem of domestic and family violence against women be included in school curricula at all levels. It also addresses the need for ongoing training for police officers on gender, race, and ethnicity.

Fifth, in contrast with the trivial sanctions meted out under the old law (9099/95), the new law states that offenders in cases of domestic violence may not be punished merely by being required to make restitution through gifts of food or other pecuniary penalties, nor can they get by with merely paying a fine.[13] This measure is intended to eliminate the state's complacency with regard to the crime of domestic violence, following the terms of the convention by broadening the concept of violence against women to include "any act or omission thereof based on gender that causes death, injury, physical, sexual or psychological suffering and moral or pecuniary damages" that occurs within the domestic unit, within the family, or in any intimate relationship.

The sixth innovation is the establishment of a broader definition of "family" and the visibility given the right to free sexual orientation. The new law affirms that sexual orientation is of no relevance in determining how the law applies. It reiterates that all women, regardless of sexual orientation, class, race, ethnicity, income, culture, schooling, age, or religion have the right to live without violence. Finally, the law calls for the creation of databases and provides for the promotion of research and the collection and analysis of relevant data—broken down by gender, race, and ethnicity—on the causes, consequences, and frequency of domestic and family violence against women. It also provides for the organization of this data and a regular evaluation of the results of the adopted measures.

Commenting on the law, Leila Barsted concludes that the history of the issue of domestic violence "reveals the important role of women's movements in dialogue with the State in its different spheres": with the executive to ratify treaties, the legislature to pass the necessary laws and regulatory rules, and the various agencies involved in law enforcement and the provision of services to address the consequences of domestic violence, including police stations and shelters. The movement must continue to lobby to ensure that these facilities are adequately funded, including funds for the collection and analysis of data. "There is no doubt," Barsted adds, "that in the past three decades, the women's movement has been a major player driving public policies on gender, including those [on] the prevention of violence. Nevertheless, in spite of the breakthroughs achieved, there is still an undeniable persistence of domestic and sexual violence against women in Brazil" (2006:288).

## Conclusion ⸙

The "Maria da Penha" law was passed in August 2006 and came into force forty-five days later. The groups in the women's movement remain in close contact with each other to confront resistance from various sectors to the measures included in the new law. Some legal experts have argued that the law is unconstitutional, claiming that "a measure that only affects violence against women is discriminatory," thereby ignoring the persistence and the epidemic proportions of this gendered pattern of violence. There are judges who contend that the creation of courts with both civil and criminal jurisdiction, as the "Maria da Penha" law demands, is unconstitutional because it is not part of the Brazilian tradition.[14] However, the women's movement has stood firmly behind the new law, emphasizing the importance of its innovations and stressing the law's constitutionality—arguing, in fact, that *not* having such a law would be unconstitutional.

The "Maria da Penha" law produced an intense public debate on violence against women. It resulted from a successful strategy by the Brazilian women's movement to identify an emblematic case of violence against women and submit it to an international court, using the power of international litigation supported by transnational activism. The women's movement used a range of legal, political, and communication strategies to bring public attention to its message. With the IACHR decision and growing public awareness, women's groups succeeded in changing the law and shaping public policy. By monitoring the legislative process and actively participating in drafting the law on violence against women, they played a direct role in passing the law, and now they are fighting for its effective implementation.

The Brazilian experience also illustrates how bringing an international legal case can focus public attention on human rights violations against women not taken seriously before. The IACHR decision caused the Brazilian government considerable political and moral embarrassment. Confronted with human rights violations in the court of international public opinion, a government is practically compelled to justify its actions.

James Cavallaro (2002) argues that well-articulated international litigation strategies differentiate merely procedural victories from substantive gains, and the "Maria da Penha" case provides an important example of the latter. Kathryn Sikkink (1993) has shown how the work of transnational NGOs makes the repressive practices of states more visible and public, requiring a response from those who would otherwise remain silent. In this case, it is clear that international attention made it easier for the Brazilian women's movement to mobilize the media, engage public opinion, and advance the cause of women's human rights (Cavallaro 2002:492). When a government recognizes the legitimacy of international interventions on the matter of human rights and when, in response to international pressure, it alters its behavior, the relation between the state, its citizens, and international actors is strengthened (Sikkink 1993:414–15). The extensive involvement of non-government organizations employing coordinated and competent litigation strategies made the international instruments Brazil had signed powerful mechanisms for strengthening human rights protections for women.

The liberating ethic of human rights requires social transformation to ensure that each person can fully exercise his or her potential without violence or discrimination. It is an ethic that views others as deserving of equal consideration and profound respect, and as having the right to develop their human potential freely, autonomously, and fully. Historically, the campaign for human rights has not always followed a linear path upward (Pitanguy 2006). But although it has not been a triumphant march forward, it has certainly not proven a lost cause. The history of human rights is a history of conflict (Lochak 2005:116; Lafer 2006) that opens and consolidates new spaces from where it is possible to continue the struggle for human dignity.

The goal of the women's movement was to give the Maria da Penha case special integrity and meaning, as well as to inspire hope, creative action, and the capacity to transform the society in which they live. Hannah Arendt (1995, 1998) emphasizes this human potential and believes that, with patience, people can tame the wilderness with the faculties of passion and action. These are lessons that can be learned from the way the women's movement in Brazil pursued the Maria da Penha case and gained a legal, moral, and practical victory for women.

Notes ❧

1   This Human Rights Watch report also reveals that, of more than eight hundred cases of rape reported to police stations in São Paulo from 1985 to 1989, less than a quarter were investigated. The same report also states that the women's police station in São Luis, in the state of Maranhão, reported that, of the more than four thousand cases of physical and sexual assault brought to their attention,

only three hundred ended up in court and only two resulted in the punishment of the accused.

2 Adopting the classification made by Guillermo O'Donnell, who wrote: "It is useful to conceptualize the processes of democratization as actually implying two transitions. The first is the transition from the previous authoritarian regime to the installation of a democratic government. The second transition is from this government to the consolidation of democracy or, in other words, to the effective functioning of a democratic regime" a process that is still in progress (O'Donnell 1992:18)

3 She writes further, "this favorable legislative situation was the result of women's long struggle . . . since the Brazilian Republic [was] founded in 1889. The restrictions on women's political rights were only fully withdrawn in the 1934 Federal Constitution; until 1962, a married woman needed her husband's authorization to exercise the most elemental rights, for example, the right to work. Until 1988, married women were still considered their husbands' collaborators, and husbands were responsible for directing the marriage. Until the late 1970s, the law, under the pretense of 'protection,' prevented women's entry into numerous sectors of the labor market" (Barsted 2001:34–35).

4 Law 9.029 of April 13, 1995, prohibits employers from requiring women to present pregnancy or sterilization certificates, or any other discriminatory practices, for the purposes of hiring or continuing employment.

5 Law 9.799 of May 26, 1999, which includes (in the section on consolidation of labor laws) rules on the access of women to the labor market.

6 Law 10.778 of November 24, 2003, requires both public and private health services throughout Brazil to notify the authorities of all cases of violence against women they have treated.

7 Foremost among them are: (1) the Inter-American Convention to Prevent and Punish Torture, on July 20, 1989; (2) the Convention against Torture and other Cruel, Inhuman, or Degrading Treatment, on September 28, 1989; (3) the Convention on Children's Rights, on September 24, 1990; (4) the International Covenant on Civil and Political Rights, on January 24, 1992; (5) the International Covenant on Economic, Social, and Cultural Rights, on January 24, 1992; (6) the American Convention on Human Rights, on September 25, 1992; (7) the Inter-American Convention on the Prevention, Punishment, and Eradication of Violence against Women, on November 17, 1995; (8) the Protocol to the American Convention regarding the Abolition of the Death Penalty, on August 13, 1996; (9) the Protocol to the American Convention in the Area of Economic, Social, and Cultural Rights (San Salvador Protocol), on August 21, 1996; (10) the Rome Statute, which created the International Criminal Court, on June 20, 2002; (11) the Optional Protocol to the Convention on the Elimination of All Forms of Discrimination against Women, on June 28, 2002; and (12) the two Optional Protocols to the Convention on Children's Rights, regarding children's

involvement in armed conflicts, the sale of children, and child prostitution and pornography, on January 24, 2004. In addition to these advances, one might add Brazil's recognition of the jurisdiction of the Inter-American Court of Human Rights in December 1998.

8 On this point, the following laws stand out: (1) Law 7.716 of January 5, 1989, which defines crimes arising from discrimination based on race or color and considers racism an "unbailable and imprescriptible" crime (prior to the 1988 Constitution, racism was considered merely a misdemeanor); (2) Law 9.029 of April 13, 1995, which prohibits employers from requiring women to present pregnancy or sterilization certificates, or any other discriminatory practices, for the purposes of hiring or continuing employment; (3) Decree 1.904 of May 13, 1996, which establishes the National Human Rights Program and for the first time endows human rights with the status of government public policy, prescribing government initiatives for the protection and promotion of civil and political rights in Brazil; (4) Law 9.459 of May 13, 1997, which modifies Law 7.716 (that defines crimes arising from discrimination based on race or color), expanding it to include punishments for crimes arising from discrimination based on ethnicity, religion, or nationality; (5) Law 9.504 of September 30, 1997, which establishes election rules, stating that each party or coalition must reserve a minimum of 30 percent and a maximum of 70 percent for the candidacies of each sex; (6) Law 8.069 of July 13, 1990, which provides for the Child and Adolescent Statute, considered one of the most advanced pieces of legislation on the subject, as it establishes full protection for children and adolescents, emphasizing their fundamental rights and the policies needed to protect these rights; and (7) Law 9.455 of April 7, 1997, which defines and punishes the crime of torture as a crime not subject to bail, mercy, or amnesty, and whose perpetrators, accessories, and those who, being in a position to prevent the crime, refrained from doing so, shall be held liable pursuant to Article 5, XLIII, of the Constitution of 1988.

9 See the shadow report on the International Covenant on Civil and Political Rights submitted to the Human Rights Committee, Geneva, in October 2005, particularly the section drafted by CLADEM (Latin American and Caribbean Committee for the Defense of Women's Rights). See also Piovesan and Pimental 2002b, 2003.

10 Language in this and the following paragraph are taken from the IACHR, -OAS, Report 54/01, case 12.051, *Maria da Penha Fernandes v. Brazil*, 16/04/01, paragraphs 54, 55.

11 The annual report of the IACHR in 2003, in the chapter entitled "Status of Compliance with the Recommendations of the IACHR" (www.cidh.org/annualrep/, accessed on February 25, 2005), reveals that the Brazilian state informed the commission on the progress of the ongoing criminal proceedings against the person responsible for the assault and attempted murder to which recommen-

dation 1 refers. In due course, the commission learned that the prison sentence imposed on the offender had been executed.

12    From the point of view of Leila Linhares Barsted: "Ten years after the approval of this law, it has been found that nearly 70% of cases heard in the Special Criminal Courts involve situations of domestic violence against women. Of all these cases, the vast majority end in 'conciliation,' without the Public Prosecution Service or the judge even becoming aware of the case and without the women getting an appropriate response from the State for the violence suffered. Given the all but discriminatory effect of this law, the women's movement has debated some solutions and evaluated the initiatives of lawmakers currently in the National Congress, as well as legislative experiences in other countries that have drafted laws against domestic violence. Drawing on this insight, a consortium of NGOs prepared a draft bill on the topic, modeled on the Convention of Belém do Pará and rejecting the application of Law 9.099/95. This proposal was presented to the Special Department of Policies for Women" (2006:280–81).

13    An article in *O estado de São Paulo* entitled "Nova lei que protege a mulher já tem um preso" (September 23, 2006) refers to a case where a man was detained who beat his wife, who was five months pregnant. According to the female arresting police officer, the offender considered his imprisonment to be "ridiculous," indicating that although laws can be changed, they must be enforced to affect underlying attitudes.

14    A Motion to Reject the Domestic Violence Law, Law 11.340/06, was approved in the Third Conference of Special Criminal Court Judges, in Rio de Janeiro, in September 2006. In the document, the judges criticize the "unsystematic and unscientific form in which various laws, penalties, and criminal procedures have been rewritten in recent sessions of the legislature." They add that "the succession of imperfect laws baffles society and increases the feeling of despair." Likewise, the majority of prosecutors and judges from the Federal District consider the law unconstitutional, particularly the provision that prevents the application of Law 9099/95 to crimes of domestic and family violence against women. On the opposite end of the spectrum, however, note the commendable and extraordinary efforts of the judge Shelma Lombardi de Kato, which led to the installation of Brazil's first Court for Domestic and Family Violence against Women, in Cuiabá, on September 25, 2006.

# 6

# Gender and Human Rights ⟨

LESSONS FROM THE PERUVIAN TRUTH AND
RECONCILIATION COMMISSION

*Julissa Mantilla Falcón*

T he main documents of international human rights law, such as the Universal Declaration of Human Rights (1948) or the International Covenant for Civil and Political Rights (1966), refer to the principle of non-discrimination and employ a supposedly neutral language that does not distinguish between men and women. However, in Vienna in 1993 the United Nations Second Conference on Human Rights declared the rights of women and girls as human rights. Since then, international documents and case law have included stronger references to women's human rights and to the need for a gender perspective, although the international community still underestimates the importance of the gender perspective to investigations of human rights violations and the processes of postconflict reconciliation.

This essay reviews the evolution of the incorporation of a gender perspective in international human rights law and looks at the case of the Peruvian Truth and Reconciliation Commission (PTRC) as an example of the impact this perspective has had in a human rights investigation.

## The Gender Perspective in International Human Rights Law ⟨

The term *gender* is often associated only with women or women-based approaches. In fact, gender should be understood as the "socially constructed roles of women and men that are ascribed to them on the basis of their sex, in public and in private life." Thus gender roles depend on a particular socioeconomic, political, and cultural context and are shaped by other factors, including age, race, class, and ethnicity (UN 1998:paragraph 16). Each society elaborates gender roles in a different way, but often in ways that curtail women's rights and freedoms, limiting them largely to the family and preventing them from assuming roles in the public sphere. Cecilia Medina argues that the subordinate position of women in society causes the violations of their rights (Medina 2003; UN 1998).

Applying a gender perspective to international human rights law requires that treaties and international documents be drawn up taking account of gender differences, and it calls on international bodies to take account of gender in choosing their membership. A gender perspective also allows us to see that human rights violations often affect men and women differently. From this perspective it becomes clear that less attention has been paid to human rights violations that affect women, making it less likely that women will receive justice or appropriate reparations. A gender approach also helps us understand that some human rights violations affect women simply because they are women. An obvious case is sexual violence during armed conflict and the use of women's bodies as a battlefield. The judgments from the international tribunals for Yugoslavia and Rwanda show that sexual violence against women was expressly planned and that women did not have access to justice. Moreover, those tribunals concluded that sexual violence could be considered torture and might constitute genocide in some circumstances.

To recognize women's human rights, it is necessary to see the ways in which conventional definitions of human rights take men and male experiences as their point of reference (Facio 1991). Hillary Charlesworth (1999) gives interesting examples of this in her analysis of international humanitarian law. Quoting Article 27 of the Fourth Geneva Convention, she shows how states are under an obligation to protect women in international armed conflict "against any attack on their honor, in particular against rape, enforced prostitution, or any form of indecent assault," implying that women should be protected from sexual assault and prostitution because these crimes affect a woman's honor, not because they constitute violence or a crime. Additional Protocol I replaces the reference to a woman's honor with the concept that women should be the object of special respect, implying "that women's role in childbearing is the source of special status" (386–87).

In the absence of international armed conflict, Article 3 in all the Geneva Conventions prohibits "violence to life and the person, cruel treatment and torture, and humiliating and degrading treatment," but it does not specifically refer to violence against women. Treating rape and sexual assault as attacks "on [the warrior's] honor or on the sanctity of motherhood" implies that they are not "of the same order as grave breaches against men, such as compelling a prisoner of war to serve in enemy forces" (Charlesworth 1999:387). A gender approach allows us to understand international law from a different and enriched perspective, identifying and giving attention to women's claims. A lobby of women activists around the world, discussions at several UN conferences, and the work of academics have drawn considerable attention to the issue, finding ways to address it explicitly and systematically at all stages of the implementation of human rights instruments, including in the ways rights and freedoms are conceptualized (UN 1998:paragraph 17).

Progress to Date ⚜

A review of the work of the main human rights treaty bodies indicates that the inclusion of women in the framework of guarantees about the equal enjoyment of rights and nondiscrimination has been increased.[1] United Nations conferences and documents make clear that the impact of women's gender roles on women's equality is recognized, including in terms of the full enjoyment of their human rights (UN 1998:note 13). Further, since the World Conference on Human Rights in 1993, there has been increased attention to the need to include the human rights of women in general human rights activities. The Beijing Declaration of 1995 created a commitment to mainstream a gender approach in all UN programs. In 1997 the United Nations Economic and Social Council (ECOSOC) adopted conclusions on "mainstreaming a gender perspective into all policies and programs in the United Nations system," which provided a workable definition of the concept of mainstreaming as well as a set of principles and specific recommendations for action by intergovernmental "machinery." These were reviewed and reaffirmed by the ECOSOC in 2004.[2]

Although there have been advances in recognizing the issue, the impact of the structural inequalities women face needs more research. As the UN report on integrating women into human rights treaties states, "there is not yet a clear acknowledgement or understanding that gender is an important dimension in defining the substantive nature of rights" (UN 1998:paragraph 98). In fact, definitions of rights themselves need to be further explored and interpreted using a gender approach. For example, the definition of the right to life should include issues such as maternal mortality, while that of the right to health should include sexual and reproductive rights. A gender perspective highlights the need to expand the definition of the human rights obligations of the state to include abuses committed by private persons, such as husbands or employers, that is, the issue of violence against women (UN 1998:paragraph 99).

International Case Law: Peruvian Cases ⸰

Peruvian cases in the inter-American system show how violations of women's rights have been increasingly incorporated into international case law. The case of Raquel Martín de Mejía (1992) provides a good example. Martín de Mejía was raped in 1992 after army officers kidnapped her husband. The Inter-American Commission on Human Rights (IACHR) analyzed the facts and concluded that the repeated sexual abuse of Martín de Mejía constituted violations of Article 5 and Article 11 of the American Convention on Human Rights, that is, of her right to physical and mental integrity.

The IACHR states that, for torture to have occurred, three elements have to be present: (1) the act must cause physical and mental pain and suffering to be inflicted on a person; (2) the suffering must be committed on purpose; and (3) it must be committed by a public official or by a private person acting at the instigation of the former.

Regarding the first criterion, the IACHR concluded that rape causes physical and mental suffering in the victim. Concerning the second, the IACHR found that Martín de Mejía had been raped with the aim of punishing her personally and intimidating her. Finally, the commission verified that the man who raped her was a member of the security forces. Thus the IACHR concluded that the government of Peru was responsible for the violation of Article 5 of the American Convention in her case. In addition, the report of the IACHR considered that "sexual abuse, besides being a violation of the victim's physical and mental integrity, implies a deliberate outrage to their dignity" (IACHR 1996).

However, the Inter-American Court treated the María Elena Loayza case differently (Inter-American Court 1997). The victim was detained on February 1993 by members of the National Division against Terrorism of the Peruvian National Police (DINCOTE) and accused of being a member of the subversive group Sendero Luminoso, or Shining Path. She was held without a judicial order. Loayza testified that she was raped by members of DINCOTE and subjected to torture and inhuman treatment, as the police threatened to drown her during the night (Inter-American Court 1997:paragraph 3d). The Peruvian state argued that Loayza did not state these facts in her declarations of February 1993 and that she did not get medical attention for those reasons (Inter-American Court 1997:paragraph 3f). In its judgment, the Inter-American Court of Human Rights argued that the IACHR did not prove that Loayza had been raped, although it did accept other violations of her human rights, such as being held incommunicado during detention, exhibited in public with a prisoner's striped clothing, held in isolation in a small jail cell without ventilation or natural light, and other mistreatment. The court appears not to have taken into account the Martín de Mejía case, which had already established that rape was commonly used as a form of torture during the Peruvian armed conflict. Unfortunately, the court did not explain its reasons for disregarding the rape.

In November 2006, in the Castro Castro case against Peru, the court did incorporate a gender perspective in its judgment (Inter-American Court 2006). This case involved the arbitrary executions of prisoners being transferred from the Miguel Castro Castro Prison in Lima. In this case the court decided to apply the American Convention of Human Rights and the 1994 Inter-American Convention on the Prevention, Punishment, and Eradication of Violence against Women (the Convention of Belém do Pará; see discussion in Piovesan, this volume). The court found that the personal integrity of the prisoners had been violated, noting that the prisoners had to crawl between corpses to avoid the bullets when the police started shooting. Applying a gender perspective, the court observed that the pregnant women had experienced additional psychological suffering since they were afraid not only for themselves but also for their children.

In taking into account that some of the women prisoners were pregnant, the court distinguished between men and women as victims of human rights violations. It used both equality and difference arguments in stating that women prisoners should not be *discriminated against* and that they should be *protected against* any form of violence or exploitation; that is, they should be supervised by female officers, and pregnant women should be treated appropriately.[3]

The court further found the conditions under which the women were imprisoned inadequate, and agreed that their forced nudity proved especially painful for them because they were women. During their detention the women prisoners had not been allowed to clean themselves and were sometimes forced to go to the restroom with an armed officer who pointed his gun at them at all times. Thus the court concluded that the women prisoners were victims of sexual violence since they were naked, covered only by a sheet, and were intentionally intimidated by armed men of the state's security forces (Inter-American Court 2006:paragraph 306). In concluding that the Peruvian state had committed gender violence against women and that such violence was used as a means of punishment and repression during armed conflict, the court referred to the final report of the Peruvian Truth and Reconciliation Commission (PTRC) discussed below.

The court also considered the case of a female prisoner taken to the police hospital and there forced by numerous men to undergo a vaginal inspection. On this point, the court followed international criminal case law and stated that such an "inspection" should be considered rape and an act of torture (Inter-American Court 2006). As a consequence, the Peruvian state was charged with the violation of the rights addressed in the American Convention of Human Rights, Article 5.2 (the right to personal integrity), and in the Inter-American Convention for Preventing and Punishing Torture, Articles 1 and 6 (the obligation of the state to prevent and punish torture) and Article 8 (the obligation of the state to guarantee that any person making an accusation of having been subjected to torture within its jurisdiction shall have the right to an impartial examination of his or her case). Finally, the court established specific reparations for pregnant women whose special needs had not been taken into account and for the women victims of sexual violence.

## Civil War and the Establishment of the Peruvian Truth and Reconciliation Commission (PTRC) ⚜

Several truth commissions (TCS) have been created in postconflict situations around the world to research and report the massive human rights violations that have occurred in a context of armed conflict or under repressive regimes. They confront and acknowledge the truth about past human rights abuses "with the hope of contributing to reconciliation, healing, and reform" (Hayner 1996:174.) Each country has developed a model of how its TC should proceed according to its own reality. For example, Argentina and Chile installed TCs after repressive military regimes, while Guatemala and Peru set up theirs after internal armed conflicts.

Although no standard model exists for all countries, TCs share some common characteristics. First, their main goal is to help a country confront its past and to prevent the recurrence of similar abuses and human rights violations. However, TCs do not replace the national prosecutor's office or the judicial branch; on the contrary, they function as additional independent investigative bodies. At the end of their work, they issue a final report with an analysis of the facts and a set of recommendations for reforms and reparations. Many TCs share another feature: they have not implemented a gender perspective, although important exceptions include South Africa, Guatemala, Peru, Sierra Leone, Morocco, East Timor, and Liberia. Each new TC is aware of the practices of earlier ones, so that each commission's experience becomes a model for the next one, as well as an example of what to avoid. The incorporation of a gender approach in a human rights investigation and in the work of TCs still constitutes a relatively new process, and very little literature exists on the matter. However, as the Peruvian example shows, a gender perspective can play an important role in the work of a TC.

Armed conflict in Peru began in 1980, the year Peru returned to democratic rule. That same year, the Shining Path, a Maoist guerrilla group with origins in the highland city of Ayacucho, burned electoral materials in Chucchi, one of the poorest regions of the country. At that time, no one imagined this would mark the beginning of the cruelest and most difficult period in modern Peruvian history.

For years the population suffered the effects of the actions of the Shining Path and the state forces sent to put down the rebellion. Later, another subversive group, the MRTA (Túpac Amaru Revolutionary Movement), also engaged in guerrilla tactics that provoked armed responses by the state. During this period, which lasted until the Shining Path leader, Abimael Guzmán, was captured and jailed in 1992, thousands of people were disappeared, tortured, executed, and condemned without due process. Successes against the Shining Path increased support for President Alberto Fujimori, who then used his popularity to impose a semiauthoritarian and politically corrupt regime.

In 2001, as the extent of the corruption was revealed, Fujimori was forced to flee the country, and Valentín Paniagua became interim president, pending elections. Intense efforts by human rights NGOs convinced the Paniagua government to create a TC to investigate the crimes and human rights violations that had occurred during the armed conflict (Supreme Decree No. 065–2001-PCM). President Alejandro Toledo was elected in 2001 and renamed the commission to include the word *reconciliation*. He increased the number of members of the commission from seven to twelve, although there were only two women among the commissioners (Supreme Decree No. 101–2001-PCM).

## THE PERUVIAN TRUTH AND RECONCILIATION COMMISSION

The PTRC's main purpose was to investigate cases of gross human rights violations, including torture, forced disappearance, arbitrary executions, and kidnappings. The PTRC's mandate did not specifically include the cases of sexual violence committed against women, in part because it was thought that such cases were not very common. It did not recognize the importance of working with a gender perspective. However, in carrying out its charge, the PTRC consulted the final reports of the TCs of Guatemala and South Africa as international precedents, leading to some changes. Among them was the decision to adopt a broad definition of sexual violence, which the PTRC defined as "the realization of a sexual act against one or more persons or when a person is forced to realize a sexual act by force or threat of force or through coercion caused by fear of violence, intimidation, detention, psychological oppression, or abuse of power used against that person or other persons, or taking advantage of a coercive environment or the inability of the person to freely consent" (PTRC Final Report 2003). This definition allowed the investigation of cases including forced marriage, forced abortions, forced nudity, sexual blackmail, and sexual slavery in addition to cases of rape.

Following through on its intent to examine these cases did not prove an easy task for the PTRC. The lack of awareness of the gender dimensions of the conflict and the lack of necessary information on cases posed problems and caused the PTRC to develop some specific strategies to address them. These included setting up training sessions on gender and sexual violence for the PTRC's personnel; establishing a gender unit to supervise the incorporation of the gender perspective in the PTRC; using flyers, posters, and radio programs to explain that sexual violence constitutes a human rights violation and should be denounced; and creating a support group for women that included representatives of human rights groups, academics, and members of women's NGOS (Mantilla Falcón 2005).

The PTRC released its Final Report on August 28, 2003. It had a major impact on public perception as few Peruvians were aware that the number of deaths caused by the civil conflict had reached nearly seventy thousand. The Final Report included chapters on gender and sexual violence against women (PTRC Final Report 2003). It recognized that the conflict had transformed gender roles as women assumed responsibility for family survival and for dealing with the displacement of entire populations escaping from the conflict (Deng 1996). Concerning the cases of sexual violence, the PTRC recognized that victims often did not denounce instances of its occurrence due to feelings of shame and fear. Moreover, the cases of sexual violence often happened in the context of other human rights violations (such as massacres, arbitrary detentions, summary executions, and torture), which tended to overshadow their sexual dimension.

Although previous reports on the conflict had not mentioned the magnitude of sexual violence in Peru, the PTRC concluded that sexual violence against women was widespread. The evidence from Guatemala and South Africa made the PTRC aware of the likely statistical underrepresentation of these cases. The Final Report concluded that sexual violence happened in at least fifteen rural towns and cities. Ayacucho, where the Shining Path originated, had experienced the most cases of sexual violence, followed by Huancavelica and Apurimac, located in the poorest regions of Peru. As is frequently the case, the victims were often illiterate or had only primary education. Most of the victims were rural women who spoke the indigenous language, Quechua; they were farmers or housewives.

Concerning the perpetrators, the Final Report found that, although the insurgent groups did commit acts of violence against women, forcing them to marry if pregnant or have abortions, most of these acts were committed by the army and the police, and they were concentrated in two years of the conflict: 1984 and 1990. The PTRC also found that the main objective of this sexual violence was to punish, intimidate, pressure, humiliate, and degrade the population. In some cases its purpose was to make the detained women blame themselves for their plight. In addition, there were many cases of sexual abuses that had no direct link to the armed conflict, although sexual violence always constituted an exercise of power in a context in which the aggressors controlled the situation (Mantilla Falcón 2005).

The PTRC also concluded that rape did not constitute the only form of sexual violence. Cases of sexual mutilation, molestation, and humiliation, and of forced prostitution, forced pregnancy, and forced nudity proved common. The perpetrators of sexual violence had enjoyed impunity, not only because women were afraid to denounce them but also because the national authorities failed to provide support. The PTRC handed some cases of sexual violence over to the national prosecutor, and these are currently under investigation. The final report included a proposal for reparations to victims of rape and their children.

Finally, the PTRC provided evidence to show that sexual violence against women was a widespread practice in the context of massacres and arbitrary executions organized by the army and the police. Rape constituted a repeated and persistent practice in a general context of sexual violence, which fits one of the criteria for the definition of a crime against humanity in the Statute of the International Criminal Court.

The Impact of the PTRC on Women's Human Rights ⸙

In February 2004, the High Level Multisectorial Commission (CMAN) to follow up the state's actions and policies on peace, collective reparation, and national reconciliation was created.[4] A year later, the National Council of Reparations (CNR) was established to put together a register of victims to be used as the only instrument for identifying the victims of the armed conflict.[5]

Victims of sexual violence have been included in the register, and they will receive economic and symbolic reparations as well as healthcare, housing, and education if they comply with certain requirements. Likewise, children born due to rapes are considered indirect victims and will have access to education, healthcare, housing, and symbolic reparations. Victims and their children could also benefit from collective reparations. Yet many difficulties remain with these cases. In some, women do not identify themselves as victims of human rights abuses, and they also fear their community's social condemnation. Cultural constraints are also a factor, especially for indigenous women. Therefore the CNR is trying to develop special methodological tools for its work.

Of the forty-seven human rights cases turned over to the National Prosecutor by the PTRC, two deal with gender violence. This may appear a small number, but it is symbolically important and a success in that the PTRC did not plan to include cases of sexual violence in its investigation when it began its work. The first of these cases is that of a student detainee who was raped and became pregnant in 1992. The prosecutor originally closed the case "temporarily" because the rapist could not be identified. When the temporary closure lasted for more than ten years, the victim, Magdalena Monteza, approached the PTRC. The second case deals with the systematic sexual violence committed against women from the towns of Manta and Vilca in the province of Huancavelica, one of the poorest areas in Peru, where the military conducted anti-insurgent operations in 1984 (Vilca) and 1998 (Manta). As a consequence of the sexual abuses, several children were born who do not know who their fathers are. In October 2007, the prosecutor accused former army members of being responsible for sexual violence as torture. This is the first sexual violence case formally denounced as a crime against humanity in Peru.

Currently several NGOs are filing cases on sexual violence that happened during the armed conflict involving about forty-six victims.[6] This, too, marks a big step forward as few NGOs dealt with these kinds of cases during the 1980s and 1990s. In fact, this development might serve as an example of the PTRC's impact in terms of showing the reality of sexual violence against women and the lack of attention formerly paid to the issue. In addition, some friend-of-the-court briefs are being prepared with the support of scholars from international institutions like the International Center for Transitional Justice (ICTJ) and from American universities, including the City University of New York and American University. These efforts form part of a broader trend toward seeking gender justice around the world.

Yet serious problems remain. Peruvian women still lack the resources needed to seek legal aid. The Peruvian criminal code still lacks an adequate definition of sexual violence, which it defines narrowly as rape. Although there is a project underway supported by the International Committee of the Red Cross and some human rights and feminist NGOs to update the criminal code to incorporate sexual violence as a crime against humanity, the process of gender inclusion is uneven. For example, the protocols for the exhumation of mass graves do not include ways to measure gender violence, and there are no guidelines that require researchers to look for or analyze such cases.

Despite the work of the PTRC, women remain reluctant to file complaints because the judicial authorities are often unresponsive and have not incorporated gender sensitivity into their work. In some cases, for example, judges have requested that women undergo medical exams for rapes that happened during the 1980s and 1990s, although this is obviously impossible. In other cases, rape victims do not want to tell their stories because they fear disclosure and a public legal process might threaten their new personal relationships. Not all communities support rape victims who want to file complaints.

However, the work of the PTRC has had an important impact not only at the national level but also in the international arena. Truth commissions formed more recently have incorporated a gender perspective in their mandate and work, as in the case of Liberia (see the Liberian TC's Web site, www .trcofliberia.org). Another example is Colombia, where a TC is doing its work while the private militias are demobilizing. The National Commission on Reparation and Reconciliation (NCRR; see www.cnrr.org.co) is not strictly a Truth Commission because Colombia is still in the middle of an armed conflict and different positions support and criticize the process. However, there is an ongoing debate in Colombia concerning gender and the importance of including women's voices and stories in the search of truth, justice, and reparation. The NCRR, inspired by the PTRC's work, has included a focus on "Gender and Specific Populations," with the term specifically referring to minority and indigenous groups.

Conclusions ⸙

As I have shown, there is a growing trend toward incorporating a gender perspective into the research on human rights violations and into the defense of human rights. In April 2007 the Argentine prosecutor, Federico Delgado, requested the investigation of cases of sexual violence that happened in detention centers during the Argentine dictatorship (1976–83), based on the testimonies of rape victims. This is the first time that sexual abuses against Argentine women will be investigated independently from other human rights abuses.[7]

However, there is still a long way to go before women's human rights can be better protected. For this to happen, it is necessary to recognize that the incorporation of a gender perspective into law protects the human rights of *both men and women*. Understanding this will require a new vision of international human rights law and a clearer recognition of the real challenges to human rights around the world.

## Notes ✦

1   For a summary of the main advances of the different bodies of the United Nations, review the 1999 report of the UN Office of the High Commissioner for Human Rights (OHCHR).

2   See E/2004/INF/2/Add.2, Resolutions 2004/4, which reviews the Economic and Social Council conclusions in UN 1997 on mainstreaming the gender perspective into all policies and programs in the United Nations system. www.un.org/womenwatch/.

3   The court refers to the Standard Minimum Rules for the Treatment of Prisoners, adopted by the First United Nations Congress on the Prevention of Crime and the Treatment of Offenders, held at Geneva in 1955, and approved by the Economic and Social Council by its resolution 663 C (XXIV) of July 31, 1957, and 2076 (LXII) of May 13, 1977.

4   The CMAN was created by D.S. N° 011–2004-PCM, and modified later by D.S. N° 024–2004-PCM and D.S. N° 031–2005-PCM.

5   Law N. 28592, as required by Supreme Decree N° 015–2006-JUS, mandates the creation of a legal list to be used for purposes of reparations. The information about the register of victims was gained through an interview in December 2007 with Sofia Macher, a former commissioner of the PTRC and a current member of the CNR.

6   These include the Asociación pro Derechos Humanos (Aprodeh), the Comisión de Derechos Humanos (COMISEDH), the Instituto de Defensa Legal (IDL), Aporvida, and the Estudio para los Derechos de la Mujer (DEMUS). This number of victims is not confirmed yet, but it was discussed in a recent meeting with the American expert Rhonda Copelon in Lima, June 19, 2007.

7   See http://www.mujereshoy.com (accessed on June 29, 2007), a Latin American website on violence against women.

✢ INTERNATIONAL AND
CROSS-BORDER ACTIVISM ✢

# International Feminisms ⸙

## THE WORLD SOCIAL FORUM

*Virginia Vargas*

> The "content of transnational action by social movements transcends the content and contexts in which national dynamics take place, although they are closely linked to them, influencing each other, empowering or disconnecting each other, exchanging strategies, reinventing others, broadening or narrowing the spaces of action."
>
> JAMES GOODMAN, "Transnational Integration and 'Cosmopolitan Nationalism'"

Since the beginning of feminism's second wave, Latin American feminists have developed rich regional and international patterns of interaction, the content, successes, and contradictions of which reflect the increasing complexity of feminist goals and practices and the tensions or "knots" that have accompanied them since the beginning. The different approaches to development in the region that have succeeded one another over time have also produced changes—economic, political, and subjective—influencing feminist strategies. The most dramatic and visible of these is the shift of the development paradigm from industrial capitalism to a global information capitalism, which has had profound economic, social, and cultural effects.

Latin American feminisms have taken multiple forms, through numberless organizations, collectives, action networks, themes, and identities. These networks and collectives have given rise to a rich internationalist dynamic, generating new forms of thought and expression. On the regional level, the most important are the feminist *Encuentros*, held first every two and then every three years from 1981 to 2005, the latest in Brazil. The dynamics of the *Encuentros* reflect feminist advances, shared strategies, conflicts of perspective and meaning, and different discourses that have produced multiple and intense linkages between the national and the international.[1] However, feminist awareness of the potential of this international space and the capacity to reflect on it was slow to develop through the decade of the 1990s.

During the 1980s, when Latin American countries were under dictatorial or authoritarian governments and then moved toward democratic governments that proved to be far from fully democratic, feminist political strategies did not connect very well with the institutions of governance, either on the national or on the global level. Instead, feminisms were oriented more toward politicizing the conditions of women in the private sphere (Tamayo 1998), recreating collective practices, and making the invisible visible. Latin American feminists devised new categories of analysis and even new language to name things that had thus far gone unnamed — sexuality, domestic violence, sexual assault, rape in marriage, and the feminization of poverty, among others — and put them at the center of democratic debates. The symbolic dimension of change, a kind of cultural ferment, formed part of feminist action, creating new dates to celebrate and recovering leaders, histories, and symbols. These transcended national boundaries and gave regional feminisms a broader, Latino-Caribbean significance.

Feminist dynamics on the regional and international levels changed dramatically between the 1980s and the 1990s. The return to democratic government created new and complex political contexts, with varying effects on the development of feminisms and feminist strategies. It became impossible to speak of feminism in the singular, not only because of the movement's expansion across the region but also because of the differences in strategies, in positions, and in the ways in which feminists confronted the new uncertainties that began to emerge within what had previously been considered classically feminist positions. The successive United Nations (UN) world conferences of the 1990s — on the environment (1992), human rights (1993), population (1994), and women (1995) — opened new arenas for action and debate at the global level and helped shape the new feminist perspectives and strategies that were taking form in the region. The democratic context also brought a new risk: that the relations between feminists and national governments, as well as between feminists and international institutions, might become too intimate (Waterman 2005).

During the first years of the 1990s, as networks became more specialized and institutional strategies took precedence, there was a tendency toward fragmentation, along with the emergence of the "me culture" promoted by the competitive and consumerist values of neoliberalism that had begun to install themselves in the social imagination. The UN conferences, especially the one on women in Beijing, opened a new space for feminist expression. A fresh and rich international praxis began to emerge. Latin American feminisms were confronted not only with the need to create a regional feminist space but also with the construction of, and contestation within, a global arena.

In the 1980s contacts among Latin American and Caribbean feminists had largely been directed toward constructing a regionwide movement that would connect civil-society groups across national borders around thematic and identity networks. In the 1990s regional and global relations drew on two streams: one based on civil societies (primarily represented by the *Encuentros* and the expansion of feminist networks) and one based on the interactions of feminists working in official state capacities. In Beijing both groups were able to cooperate while also confronting each other, making similar demands yet following their own distinct dynamics. The feminists who came to Beijing arrived with experiences gained in key civil-society organizations and secure in the gains achieved at previous UN conferences, especially the human rights conference in Vienna and the population conference in Cairo, where expert organized networks had helped shape the conference agendas and platforms.

Beijing brought together expert networks as well as identity groups and NGO feminists who came with little experience in lobbying governments and even less in lobbying transnational institutions. Beijing provided an enormous opportunity for learning, but it also revealed the new tensions arising from NGO-ization as feminist organizations became increasingly institutionalized.

The consequences of the paradigmatic shift to neoliberalism, which had become clear by the new millennium, altered the possibilities for feminists as much as they did for other groups facing the challenges of neoliberal hegemony, turning feminist attention toward issues of class, diversity, and sexuality. The increasing power of conservative and fundamentalist groups provided a new challenge, as these sectors deepened patterns of exclusion and directly challenged women's rights and sexual diversity. The UN, which from the start of the Women's Decade (1975) to Beijing (1995) had provided ample space for debate and negotiation to global feminisms and broadened the meaning of women's rights, is no longer the organization it was in the 1970s and 1980s. Its autonomy is now severely weakened, overtaken by the scandalous unilateralism of the United States and the domination of global politics by the powerful economies. It has lost credibility. At the same time, strong new movements of global solidarity are emerging to seek an alternative globalization to the one promoted by neoliberalism. Many feminist groups are playing active roles in this effort.

Feminist Dynamics for a New Millennium ⚐

Peter Waterman writes that, in the "series of levels and spaces" of the international world today, "women's movements of Latin America have a permanent and challenging presence." Their commitment and the seriousness of their reflection on globalization "have lessons for other radical democratic movements, theories and ideologies" (Waterman 2005).

As Millie Thayer observes, in the past, inequalities among women in different classes and cultures "seemed like unchanging facts to be mediated through the political system and the economy." Today, however, "the increasing density of transnational connections has transformed the grounding of social movements." This is converting the "apparently hard and fast 'facts' of inequality" into "sets of direct experiences with relations of power among allies, male and female, who are part of a larger pattern of global inequalities and geographic disturbances" (2001:106).

In the new millennium, diverse feminist streams are experiencing fundamental modifications in their ways of thinking and acting and are becoming more complex and nuanced in the struggles they take on. There are new interpretive frames for action (Jelin 2003) that have affected both the content of feminist agendas and the spaces from which feminists choose to act. This has broadened their global transformational horizons.

This new political cultural climate is more flexible and inclusive. The historical conjuncture that brought the hegemony of global neoliberalism has also produced the disintegration of old paradigms (Waterman 2006). There is an urgent need to create a new reality by envisioning radical new approaches to address global change. This can be seen in new ways of thinking about the state and capital on both national and global levels—ways of thinking that oppose the messianic, universal narratives of past movements. Conditions are ripe for the emergence of new forms of political culture or, better yet, for countercultural proposals that challenge the neoliberal logic of power now extant at the global level and strongly influencing the local.

One fundamental aspect of this new political culture is its assumption that the transformation of the world depends on a transformation of vision (Beck 2004). For me, this new way of looking at the world implies changing one's imaginative focus from the nation-state to a more cosmopolitan view. This does not limit but relocates the global-local opposition, avoiding the loss of social experience characteristic of abstract models (De Sousa Santos 2006). In contemporary international society the levels of local, national, and global sociability are interconnected, and privileging one level over another constitutes a political, not an empirical, decision. For his part, Ulrich Beck assumes that these levels are complementary, which allows us to dissolve the fiction that any one of them represents "reality." Instead, the cosmopolitan vision comes closest to reality because it opens up possibilities that a national perspective, taken alone, excludes.

This cosmopolitan vision offers the key to understanding the new ways in which social movements are acting and interacting in global-local space, with a range of struggles and emancipatory concerns. Critics have claimed that these movements have produced fragmentation and localized conflicts; they have been accompanied by what Norbert Lechner has called the "privatization" of social conduct, which is seen in the resistance of people to involvement in collective action (2002). It is also true that new forms of interaction are occurring in what Manuel Castells calls the "networked society" (1999). These are expressed not by unified actors in a well-defined social or even multicultural context, but rather as dimensions of a broad "field" of social interaction, one that is diverse and constantly expanding and transforming itself (Jelin 2003), producing new frameworks of meaning. In this field, the radical break that many have posited between "old" and "new" social movements no longer emerges very clearly. There are other dynamics that have just begun to be felt: campaigns for global justice arising from new and different sources, and efforts to free ourselves from obsolete paradigms without yet knowing what will replace them.

These struggles do not erase the differences among groups; on the contrary, what emerges is a multiplicity of meanings as the social space of experience expands both locally and globally. And all these struggles, except for those that arise from an essentialist viewpoint, shape only a part of one's identity. In the case of feminism, the classical campaigns calling for a different view of sexuality and for changing the relations of power between men and women are merged with other struggles in a global process of transformation that opposes neoliberalism, militarization, and fundamentalisms of various kinds.

In relation to the question of the spaces from and in which feminisms now act, one can observe two significant and promising changes. The first is the possibility of recovering a politics not located solely in "the state" but also in society and in daily life. The second is the prospect of transcending one's own location to connect and debate ideas with other groups oriented toward change, which broadens the emancipatory horizon and has the potential to create a counterpower to confront (and offer alternatives to) the hegemonic power and discourses we face.

As for the content of feminist agendas, feminists have begun to widen their political categories, such as democracy, and to make them more complex. The search for a concept of democracy that is plural and radical remains central to their thinking and attempts to recover the diversity of experiences and aspirations that the neoliberal model, which emphasizes elections and minimizes the redistributional responsibilities of the state, denies. It nurtures democratic, secular, untutored visions that are transcultural rather than Western and works on different scales and dimensions, incorporating subjectivity into the transformation of social relations and generating multiple sites from which emancipatory democratic agendas can emerge. In this process, struggles *against* material and symbolic exclusions and *for* redistributive justice and recognition create a new politics of the body. Dialogue among diversities constitute one of the ways in which feminist and women's movements are seeking to have an impact.

This perspective has also expanded the human rights paradigm, incorporating new rights to respond to new risks, subjectivities, and citizen demands. Countercultural strategies put the recovery and broadening of economic rights (those most devalued by neoliberalism) and sexual and reproductive rights (those usually resisted by official governing bodies) at the center of feminist praxis. At the same time, various feminisms seek to impact the many dimensions of global transformation, resisting the neoliberal model, with its exaggerated individualism and consumerism, and opposing the growing militarism increasingly attributable to actions of the U.S. government. There is a sustained battle against fundamentalisms.

One critical effort means to show how discriminations by race, ethnicity, class, gender, age, and sexual orientation are linked as constitutive elements of a nucleus of domination. To achieve this, feminists seek to understand and draw attention to the interpretive frameworks used by other social movements, but also to engage them in dialogue to raise issues insufficiently incorporated into their transformational agendas. Women's "impertinent forms of knowledge" (Mafia 2000) can undermine traditional discourses and must be present in the efforts to bring about change.

Many feminisms interacting internationally share the goal of fighting fundamentalisms. In their multiple expressions—whether in the name of God, the market, or tradition—fundamentalisms defend a set of immutable ideas about the world that are held up as norms for society, often with horrendous consequences for the bodies and lives of women. In the struggle against fundamentalisms, the body serves as one of those "impertinent forms of knowledge" that can broaden the terms of transformation. The body has become an "endowed space of citizenship" (Ávila 2001). The rights of the body mark the disputed element in the struggle for sexual and reproductive rights; in the battle against HIV/AIDS (which is also a battle against patents and transnational pharmaceutical companies); in the fight against militarism, which makes women's bodies war booty on all sides; and in the resistance to racism, the real and symbolic discrimination based on skin color that has perverse consequences for women's sexual bodies. It is the battle against injustice and hunger, which permanently limit the bodily capabilities of new generations.

The body thus conceived recovers the connections between the public and the private; it confronts capital and the state, as well as national and international institutions. The body is a concept with democratic potential,[2] challenging commonly held beliefs and supporting those who wish to reclaim personal politics as integral to global emancipatory strategies. Examining the impact of global forces on bodies provides a central fulcrum of analysis, although it has not yet produced a shared transformatory meaning for all groups.

The World Social Forum: Contested Space in the
Construction of Counterpower ⚜

Cándido Grzybowsky has argued that feminism has a critical role to play in the World Social Forum. "'Another world is possible' is the motto of the World Social Forum," he writes, but "seen from a feminist perspective, the task is much larger than it appears." The wsf is "making the dominant ways of thinking uncomfortable," but also, he asks, "Are we also making ourselves uncomfortable with our machismo, racism and other forms of intolerance?" The dialogue among diverse perspectives in the wsf "gives the Forum its originality and power in the construction that globalizes the various citizenships of Planet Earth," he argues. "But the road is long and full of obstacles. I hope that women will make us radical, acting as they have up to now: asking what is due and making us uncomfortable" (2002).

The World Social Forum (wsf) constitutes a new global space that slowly has turned into an arena for the construction of linkages, knowledges, and global democratic thought among social movements. As Betania Ávila writes, this is a space where feminism finds a fruitful place to weave its alliances and connect with others who are seeking change and to contribute to the democratization of politics. Movements and this global space are in "a dialectical relation, in which the movements produce a process that reconfigures the shape of each movement and of all movements together" (Ávila 2003:3).

Feminisms have contributed to this alternative process of globalization. With a long and rich history of international solidarity, which has grown cumulatively out of the feminist *Encuentros* and involvement in expert networks and identity groups, feminisms express themselves at regional and global levels. Many interactions began at the un conferences, weaving the fabric of international connection. As Peter Waterman suggests, the support of feminist thinkers in the 1970s and 1980s undoubtedly proved critical to what is now considered a global movement for social justice. Their roles in new movements today can be traced back to earlier feminist practices on the international level (Waterman 2005).

Many feminisms come together in the WSF, which opens spaces for a variety of approaches and emphases in confronting neoliberal globalization. In the forums held to date (six world social forums, three polycentric forums, innumerable regional, thematic, and national forums), feminists have shown different kinds of presence and expression. They have been active in the organization of workshops and panels, in exchanges and alliances with other movements, in the development of global campaigns, and in the management of the WSF, including work on the International Council (IC).[3] Feminist networks, from Latin America and elsewhere across the globe, although few in number, have been active since the first WSF in bringing broader perspectives to bear on the processes of transformation that the Forum is designed to bring forward and debate.

At the WSF, regional and global networks of women connect with each other and with other movements. They have supported important global campaigns in each of the Forums, including that of the Marcha Mundial de Mujeres (Women's Global March) calling for a "global women's map." A campaign named Against Fundamentalism, People Are Fundamental has been brought forward by the Latin America–based Articulación Feminista Marcosur (AFM) to broaden the concept of fundamentalism to include "all religious, economic, scientific, or cultural expressions that deny humanity its diversity and legitimize the violent mechanisms by which one group subjects another, or one person subjects another" (AFM 2002).[4]

The WSF puts fundamental aspects of women's struggles onto democratic and transnational agendas. Feminists have organized panels including "Abortion in the Democratic Agenda," "The Effects of Neoliberalism on the Lives of Women," and "Women against War; War against Women." Special mention should be made of the panel "Dialogue among Movements," organized by a group of networks from different regions in the most recent Forums,[5] beginning in Mumbai in 2004 and repeated in Porto Alegre in 2005. This panel brought unionists, untouchables, peasants, gays, lesbians, and transsexuals into dialogue with one another to discuss their differences but also to share reflections on how to expand each group's perspective on transformation and thereby enrich their common ground for action.[6]

In 2007, at the Sixth World Social Forum in Nairobi, the feminist organizing group Feminist Dialogues (or Diálogos Feministas), comprised of twelve regional and global networks, organized several actions. A march coorganized by the Women's March for Freedom and various African feminist groups constituted the Forum's largest and most visible demonstration. The Young Feminists, along with the African Committee and African feminist organizations, coorganized the "Central Panel of Women" (a series of large thematic panels); organized the "Panel of Dialogue and Debates" that brought feminist antiwar and antifundamentalist perspectives onto the agenda; and presented proposals to the wsf for actions to be carried out during the rest of the year.

Are there aspects of the feminist presence that make the wsf more radical, as Cándido Grzybowsky has argued it should be? The wsf provides an umbrella for a multiplicity of movements whose common concern is the struggle against the catastrophic consequences of neoliberalism for the world's people. However, a univocal vision of the impact of neoliberalism, or of the dynamics of social change more broadly, can exclude important debates and contestations over meanings and cultures and obscure the subversive ways in which democratic change occurs locally and globally. A univocal vision can also deny recognition to new social actors who have the capacity to carry on the struggle in different arenas. These are the visions that various feminist and other movements (youth, gays, and lesbians) have been disputing and debating since the first wsf. There have been important gains, but also some resistance.

Resisting Diversity ⚜

The statements of Fray Beto, a well-known progressive theologian committed to social movements, offer an example of a problem the wsf faces in this regard. At a panel at the Fifth World Social Forum in Porto Alegre he argued that the feminist movement rose and fell in the twentieth century and that feminists should no longer be considered international actors or as committed to the transformations called for by the struggle against neoliberalism. In response, Brazilian feminists presented an open letter, objecting that Fray Beto had arbitrarily condemned a vibrant movement, one active in the wsf, to oblivion. "To make a political subject invisible is a serious sign of an enormous arbitrariness, and goes against the democratic practices of social struggle" (Articulación de Mujeres Brasileras 2005).

Perspectives that disregard the existence of movements like feminism claim power for some groups at the expense of others. But Fray Beto's narrow viewpoint cannot erase the experiences of feminists, gays, lesbians, and transsexuals, or dismiss the specific struggles that, for example, the black feminists of Latin America have carried out in their own communities and cultures. To think in exclusionary terms is to employ a view of emancipation that profoundly contradicts emancipatory goals.

Against these exclusionary dynamics, feminists within the WSF and its governing International Council have carried on a tenacious struggle to increase their visibility, democratize participation in WSF's panels and activities, and reinforce gender and diversity as basic principles. Their vision is not partial but global. Openness to diversity identifies new dimensions of struggle, not for a better *world*, in the singular, but for other better *worlds* that will reflect many emancipatory perspectives.[7] Confronting exclusionary viewpoints is important to feminists, but it is also important to other actors. This became clear, for example, when the Youth Camp of the 2005 World Social Forum brought forward issues and perspectives not anticipated by the WSF's coordinating groups. They objected that youth was given little space in the way the WSF had been organized and that the Youth Camp itself had been located on the margins of the Forum's meeting space, symbolizing the lack of interest in the ideas and concerns of youth on the part of the older generations, from whose ranks the WSF leaders were drawn.

Differences also exist in regard to the place from which one speaks. If many groups and social movements agree on the need to struggle against neoliberalism and militarism, then reflecting on how neoliberalism and militarism affect women and gender relations will yield better ways to approach this agenda.[8] Women are affected by global economic change and suffer in wars by being displaced from their homes and families. They are often victims of rape and constitute many of the civilian dead. Feminists can take up the issues of globalization and militarism, but some feminist issues are not as easily taken up by other movements. The struggle to have their issues recognized therefore requires opening spaces for further discussion and communication. The struggle against fundamentalisms, which finds the relations among sexuality, production, and reproduction relevant at both the symbolic and the material levels, offers a key example. These movements may form part of the opposition to neoliberalism, but they are also examples of social relations of exploitation and domination on other grounds (Ávila 2003). The struggle against fundamentalisms recognizes a diversity of connections, life experiences, and subjectivities, and feminists have important perspectives to offer.

But these perspectives have not been fully recognized as important dimensions of the transformative proposals put forward by both men and women in the WSF. A statement to the press by the AFM on January 31, 2005, addressed this issue. Speaking from the "Women's Ship" (Barco de las Mujeres), AFM declared:

> The fight for sexual freedom and abortion is one of the most advanced forms of opposition to fundamentalisms within the framework of the WSF. . . . Until now it has not succeeded in making the Forum equal; the focus on the "important" activities of the "important" men shows how necessary it is to make the Forum more democratic. . . . The AFM believes that the WSF should be a place of lived radical democracy, with equality among diverse people.[9]

At the 2007 WSF in Nairobi, which boasted an unusually large presence of church groups from Africa and around the world (including a United States–based pro-life organization), a dramatic confrontation occurred. Several of the church groups had organized an antiabortion march. In addition, during the closing ceremony, a verbal attack occurred against a speaker who was a lesbian activist. This produced diverse expressions of resistance from both men and women on the International Council (IC), some noting that the Charter of Principles affirmed the WSF as a nonconfessional space. After the WSF, in response to the situation, a group of networks and institutions sent a statement to IC, which read in part:

> By this document we affirm that the struggles of our sisters (nuestr@s herman@s) for sexual and reproductive rights throughout the world are also our struggles. And therefore, calling on the principle of diversity that we believe is fundamental to the goal of constructing other possible worlds that are more solidary and just . . . [and] given that the struggles to create these other worlds can only be successful if they recognize the diversity of identities and political positions, we affirm that the WSF is open to all who recognize this diversity. Organizations and individuals who promote the marginalization, exclusion, or discrimination of others cannot be part of this process. . . . We call upon the International Council, and on the

various organizing committees, to promote and support the integration of the struggles for sexual and reproductive rights in each Social Forum that takes place around the world. We understand the diversity of cultural and political contexts, but the right to fight for the autonomy and liberty of nuestr@s herman@s is not negotiable. (En Diversidad, Otro Mundo Es Posible 2007)[10]

Diversity and Democracy ⚡

Providing space for debate is one of the most precious founding principles of the WSF. The tensions and contradictions and the different levels of their expression are fundamental to the recovery of the range of sensibilities and challenges to new stages of globalization. Inequalities perceived and named become the basis for more daring proposals that can broaden and connect particular viewpoints.

Such debates have expanded our understanding of democracy. Boaventura de Sousa Santos speaks of "demo-diversity" as a useful antidote to rigid and univocal conceptions of democracy. Demo-diversity is "the peaceful or conflictive existence, in a given social field, of different models and practices of democracy" (De Sousa Santos 2006). To have an impact on this new conception of democracy, it is necessary to make one's own position clear. Multiple feminist strategies arise from difference as we support and commit ourselves to the struggles that have given rise to other social movements as part of the process that drives the WSF. Feminist political visions of democracy and change must be incorporated into this debate, creating a space for dialogue that is sensitive to differences and seeks points of convergence. This democratic vision incorporates struggles for recognition. For recognition to have space, Marta Rosenberg maintains, it is necessary to politicize differences, celebrating equality as the vehicle of justice while protecting expressions of difference as acts of freedom (Rosenberg 2002).

For this conception of feminism, democracy in diversity implies the recognition that multiple forms of struggle for justice and freedom are valid, and that their expression broadens the democratic base. Once we accept this idea, the subjectivities and recognitions vital to diversity can be transformed. Differences perceived and named, rather than ignored or repressed, become the raw material for audacious proposals. The acceptance of diversity through recognition can subvert the fragmentation neoliberalism produces, even while maintaining a coherent alternative to the neoliberal view of the world and its future.

## Feminist Dialogues from Difference ⸖

A group of feminist caucuses (*articulaciones*), and organizations from different regions of the world have taken on the task of organizing a space for recognition and dialogue among feminists in the WSF. A meeting under the trees, organized by AFM during the 2003 WSF, led to the Feminist Dialogues initiated in 2004 in Mumbai and continued in Porto Alegre and Nairobi. Women from all over the world meet for three days prior to the forum: we were 180 in Mumbai, 260 in Porto Alegre, and 180 in Nairobi. Although we all had regional or transnational feminist connections, few of us had engaged in such discussions before at the global level. One of the constants of the Feminist Dialogues is finding feminist ways to approach the basic goals of the WSF — confronting neoliberalism and militarism — while also emphasizing the importance of opposing all fundamentalisms. Making the body an analytical focus has the potential of integrating disparate views and inspiring a radical democratic vision.

This idea is expressed in the following "Conceptual Note" from the 2005 meeting:

> Conscious as feminists that our bodies are full of cultural and social significance, we also experience our bodies as key sites of political and moral struggles. Through the bodies of women, the community, the state, the family, fundamentalist forces (state and non-state), religion, and markets define themselves. These forces and institutions, using a plethora of patriotic controls, transform the bodies of women into expressions of relations of power. The bodies of women, therefore, are at the center of authoritarian or democratic projects.

In 2007, the Third Feminist Dialogue issued the following "Note on Political Perspectives for a Radical Democracy":

> The feminist movements of the new millennium are committed to the enrichment of the radical political-democratic project, in which diversity must be recognized, internalized, and negotiated in ways that create subjects, rather than be considered something merely to be tolerated. We look

for spaces where women can express and enrich themselves by a process of learning and experimenting with change, giving rise to the mutual recognition of and relations among other local, national, regional, and global democratic struggles. This in turn will enrich the emerging democratic cultures, which will express themselves in an explosion of new themes, identities, and social actors. . . . A different world will not be possible without a different conception of democracy. And a different democracy is possible only through a process of personal and subjective revolution, involving both men and women, which actively recognizes diversity and takes the intersectionalities of these different struggles as a collective end. (Diálogos Feministas 2007)

Feminists who participate in the WSF, from their multiple differences and without any prior relationship among them, share a referential horizon expressed in their choice of the WSF as a place of participation and action. With different emphases, they share a commitment to struggles for redistribution and for recognition and to interacting in pluralist spaces with other social actors, male and female. They want to "strengthen feminist political organization beyond borders," in the words of the Global Report of the Second Feminist Dialogue in 2005 (Diálogos Feministas 2005). In the WSF, feminists are in dialogue and debate to transcend their own limits, democratizing their interactions and avoiding their own "fundamentalist" or single-minded versions of what is possible.

Those who participate in the Feminist Dialogues are active in many networks and organizations in addition to the WSF. Yet the WSF offers a distinct space for ongoing learning and interchange that can create new visions of democracy and strengthen global democratic forces. Women's interactions in feminist spaces before coming together in the WSF facilitated our discussions and aided our vision, but it has also made our dynamics more complex. The reflections that nurture the Feminist Dialogues form part of a critical repositioning within feminism.

Nandita Gandhi and Nandita Shah (2007:2) have argued that for those who participate, "feminism goes further than the popular liberal understanding of equality between men and women." In the Feminist Dialogues, feminism sees oppression and women's agency both within a patriarchal structure and "within neoliberal economic, social and political systems." It is a feminism "against fundamentalisms, global capitalism, and imperialism," which "allies itself with the marginalized and indigenous," "develops its practices every day of our lives," and "seeks to work collectively and democratically." The point is not to "privilege" either the particular or the universal, "but to universalize our visions and goals as women's movements."

We recognize that the past few decades have rendered the old paradigms obsolete and that it is necessary to recreate or construct new concepts and connections, working with others to construct an alternative globalization from a radical democratic standpoint. Gender identities must be seen in constant interaction and articulation with other identities. Forms of discrimination based on race, ethnicity, age, sexual orientation, and geographical location are all expressions of global systems of domination.

We must be clear: there are many struggles. Rather than make differences invisible, we must use them to provoke a multiplicity of responses that can expand the space of social experience at the local and global levels. The old distinction between local and global has lost much of its meaning, and this in turn requires a change of perspective, as Beck argues, from the national to the cosmopolitan. As he observes, conflicts over gender, class, ethnicity, and sexual preference have their origins in the nation, but they have long escaped that frame and now overlap and interconnect globally (Beck 2004).

For Latin American feminists who participate in the WSF, the Feminist Dialogues have added a new dimension to their international experience, which has moved from the regional level of the Latin American and Caribbean feminist *Encuentros* to the global spaces of the UN world conferences on women to this new arena of interaction with feminists and with other social movements at the global level. Their strategies are shifting from advocacy to the creation of counterpower and counternarratives against neoliberal ideology. Both strategies were present at Beijing, but advocacy, not opposition, characterized the second half of the 1990s.

In contrast to the regional *Encuentros*, however, where all feminists who wanted and were able to participated, these new global spaces do not manifest as strong a feminist presence as other forums, nor as strong a one as possible. We are a small group, which is due as much to the low levels of activist interest in global issues as to the cost of international travel. The advances, new understandings, and new questions gained from our WSF experiences still lack channels of expression and analysis at the national-global level. It is important for us to infuse our actions with insights from these multilevel discourses. Seen from any particular point on the planet, the global is always local.

In the past four years, the Feminist Dialogues have changed. From the beginning it proved difficult to find a way to proceed, and we learned as we went, helped by the criticisms of the feminist participants and the self-criticism of the organizing team. Seeing that the approaches used in previous meetings had failed to provide an environment in which we could express our similarities and differences and work toward future perspectives,[11] we proposed that the 2007 WSF in Nairobi give more attention to the discussion of feminist political agendas in relation to the goals of the WSF, and to the construction, from many perspectives, of global feminist agendas. The call to participate in the Feminist Dialogues was directed to "feminists with a strong interest in the political project of constructing a movement . . . recognizing, of course, that the notion of 'a movement' is dynamic and filled with diversity and contradictions" ("Methodological Note," Diálogos Feministas 2007).

In addition to discussions of democracy, citizenship, and neoliberal, fundamentalist and militarized states, the meeting emphasized the goal of creating global feminist strategies, hoping to generate critical perspectives and diverse reflections from the different feminisms represented by the participants ("Conceptual Note on Feminist Strategies," Diálogos Feministas 2007). Furthermore, for the first time the organizing team decided to take positions in the WSF, supporting some of the initiatives already discussed, including the Women's March for Freedom, the Feminist Youth Tent, and the opportunity to collect and propose ideas for the list of actions the WSF as a whole would agree to carry out during the rest of the year. One of these initiatives was to participate in a so-called Global Day of Action in the third week of January 2008, organizing actions, mobilizations, panel discussions, and other events around the three common issues of militarism, neoliberalism, and fundamentalism.

Significant changes also occurred in the WSF itself, which moved toward greater democratization and the more effective inclusion of different perspectives within the framework of the Charter of Principles, making strategic spaces like that of the Feminist Dialogues and others more relevant. Feminists reacted to the active presence of participants linked to conservative churches by entering into dialogues on many issues; they challenged conservative agendas using their feminist focus on the body to argue their case. Various panels were organized by the AFM to focus on "the body in the democratic agenda." Participants with religious beliefs were invited, and they accepted—a positive expression of the type of dynamic the WSF facilitates.

But the new presence of people who came to the forum primarily as representatives of church organizations brought a narrow view of human rights to the WSF, exhibiting a moralism positioned against humanistic and emancipatory thought and a commitment to denying the rights, liberty, and autonomy of women, gays, lesbians, bisexuals, and transsexuals. This affected not only women and homosexuals but also diluted the spirit of democratic pluralism that had marked the WSF. For the first time, there was a pro-life exhibit and an antiabortion march. And for the first time, a speaker suffered verbal attacks in the closing ceremony because she was a lesbian and opposed by a significant number of Forum participants. The visible presence of African groups supporting sexual diversity in Nairobi constituted a welcome counterbalance, but it is clear that sexual and reproductive rights have become one of the disputed divides at the global-local level represented by the WSF.

Conclusions ⚘

The Feminist Dialogues have proven an intense learning experience for the group that first promoted them, and that group has grown larger.[12] Political and practical lessons have been learned: the discovery of other perspectives and knowledges, of new ways to interrogate reality, and of the awareness that the same strategies can produce different effects in different situations. A telling example, which emerged from discussions in Mumbai, is the contrasting ways in which the right to abortion is seen in different contexts. Latin American feminists tend to see the right to have an abortion as the strongest expression of the struggle to broaden the margins of choice women have in their lives; it constitutes an important political goal as abortion remains illegal in most of the region, although estimates suggest that several million illegal abortions are performed, endangering the health of women, particularly of poor women. In India abortion has been decriminalized, but Indian feminists must confront the fact that this opening of greater space for choice has been used against women, because families overwhelmingly choose to abort female embryos. Reproductive rights are recognized by law in India, but they have given power to the state—which uses them to impose far-reaching policies of birth control—and not to women.

Other cultures, other resources, and other "lacks" mean different problems; and with regard to problems that women have in common, there are often different solutions with different risks. It is enriching to know that the common goals of justice and liberty cannot necessarily be pursued using the same strategies, and that similar strategies often produce quite different results. This knowledge extends the limits of what we can imagine as possible, but it also complicates feminist proposals at the global level. Finally, it raises the fundamental question of whether there can ever be universal solutions — or universal ways of thinking about them.

## Notes ✢

1   The regional-global connections and interrelations have become more complex to the degree that the number of feminisms in the region also multiplied. Initially feminists were relatively homogeneous, with similar perceptions of the importance of autonomy. As time passed there were more differences among feminists, less in their strategies and more in the ways in which they incorporated diversity. These reflected the different periods when groups became active, and also subregional differences, including those between South American feminisms, which were more developed and hegemonic, and the Central American movements that emerged from the region's civil wars. Feminists are increasingly differentiated by their opportunities and access to political powers; by their urban or rural bases; and by the degree to which they recognize diversity (e.g., lesbian feminists began to hold their own *encuentros*, often preceding the regional ones). The tensions seen at the end of the 1980s between "institutionalized" (NGO) and "voluntary" feminists foreshadowed more serious conflicts in the 1990s.

2   The campaign for an inter-American convention of sexual and reproductive rights forms part of this strategy, reflecting new forms of interaction and dispute with international organizations, as the initiative does not come from the UN but from organized feminist groups.

3   The IC boasts the active presence of feminist networks that support democratization and the permanent broadening of the World Social Forum. Among these feminist groups are the Articulación Feminista Marcosur, la Marcha Mundial de Mujeres, Red Mujeres Transformando la Economía, Dawn Network, Red de Educación Popular entre Mujeres (REPEM), Red Ashkara, and Red LGBT Sur-Sur, among others.

4   Initiated in the 2002 WSF by the AFM, the campaign against fundamentalisms is now a global one.

5   The organizations and networks that initiated this panel are: Ashkara, from India; Women's International Coalition for Economic Justice (WICEJ) and AFM from Latin America; Feminist Network (FEMNET) from Africa; DAWN, red global (global network), and INform from Sri Lanka.

6   This experience is in keeping with the new approach of the WSF, which seeks to put different networks in dialogue and to cement relations among groups interested in the exchange of strategies and proposals.

7   This dispute has been evident since the first WSF, where women outnumbered men and yet few more than ten women participated in the panels. In the second WSF some feminists succeeded in organizing panels, but the responsibility for organizing the themes or "axes" (groupings of six or seven large panels) remained in male hands. At the third WSF two of the five axes were organized by feminist networks: the AFM and the Marcha Mundial de Mujeres.

8   In the case of militarism, besides confronting a warlike culture that privileges war, women point out what the logic of war implies for women's bodies. Neoliberalism not only increases part-time and outsourced domestic piecework, but also makes the private sphere responsible for social-welfare obligations that states ought to provide, which in turn increases the burden of women's work and their responsibilities as caretakers.

9   The ship was organized by the Campaign against Fundamentalisms, providing a space for diverse activities, workshops, discussion groups, and presentations about topics that ranged from water as a scarce resource to discussions with and about transvestites and transsexuals.

10  This letter, initially signed by the Program of Democracy and Global Transformation of the University of San Marcos, Lima, the AFM, the Flora Tristán Center, Asociación Brasiliera de Organizaciones No Gubermentales (ABONG), and the Paulo Freire Institute, has received a large number of additional signatories.

11  The fact that the organizing team did not want to seek consensus on actions or agendas helped produce this outcome.

12  To the initial group, which included the AFM, INform, National Network of Autonomous Women's Organizations (NNAWG), DAWN, WIECEJ, Isis Manila, and FEMNET, Akina Mama wa A'frica (AMWA), the Latin American Committee for the Defense of Women's Rights (CLADEM), the Latin American and Caribbean Network of Young People for Sexual and Reproductive Rights (REDLAC), and the Popular Education Network of Women of Latin America and the Caribbean (REPEM), Women Living under Muslim Laws (WLUML), and Women in Development (WIDE) later added their endorsement.

# 8

# Social Accountability and Citizen Participation ⸙

## ARE LATIN AMERICAN GOVERNMENTS MEETING THEIR COMMITMENTS TO GENDER EQUITY?

*Teresa Valdés and Alina Donoso*

In the past few decades, the countries of Latin America have lived through important political, economic, social, and cultural changes, ones marked by democratization and globalization. Along with new possibilities for growth, the current development model has created new tensions, inequalities, and forms of discrimination at the national and international levels. The search for equity has been left to public action by civil society as well as by the state. Governments have also shown an increasing concern for gender equality and the advancement of women. This newly gained awareness has resulted from pressure from women's movements, international agencies, civil society, and gender units within governments. It manifests itself in political mobilizations, in the development of binding international laws (through international conventions and accords), in the emergence of nonbinding norms (developed from summits and conferences), and in the design and implementation of social policies, constitutional reforms, and laws.

Monitoring how states fulfill the international commitments they have made has become an important goal for civil-society organizations, especially where the government has made a public commitment but is not legally bound. Meeting these commitments requires political will, which may not last after the documents are signed and the government representatives return to their countries. In addition, governments are likely to face resistance from sectors of their populations that do not agree with the content of the accords they have signed onto. But the consolidation of an international agenda for gender equity, constructed with the active support of national governments, has created a new arena favorable to women's movements and organizations seeking new ways to engage in political action on these issues. One way to promote change is to organize to monitor the degree to which governments are fulfilling their commitments, a process known in Spanish as *control ciudadano* and in English as social watch or social accountability.

In Latin America, that governments have made these commitments has permitted women's organizations to carry out a series of actions, among them the construction of an Index of Commitments Fulfilled (Indice de Compromiso Cumplido, or ICC) to monitor the progress made on the goals set out in the Platform of Action of the Fourth UN Conference on Women, held in Beijing in 1995 and the Program of Action from the Cairo conference on population, in 1994. By 2005 eighteen countries had participated in the project.[1]

### The Strategy of *Control Ciudadano* ⚜

The term *social accountability* applies to a number of individual and collective actions intended to monitor the acts of public authorities and the policies, programs, and measures that affect people's rights (Instituto del Tercer Mundo 1999a; Arteaga 1998). These actions are undertaken by citizen activists interested in creating a better society through participating in specific activities that contribute systematically to holding governments accountable. Going beyond a formal citizenship, the concept of active citizenship places a high value on rights, but also on the responsibilities individuals have to the political communities to which they belong. Active citizenship means participating in public affairs and being part of the debates on issues that affect individual citizens. It gives people a new sense of themselves and their goals, generates awareness and new practices, strengthens civil society, and broadens the connection between rights and responsibilities that is implicit in the idea of citizenship. It attempts to extend the understanding of both democracy and citizenship beyond the role of a citizen as conventionally understood in representative democracies (Bonino 1998). Active citizenship assumes citizens will take leading roles in civil society and in public action to develop new ways of relating to the state. This concept of citizenship sees women's organizations as political subjects, capable of making significant but realizable demands and of developing practices that are autonomous, deliberative, and participatory.

The idea of finding ways in which civil society, and particularly NGOS, could monitor international agreements came out of the UN Social Development Summit, held in Copenhagen in 1995, and gained momentum in a number of countries.[2] After the UN conference on women in Beijing, many women in Latin America were very concerned about the implementation of the Platform of Action, which reflected the agenda of the women's movement but lacked mechanisms to ensure that the goals of the platform be carried out. For this reason, the Regional Coordinating Group of women's NGOS made it one of their goals to monitor the implementation of the Platform of Action. It proposed to create a regional ICC focusing on key indicators that would reflect the degree of progress states were making toward meeting their commitments. Although women's groups were highly enthusiastic and had developed good relations with government authorities, they remained very concerned that the platform would remain a paper document, rather than an effective guide to policies and programs.

The framework for social accountability is the set of commitments that states themselves have made both nationally and internationally, particularly at UN conferences on global issues in the 1990s.[3] The approach tries to identify and evaluate the degree to which each government is fulfilling its promises. When the method identifies problems, actions, or lack of action on the part of the state, the information can become an effective tool for pressuring the government to make the necessary changes (Instituto del Tercer Mundo 1999a).

The development of social-accountability actions in the area of gender has been reinforced by the UN conferences' incorporation of women's organizations into the process of developing their goals and the encouragement of women to take active roles in ensuring implementation of the goals. Some groups have received funding from international organizations to do so, and some Latin American governments have created special commissions to monitor the implementation of the commitments they made in Beijing. Many of these commissions have encouraged the participation of groups from civil society, and they have developed the technical means to monitor progress (CEPAL 1999). In some cases, for example during the conference on population and development in Cairo in 1994, governments approved the participation of civil-society groups in the conference itself.

Becoming active citizens proves a major challenge for women, given the persistence of a political and institutional culture deeply imbued with authoritarianism and hierarchy and given the effects of the neoliberal model of growth, which weakens social ties and makes it difficult to push for new rights or to debate issues of economic organization. To change these conditions, women's organizations must be political subjects, that is, be capable of making realizable demands of carrying out autonomous, participatory, and deliberative ways of organizing and acting that go beyond formal or legal definitions of citizenship.

A key precondition for active citizenship is autonomy, the degree to which political subjects are able to appropriate their own energies and direct their own lives. Autonomy depends on multiple, complex processes such as individuation, the construction of identities, and empowerment. To develop autonomy, individuals must be able to see things from a critical point of view. That in turn implies knowing how to recognize power relations and being able to change them through individual and collective decisions and actions. Autonomous citizens must also have sufficient economic resources to make political action possible (Vargas 2000). They must have the confidence and freedom to monitor state actions and challenge the government when necessary. Women must recognize that gender issues are public issues, and they must acquire the capacity to keep track of the resources that governments have pledged to address gender issues. They must be ready to take advantage of opportunities to press for change.

Participation in this form of citizenship requires an awareness of one's rights. Yet many women do not see themselves as the subjects of rights, or recognize their "right to have rights," without which they cannot be active creators of a more egalitarian society. For this reason the empowerment of women as social actors must be a task of the highest priority. *Control ciudadano* requires a women's movement with the political capacity to make its own demands and link its demands for gender equity to broader demands for social justice. It must be able to engage in dialogue with other social sectors and movements and find ways to coordinate actions that address shared agendas. To be successful in monitoring progress, women's movements must also be able to negotiate with and find areas of agreement with government authorities. A "political strategy" alone is not sufficient; it is necessary to proceed with an idea of rights that can enable the state to express popular sovereignty in ways that go beyond its own technocratic and bureaucratic dynamics.

The Index of Commitments Fulfilled (ICC)
as a Means to Citizenship ⚜

Following the recommendation of the Regional Coordinating Group to monitor post-Beijing follow-up efforts, in 1996 a Chilean network of the main NGOs and an academic center specializing in gender became the Initiating Group of Chilean Women. Basing their activities on the experience of some of its members, the group took on the task of constructing an ICC for Chile as part of a social-watch strategy that included work with the media and the establishment of political forums for discussion and negotiation with government authorities.

To monitor the state it is necessary to have access to information that allows citizens to compare what is actually happening to the goals the state set for itself. With this as its objective, the Initiating Group of Chilean Women developed an ICC to measure the degree to which the Chilean government was fulfilling its international and national commitments to gender equity.[4] The ICC was also conceived of as a negotiating tool, as a way to strengthen women's organizations to demand that the government show political will and make measurable advances in the areas under observation, and to provide women's groups with the concrete evidence on policies and programs that they would need to question politicians and government officials. Both strategies were intended to make gender equity issues more visible in Chilean politics.

The thematic and political priorities represented by the ICC were decided on in discussions and debates that took place throughout the country in 1997, and they were operationalized in a set of indicators and a gender-equity goal for each (such as parity in the case of women's political representation) with the help of experts in each issue area. It was not difficult to decide on the thematic priorities, but it turned out to be hard to find statistical information of sufficiently high quality to assure the assessments' rigorousness, validity, and trustworthiness. The lack of statistics in some areas made it difficult to include in the ICC some of the themes originally proposed.

The ICC is a set of related indicators that allows for comparisons over time. It is expressed as an index (as numerical values on a scale) representing the degree of progress toward a specified goal. The ICC is set in a conceptual frame that uses indicators of social phenomena that change in response to pressures and policies as measured against the standard that the index defines as optimal. This approach makes it possible to grasp a complex social process with a multiplicity of actors. It seeks to understand changes in social organization in a culture that has traditionally relegated women to subordinate positions and discriminated against them in many different spheres of social life.

At the same time, the ICC is a political instrument that originates in a participatory process. It involves discussions among women in organizations who identify needs, establish priorities, select the variables they will monitor, and after a process of consideration and consultation with experts, construct a composite measure that, when combined with other, similarly arrived-at variables, creates an index. This approach assumes that working alliances exist between women in organizations and academics and professionals who themselves are committed to the democratic and democratizing process. The political dimension of the ICC comes into play each time it is used by citizens to monitor government actions.

The ICCs focus on three strategic areas for women: participation and access to power; economic autonomy and poverty; and health (including violence) and sexual and reproductive rights. Each area can be represented by a series of indicators that can be combined into an index; grouping those together creates an index that can be constructed for the entire country.

The specific frame of reference for the ICC is the set of commitments that governments signed onto in Beijing (or at other international conferences) in each of these thematic areas. Using these as the basis for setting the goals, it is possible to ask questions and to establish indicators to monitor how well the government is carrying out its commitments. Statistically, the ICC follows a model similar to the one developed by the UN Development Program (UNDP) to create the Human Development Index and various indexes of gender equity, but it focuses attention on the economic, social, and cultural aspects of the path to gender equity. In contrast to the UNDP approach, which relies solely on experts, the ICC is developed by groups in civil society who then consult with experts. The spirit of the ICC is citizen participation.

The use of gender indicators requires data disaggregated by sex to operationalize concepts of gender inequality and measure changes over time. Seeking concrete data, in addition to democratizing citizens' access to information, allows civil society groups to assess the results of government policies directly, rather than relying on governments' rhetoric about their intentions and programs. The ICC makes it possible to evaluate changes as they are occurring, and to know what the specific consequences are for women and gender relations.

Once the ICC was developed for Chile, women and women's organizations from other Latin American countries who were interested in monitoring the progress of their governments on international treaties and who saw the value of social accountability as a means to do so were invited to use the Chilean methodology to develop their own ICCs. Between 2000 and 2002, organizations from Argentina, Uruguay, Paraguay, Peru, Ecuador, and Colombia participated in this process, and eleven other countries did so between 2002 and 2003: Bolivia, Venezuela, Brazil, Panama, El Salvador, Honduras, Nicaragua, Costa Rica, Guatemala, Mexico, and the Dominican Republic.[5] Indicators for each country were chosen from areas with clear and visible areas of deficit, for which there were government commitments in areas susceptible to measurement, and for which data was available. Thus the ICC constitutes a country-specific instrument, shaped by the needs and priorities identified by women's organizations.

Conceptual Framework ⚜

The ICC is based on the concept of gender, which conceives of the relations between the sexes as a system of differentiation that produces inequality (Scott 1996; Lamas 1990; Rubin 1990; De Barbieri 1992). The mechanisms of discrimination created by the sex-gender system include the division of labor by sex, sex-differentiated socialization processes, and the construction of male and female social spaces. These are crystallized in the representations and social value assigned to masculine and feminine and through legal and social norms, which regulate social behavior.

The political concept that frames the ICC is the pursuit of gender equity both as an ethical issue and as a matter of social justice, which is the foundation of democracy. It recognizes that contemporary societies are divided by socioeconomic and cultural inequalities strongly rooted in processes and practices systematically disadvantaging certain groups relative to others and that these hierarchies are reinforced by a symbolic order that legitimizes these differences. Women as a group are hierarchically inferior to men, but intersectionality (the fact that many women are also subjected to race, class, and other forms of hierarchy) means that the sex-gender system has a harsher impact on some groups than on others. The political vision behind the ICC recognizes a paradox: although Latin American countries share widely accepted discourses calling for universal access and the elimination of hierarchies, strategies of discrimination on the basis of gender, race, ethnicity, and class, among others, are constantly deployed (Fraser 1998).

The ICC framework is egalitarian, but it also recognizes differences between men and women, especially the reproductive capacity of women and its consequences, and it also reflects awareness of differences *within* each gender. The diversity of experiences of race, class, nationality, ethnicity, and age among both women and men can be considerable. It does not suffice to analyze the condition of women by describing and naming gender differences. It is also necessary to observe the differences *among women* as a key element in the analysis of economic and social inequalities, differential access to rights, and different market roles.

In this sense, following Nancy Fraser (1998), the ICC framework assumes that gender equity cannot be measured by a single variable or norm, whether that is equality, difference, or something else, but that it must be understood as a complex notion encompassing a plurality of normative principles, some associated with the egalitarian side of the debate, and others with defending difference. For this reason the challenge in constructing the ICC is to credit egalitarian advances in areas where that criterion applies, but also to take account of difference, to be aware of the gaps and social distances extant between men and women, as well as among women.

International Commitments and Thematic Areas ⚜

The framework for social accountability using the ICC is based on the obligations that the state itself has taken on at the national or international level: the UN Convention on the Elimination of All Forms of Discrimination against Women (CEDAW), the Beijing Platform of Action (1995), and many of the agreements reached in the Plan of Action of the Cairo Conference on Population and Development (1994). The thematic areas chosen for inclusion in the ICC were defined in Chile by debates among women's organizations after Beijing, and they resembled the issues given priority by NGOs at the Latin American Regional Conference held in Mar del Plata in 1994.

Each area marks a strategic dimension of women's status. Access to power has an impact on the overall situation of women; economic autonomy gives women greater power in all other spheres; and health, when enjoyed along with the capacity and resources to make one's own decisions about sexual and reproductive life, is a basic good that supports women's empowerment in all other areas.

Participation and Access to Power ·ᢤ

Power allows for the construction of a desired social order, but women have been absent from institutionalized power for centuries. Over time, political action has produced—and reproduced—a form of social organization in which the sexual division of labor—man as producer, woman as reproducer—sets norms and shapes identities that stereotype and discriminate against women (Astelarra 1990). This limits women's ability to exercise full citizenship or to negotiate with other social actors.

Although women have demonstrated the capacity for social leadership, the traditional images of male and female reinforce the tendency to put political decisions in the hands of men. The data shows that men control most positions of greater decision-making power, and that gaining and maintaining access to power always proves precarious for women. Levels of female political participation can be measured to show the degree to which gender discrimination exists in political representation. In general, the capacities and skills to which women are socialized do not make them competitive in the political and public worlds, which have been defined by masculine parameters, styles, and rules. Women have responsibilities and tasks in which they excel, and they may be more aware of the needs of their families and communities than men are, or they may be more inclined to relate in ways based on tolerance, negotiation, and consensus, but these qualities are devalued in the public sphere. Discrimination against women in social participation and political life makes women feel that their interests and demands are not being taken seriously by those who say they represent them. And because they are ignored, women are less likely than men to be committed to active participation.

Overcoming the difficulties that women confront requires eliminating the barriers that now exist and creating new institutional and normative conditions that promote an equitable division of power. Women's access to decision-making positions, their becoming candidates for political office, and their election to office are essential to a progressive process of empowering women. This process must begin in early childhood socialization and be carried through the entire educational process. Progress toward the equitable participation of women in politics and power will be reflected in a growing number of women in public roles. This is an egalitarian goal that can also increase the transparency of the political process and deepen democracy.

Economic Autonomy and Poverty ⚡

Over millennia women have been assigned the tasks related to reproduction and men the work of production. But for decades women have become increasingly incorporated into the labor market, breaking with the conventional view that women belong in the home. The conventional view ignores the fact that women's productive work has supported national development, and the maintenance of themselves, their homes, and their families.

Nevertheless, women in the labor market have faced discrimination and subordination, evidenced in the number of women who work in jobs that are poorly paid, lack job security, require fewer qualifications, and usually do not have social security, conditions that are especially true for the poorest, for young women, and for temporary and piece workers. Unemployment is also higher among these groups, particularly among young women. At the same time, these women face strong barriers to their participation in the labor market as a result of increasing educational requirements (to which women may not have access), cultural orientations, family pressures, opportunity costs, and the need to care for young children (Fundación IDEAS 1999). Women's employment, the types of work they do, and the wages they earn are reflected in statistics that the government collects, as is their access to education and, although less reliably, the availability of child care outside the home.

A global consensus today sees health not as the absence of disease but as a more holistic combination of physical, mental, and social well-being (UN 1994). This means that people have a right to the highest level of health care and to enjoy the benefits of scientific progress in this area. Reproductive health, in particular, must be understood to include the capacity to enjoy a sexually satisfying life as well as procreation. Sexual and reproductive rights mean that individuals and couples should be able to enjoy sex without the risk of an undesired pregnancy or of contracting sexually transmitted diseases including AIDS, to decide freely how many children to have and when to have them, and to have access to the information necessary to do so. Women should have access to adequate gynecological attention during pregnancy, during birth, and after birth, and to the prevention and treatment of infertility. These rights lie at the center of the debate on women as autonomous subjects with responsibilities for and the capacity to make decisions concerning their bodies, their sexuality, and their fertility.

The patriarchal sex-gender system puts women at a disadvantage; it is ironic that the capacity to reproduce the human species, which depends on women's bodies, has become the source of women's subordination. It has justified a set of cultural values that for thousands of years has reduced women to their roles as mothers and reproducers, and it has socialized them to fulfill this task. Women are especially vulnerable to illness as a result of their reproductive roles, yet they also are disadvantaged in terms of access to and the utilization of health services. As the social constructions of male and female differ, so do the health profiles of men and women (De los Ríos 1993). The health system is organized to treat "people" defined as men, and the field favors male professionals. Doctors are privileged over nurses, and socialization directs men and women into different roles. The medicalization of the normal processes of life and the way in which women interface with the healthcare system as users of health services also have gender-differentiated effects.

The full exercise of sexual and reproductive rights implies respect for the integrity of persons, shared responsibility in the sexual and reproductive behavior of the couple, and mutual consent, among other considerations. For this reason women must be able to make decisions about their sexual and reproductive lives free from coercion, and they must have alternative ways of realizing their reproductive goals. These are essential elements in any effort to empower women to exercise their rights. Here, too, there are statistics on women's health that allow comparisons over time, and it is possible to track policies on women's reproductive rights.

Developing the Goals ⸙

The icc provides a way to show the degree to which progress has been made toward goals defined by the creators of the index as optimal in terms of equality and social justice. With this objective in mind, each indicator selected should be a measure of gender equity or social equality. The particular index developed for each thematic area depends on the kinds of issues that seem most important to the group constructing the index and on what is technically possible to achieve, given the data. In the case of participation and access to power, the indicators generally measure the achievement of sociopolitical equity between men and women. Equity is constructed from two complementary perspectives: equality of access and equality of results. For equality of access, for example, one may ask if women and men are equally able to put themselves forward as candidates and under similar conditions. With regard to equality of result, the ideal is parity—an equal number of men and women in representative or decision-making positions, reflecting the fact that women and men each represent 50 percent of the population. Parity can be considered the definitive measure of equality in the division of power among men and women.

In the area of economic autonomy and poverty, the indicators used to measure progress toward equality are labor rights, conditions of work, access to resources and training, and, to reflect antipoverty principles, the absence of exploitation and income equality (Fraser 1998). The indicators must reflect inequalities *among* women, as well as gender differences. Economic autonomy is related to the distribution of income, but it must also take into consideration differences attributable to class, geography, and race and ethnicity, among other things.

For the area of women's health and sexual and reproductive rights it is necessary to find measures that allow women to have their human rights fully recognized in all stages of the life cycle: freedom of choice in the questions of sexuality and reproduction, nondiscrimination, and social equity. This assumes respect for differences among women and equal access to services for women in different social sectors. Improvements in women's health must also mean that gender differences making certain women vulnerable to diseases associated with their socially assigned roles are recognized and taken into account.

Constructing the ICC ⌇

The ICC links several different indicators to provide an integrated understanding of the situation of women in each thematic area. However, some indicators are more reliable than others, and for this reason the process of deciding the mix of indicators begins with their evaluation by experts, both men and women. The value assigned each indicator defines its relevance in comparison with the other indicators used to measure progress in a particular area. The process results in a scale that reflects the importance women of a particular country give to particular issue areas.

An index is constructed as a series of steps undertaken in each country:

- a training workshop to transmit the methodology to the organization or NGO that has taken on the task of developing the index in each country
- opportunities for discussion within the women's movement to determine the needs and demands of women
- a conceptual discussion of the extant forms of gender discrimination and types of gender inequalities, including their manifestation in the lives of both men and women
- the identification of the obligations the national government has assumed with regard to these needs and demands at the international and national levels
- the selection of appropriate indicators
- a discussion of the selected indicators with experts
- a definition of hoped-for outcomes in the areas for which indicators have been selected, with due attention to gender equity and equality
- the search for data, using 1995 as the base year
- processing the data to produce the value of each indicator
- a consideration of each indicator in the index, in consultation with experts

- a consideration of the goals
- a calculation of the index by thematic area
- a calculation of the overall index

The following section of the essay reports on the ICC indicators in Brazil, Venezuela, and Mexico, very different countries that have made varied progress toward the goal of gender equity. Each step taken by the groups in Brazil, Venezuela, and Mexico was shared with the Regional Coordinating Group, located in Chile, to ensure the accurate application of the methodology to allow consistency and comparisons across countries. Once the calculations were finished, each country drew up a final report, which was published for public distribution and for use in social-accountability actions.

The Results ⁙

The data discussed in this article and synthesized in its tables are a brief summary of the results obtained in the ICCs of Brazil, Mexico, and Venezuela. Each country took measurements in 1995, 1998, 2000, and 2003, which cover the nine years since the Beijing conference. Each of the three countries shows progress for women in the three thematic areas represented in the ICC—participation and access to power, economic autonomy and poverty, and women's health and sexual and reproductive rights—and each shows an improved degree of consolidation and institutionalization of public policies with regard to gender equity. The existence of international commitments has made it possible for women's organizations to put their issues on the political agenda—though not without difficulty.

The advances are largely due to the efforts of women's groups. Through the creation of women's ministries and offices, which the UN calls "national machineries," they have been progressively strengthened. This strengthening and institutionalization, which was called for in the CEDAW, has been one of the most important gains of the women's movement, one further emphasized in the Beijing Platform of Action, which says that "national machineries for the advancement of women are key to the coordination of government policies. Their principal task is to support the incorporation of the concept of equality between men and women into all spheres of policy and at all levels of government" (UN 1995).

National machineries have made women's needs visible and have (with different emphases, discontinuities, and obstacles in different countries) promoted the implementation of measures for the advancement of women through the design, application, implementation, and evaluation of public policies. However, the establishment of government mechanisms for the advancement of women has not proven sufficient; their reach has remained limited, most have been underfunded, and they do not have consistent access to the centers of policy making. One reason is the turnover of democratic administrations since 1995. Although the state itself may assume the obligation to promote gender equity, the particular policies adopted by one administration are often forgotten or their implementation postponed when elections are held and a new group comes to power.

The results across countries are not directly comparable because each ICC was based on different indicators for each area, but they are useful for measuring change over time within one country. Looking at them together suggests questions that are common to the three countries. Mexico, Brazil, and Venezuela have experienced important processes of democratization in the past twenty years, with different shadings and results, but in all three countries high levels of poverty and inequality persist, revealing the tensions between the economic model and the expansion of democracy. The achievement of equality is the biggest problem these countries face, and women's groups share these concerns. Their actions have been important in tackling the challenge of democracy in a multidimensional way, which is not limited to a functional view of the political system or a minimalist view of the role of the state. Women's groups in Latin America support a vision of a democratic society that brings a greater degree of equity to all spheres of life and for all groups.

The indicators chosen for each country, and the results obtained in each area, show that together these countries are engaging in processes that go beyond a single national context. There is a sustained increase in the economic participation of women, and the structure of the labor force is unequal and segmented for both men and women. The application of structural adjustment programs and the policies of "flexibilizing" the labor force make jobs and benefits less secure. Globalization and economic opening may have brought employment opportunities to a large number of women—and with that, an improvement in their economic autonomy—but this has not had an effect on traditional patterns of horizontal segregation. Women are still primarily working in personal services, particularly in domestic service, and

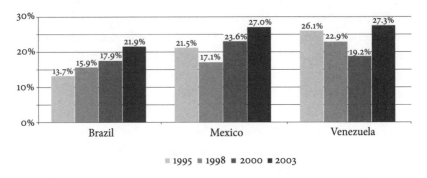

Brazil — 13.7%, 15.9%, 17.9%, 21.9%

Mexico — 21.5%, 17.1%, 23.6%, 27.0%

Venezuela — 26.1%, 22.9%, 19.2%, 27.3%

■ 1995 ■ 1998 ■ 2000 ■ 2003

1 Participation and Access to Power (*success in reaching goals by area and country*)

in industrial occupational categories that are traditionally female. As a result, new distinctions are created among women as workers, and these incorporate and make more complex existing gender inequalities.

In the area of participation and access to power, the ICCs of these three countries indicate that only 13 to 27 percent of the goal of parity has been met (figure 1). Each of these countries experiences a serious underrepresentation of women in decision-making positions, whether in the executive, legislature, or judicial sectors, indicating a strong persistence of gender discrimination in the political sphere. It is possible to see two tendencies: Brazil has made sustained but slow advances from one period to the next, while Mexico and Venezuela show an unstable pattern, with advances and losses within the time periods measured. The latter particularly suggests the fragility of the progress in women's political empowerment and the persistence of barriers to women's entry into electoral competition on an equal footing. It is the area of the greatest gap between performance and goal and reveals the difficulties women continue to face in gaining equitable representation and in bringing their concerns into the public sphere.

Quota laws, although they can be an effective mechanism for opening political spaces for women, are not in themselves enough to assure a sustained improvement in women's representation. Both Mexico and Brazil adopted quota laws after 1995. Mexico's 1996 law calls for 30 percent women in the Lower House and the Senate, and the number of women in both houses has slowly increased. Brazil's 1997 law applied to the Lower House, but no significant improvement has occurred there due to the lack of sanctions against parties that do not comply with the law. In Venezuela, a quota law passed in

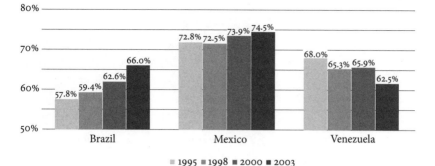

2 Economic Autonomy and Poverty Reduction (*success in reaching goals by area and country*)

1998 was withdrawn before it could be applied in an election, and subsequent laws have not been fully implemented (see Espina, this volume).

In the area of economic autonomy and poverty (figure 2), Venezuela shows decline since 1995 (although these figures may have recently been improved by the emphasis on social spending over the past few years). Brazil shows a sustained improvement, and Mexico shows a slight decline in 1998. In this area, groups in all three countries chose the same indicators: average incomes and salaries; degree of formality/informality of employment; participation in traditionally feminine occupations such as domestic service; and the number of women-headed households living in poverty. All three countries manifested trends toward more insecurity in women's work conditions, and movement into the informal sector tended to be permanent. Women's incomes decreased relative to men's.

In the area of health and sexual and reproductive rights, the ICCs show that, although the goals in this area are disputed by powerful forces including churches and conservative religious groups, the efforts of women's organizations have borne fruit in bringing their countries into a relatively high state of compliance with their commitments (figure 3). Brazil recorded sustained advances since 1995, but in Mexico there is some falling back, although the Mexican Congress passed a law decriminalizing abortion under certain circumstances in December 2006. There are large differences in the degree to which goals have been met, as well as in the magnitude of change.

In broad terms these three countries show advances since 1995 (see figure 4). In Venezuela and Mexico the changes since 1995 have been mini-

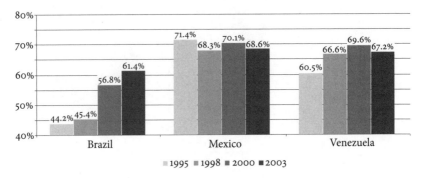

3 Women's Health and Sexual and Reproductive Rights (*success in reaching goals by area and country*)

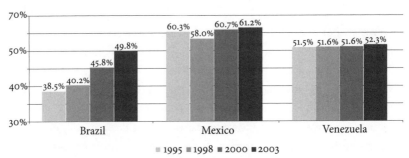

4 Average ICC Totals (*success in reaching goals by area and country*)

mal; however, we need more recent data on poverty to take account of the rapid increase in social investment in Venezuela since 2003 and, in the case of Mexico, results have fluctuated from 1995 to 2003. Advances have occurred in those areas where there is greatest consensus and little public debate. The areas that have consistently fallen behind are sexual and reproductive rights, which draw the attention of influential conservative sectors, making it difficult to develop policies to address them, and in women's access to political power, where machismo continues to play a role.

## Successes and Challenges ⁂

From a *technical* perspective, the possibility of constructing an index like the ICC depends on the availability of data, a great obstacle the ICC has faced. The ICC methodology requires statistical information that is of high quality, published regularly, and differentiated by sex as well as by other variables such as class and geographical location. The data utilized has come exclusively from recognized and valid government sources. The process of obtaining data has been slowed by problems of access to government statistics and the lack of time series data that is of good quality and disaggregated by sex.

In *political* terms, difficulties occurred in the ability of organized women to express their political priorities and goals in terms of equity, and in the creation of alliances with experts who could turn these goals into indicators that could be measured statistically.

However, the ICC experience has made a series of contributions that go beyond the successful monitoring of how governments are succeeding or failing to meet their commitments with regard to gender equity. The ICC has given women's groups new opportunities, broadening their scope for action and giving them tools to engage in focused dialogues with their respective governments. It helps women's groups overcome their exclusion that results from information largely being under male, technocratic control. Women can make the ability to understand and use statistics part of the political agenda and show that it is a reachable goal.

The ICC experience has also strengthened a network of women's organizations and NGOs, and it has trained a core of experts in the development of a methodology with the potential to go beyond monitoring these particular conferences and commitments. It has promoted a debate among women in organizations with regard to their needs and to how they relate to the commitments made by their governments. It has given their leaders new credibility to negotiate with diverse political and social actors—including economists and physicians—using a technically rigorous instrument.

At the national level, the ICC process should be considered a useful instrument for women's organizations, and the groups involved will continue to measure advances and setbacks. In the countries that now have an ICC, groups have used it to engage the executive and legislative powers with variable success depending on the level of activity, the degree of coordination, and the political weight of the organizations involved.

The successes of the ICC approach can promote strategies that push state authorities toward more effective action in favor of gender equity. The strategies that have been used thus far include press releases and press conferences, meetings with women's groups to publicize the results, and presentations to executive and legislative representatives to request pertinent information.

One example of the positive effects of the ICC is a statement made by Gender Equity, A.C., the organization that developed the ICC in Mexico, in its final report:

> Our organization has begun to link this tool of social accountability to the way we operate day to day, in the areas in which we work: [women's] budgets and sexual and reproductive rights. We have also found it useful in adapting and sharing the methodology with other organizations with which we share management and negotiation tasks, especially in the area of funding for the promotion of sexual and reproductive rights of Mexican youth. The ICC methodology is an important tool that meets the need to have instruments to obtain statistical or "hard" information, which can be used to support legal arguments in the defense and promotion of equity and in pursuit of better conditions of life and development for women.

Rosana Heringer of CEPIA (Cidadania, Estudo, Pesquisa, Informaçao, e Açao), the ICC coordinator in Brazil, believes that the ICC facilitates ongoing dialogues with the government. "We need accurate and high-quality information on the situation of women in Brazil to develop our strategies of action. Since the Beijing conference in 1995, Brazil has moved forward in guaranteeing rights to women, but the intensity of this effort was lacking" (Heringer and Dayse 2004). Examples are the Brazilian quota law for positions in the legislature and programs for the prevention of violence against women (see Piovesan, this volume). "We need to accelerate our victories and the pace of change."

It is obvious that success in using the ICC requires persistence and organizational commitment. But the ability to produce data to back up demands that would otherwise be dismissed as anecdotal or polemical can make a critical difference in the minds of policy-makers, while also providing evidence that can be used to build public support for change.

Notes ⁊

1 The countries that participated in the ICC Project between 1997 and 2005 are Argentina, Bolivia, Brazil, Colombia, Costa Rica, Chile, Ecuador, El Salvador, Guatemala, Honduras, Mexico, Nicaragua, Panama, Paraguay, Peru, the Dominican Republic, Uruguay, and Venezuela.

2 In Latin America since 1996, the Third World Institute in Montevideo, Uruguay,

has taken on the idea of social accountability and created a system to monitor the commitments made at Copenhagen and Beijing, as well as to publish reports periodically.

3 Governments made important international commitments at the UN conference on the environment (Rio de Janeiro, 1992), that on human rights (Vienna, 1993), on population and development (1994), on social development (Copenhagen, 1995), and on women (Beijing, 1995). See United Nations 1997.

4 The construction and calculation of the ICC was coordinated by Teresa Valdés of the Gender Studies Area. of FLACSO-Chile, in collaboration with Ximena Valdés of CEDEM (Center for Democracy and Human Rights). The project was developed based on a debate with women's organizations throughout the country, with the technical support of experts to ensure the methodological rigor that the project required.

5 This was made possible thanks to the support of CEPAL (the Economic Commission for Latin America and the Caribbean) and of IWHC (International Women's Health Coalition), the Ford Foundation, UNIFEM (UN Fund for Women), UNFPA (UN Fund for Population Activities), and the William and Flora Hewlett Foundation.

# 9

# Violence and Activism at the Mexico–United States Border ⚡

WOMEN, MIGRATION, AND OBSTACLES TO JUSTICE

*Kathleen Staudt and Gabriela Montoya*

Violence against women does not begin or stop at international borders, as nation-state analysts might imagine. Transnational problems are particularly evident in metropolitan regions that span the borderline. The two thousand–mile border zone that divides the United States and Mexico is home to 14 million people, and 80 million people live in the ten border states of both countries (Staudt and Coronado 2002:chap. 1). Border regions have been called hybrid and "in-between" places (Anzaldúa 1987; Bhabha 1994; Staudt and Spener 1998) wherein residents share cultures, languages, and interests. Yet the Mexico–United States border separates sovereign countries, each with its own political institutions, representatives, and constituencies. National sovereignty and multiple governments complicate transnational, cross-border politics and coalitions in local border regions.

In this essay we focus on the metropolitan region of Ciudad Juárez–El Paso, where over 2 million people of mostly Mexican heritage live, work, and relate to one another through kinship, marriage, and friendship.[1] Our essay theme is violence against women, with a special focus on migrant women — both women who cross the border, temporarily and permanently (as immigrants), and women who migrate from Mexico's interior to *la frontera norte*, the northern border, where plentiful but low-paying jobs are available in maquiladoras, foreign-owned export-processing factories. We argue that migrants face particular and unique obstacles to justice, lacking legal literacy, citizenship rights, and social capital. Until recently, transnational, cross-border antiviolence activists framed their feminist agendas around the shocking number of women who have been murdered on the border, rather than on the high levels of domestic violence that can lead to death, and to which immigrant women are particularly vulnerable.

Despite differences among women on both sides of the border, such as wage inequalities, border women share interests in ending the sexual and physical violence in their lives, whether in homes or on the street. In both the United States and in Mexico at least one in four women experiences domestic violence (U.S. Department of Justice 2001; INMUJER and INEGI 2003). Although violence cuts across all ethnic and class groups, poverty produces stresses and strains in household relationships that can trigger violence. The murders of over four hundred women in Ciudad Juárez since 1993, known as femicides, have provoked international outrage, resolutions, and widespread global-local transnational organizing—but only a limited response from Mexico's government and police. Sexualized killings, via gruesome rape and torture, characterize a third of these murders. Antiviolence organizations have addressed this as a "feminist" project, even though activists sometimes use the "human rights" or "public safety" labels to broaden their constituencies and provoke change in nonresponsive government institutions.

The border is like a magnet: for jobs, for border crossing, for trafficking, for violence, and for escape. In a transnational border context, people seek justice, and abusers elude justice by crossing from one side to the other. This essay analyzes the challenges and opportunities that feminist activists face in cross-border, transnational organizing efforts. Existing research on transnational feminist activism (Keck and Sikkink 1998; Moghadam 2005; Liebowitz 2002) has focused on distant networking among well-resourced activists, most of them in established nongovernment organizations (NGOs) that can avail themselves of electronic communication and Internet access. Kathleen Staudt and Irasema Coronado (2002) looked at U.S.-Mexican cross-border activists working for social justice in several areas, noting activists' close and personal networks in the peculiar local political terrain that the border creates. Here we focus specifically on the networks that have organized around migrant women.

Both of us are academics, but we both also participate in a cross-border organization, the Coalition against Violence toward Women at the Border. We are *fronterizas* (borderlanders) by identity, with Gabriela living in Ciudad Juárez but commuting daily across the border to attend the University of Texas, El Paso, and Kathleen living in El Paso for a quarter century. Her cross-border research efforts have included a long-term relationship with the Federación Mexicana de Asociaciones Privadas (Mexican Federation of Private Associations; FEMAP), a health and microenterprise NGO with a thirty-year track record. We are also participant observers in community nongovernment organizations that deal with immigration, civil rights, victims, and family violence, such as the Center against Family Violence, faith-based groups and services, and the Paso del Norte Civil Rights Project.

In this chapter we describe the setting: Mexico's northern border and the American Southwest, once part of Mexico until half that country's territory was lost to the United States under the 1848 Treaty of Guadalupe Hidalgo. We examine how domestic violence, less visible and less dramatic than femicide, has been normalized and largely ignored by institutions on both sides of the border. Drawing on a sample from Ciudad Juárez, we identify women at great risk, ones isolated and lacking social capital: migrants in a city of migrants from Mexico's central and northern states. We also look at immigrant women in El Paso who are vulnerable to domestic violence but lack citizenship, resources, and rights except for the limited provisions of the U.S. Violence against Women Act (VAWA) of 1994, which grants protections to immigrant women victims, but only if they succeed in accessing them through a complex, heavily bureaucratized process. The Catholic Church, although hardly a bastion of feminist activism, has joined with several faith-based groups and antiviolence nonprofit organizations in El Paso to support immigrant women who file official reports and seek protection under VAWA. We look at the barriers these groups must overcome to address the problems of violence against immigrant women and conclude with analyses of the obstacles to justice that migrant and immigrant women face on the frontier.

But we do begin with the femicides, the dramatic rise of female murders in Ciudad Juárez that started in the early 1990s and continues today, tapping the title of Amnesty International's monograph of 2003 in the heading below.

Intolerable Killings: Ten Years of Abductions and Murders
of Women in Ciudad Juárez and Chihuahua ⚘

The decade of female homicide, or femicide/*feminicidio* as it is known throughout Mexico, began in 1993. The era has also been called a decade of police impunity. Murderers have killed about thirty more women annually since 2003. Approximately one third of the deaths are sexualized, involving rape and torture.

In the early 1990s murder rates began to rise in Ciudad Juárez for both women and men, but unlike men-killing, often execution style, a third of women-killing incidents involved rape and mutilation (such as cutting off breasts).[2] Because the Mexican press was relatively free, the public became aware of the many young women who met their deaths in horrifying ways, their bodies disposed of in the desert (Benítez et al. 1999; Monárrez Fragoso 2002; Washington Valdez 2002, 2006; Staudt and Coronado 2002, 2007; for an official view, see Morfín Otero 2004). Victims' mothers sought police assistance, but they faced incompetence, corruption, and disregard, a bundle of characteristics recognizable as police impunity in Mexico's problem-laden law enforcement system. Lourdes Portillo produced a documentary in Spanish and in English, *Señorita Extraviada* (Lost Girl) (2001), which focused on the victims' mothers and was shown widely in Mexico and the United States, partly as an organizing tool.

Feminist and human rights activists worked with the victims' mothers to increase awareness and to expose the lack of police response using dramatic symbols, colors, and icons, including quasi-religious shapes such as crucifixes in pink and black and movement colors adorning streets, buildings, press conferences, rallies, and protest marches. Activists organized and framed their movement around the word *femicide*, emphasizing the gender dimension of the horrifying murders.

As women-killing patterns increased and became visible, in the mid- to late 1990s, victims' mothers began to organize in multiple groups with different names: Voces sin Eco (Voices without Echo), Mujeres de Negro (Women in Black), Nuestras Hijas de Regreso a Casa (That Our Daughters Return), among others. Working-class women crossed class lines to collaborate with wealthy, professional women to challenge police impunity and to press the government for a response. Explicitly feminist voices emerged, such as those of Esther Chávez Cano from Ocho de Marzo (8th of March), an organization named for International Women's Day. In 1998 Chávez Cano established Casa Amiga (Friendship House), a women's counseling center, during the long and historic vacuum of government disinterest in violence against women. The antiviolence activist Victoria Caraveo, a wealthy woman, was appointed to the state government women's institute, but she soon adopted the government's point of view that downplayed the significance of the killings.

In 2001, when killers brazenly dumped the bodies of eight women in a city field near the maquiladora industrial plants, activists galvanized transnational networks across the border and in other cities: Amigos de las Mujeres de Juárez (Friends of Mothers of Juárez, based in Las Cruces, New Mexico) and the Coalition against Violence toward Women at the Border. Since 2003 the coalition has been cochaired by an academic activist (female) and a retired labor union organizer (male). Both cross-border organizations tread a careful line, avoiding involvement in each other's "politics." Under Article 33, Mexico's Constitution forbids foreign involvement; international activists have been ousted from southern states like Chiapas under this provision.

Many theorize, both carefully and wildly, about reasons for the rise in femicide. An Egyptian engineer has been blamed, along with gangs, drug cartels hunting women for sport to celebrate their profits, renegade police, snuff filmmakers, "los juniors" (sons of rich families, who are politically untouchable), and organ harvesters. While some theories are more plausible than others, few are confirmed. (The Egyptian engineer, Sharif Sharif, was convicted and died in jail.) In the meantime, it is important to understand the context: a large, industrial city in the global marketplace that also happens to be located at the major south-north drug trafficking gateway on the Mexico-United States border.

The Border Context: Industrialization, Democratization, and Drug Trafficking ⚜

Known as Paso del Norte for four centuries, Ciudad Juárez and El Paso only began to grow rapidly in the latter part of the twentieth century (Staudt 1998). Both cities depend closely on one another for business, kinship and friendship connections, work, and consumption; the historian Oscar Martínez calls the area an "interdependent" border (1994). The cities are part of two different sovereign countries, although both countries have signed common treaties and agreements, including the North American Free Trade Agreement (NAFTA).

*LA FRONTERA NORTE*

In the early 1960s the Mexican government sought to decentralize industrial development away from Mexico City by creating the Border Industrialization Program. Mexico's northern border with the United States became a magnet for migrants from Mexico's interior. Formal employment in assembly-line opportunities expanded, and women workers filled approximately 80 percent of the positions in the first decade (Fernández-Kelly 1983; Gray 1986). Ciudad Juárez epitomizes the maquiladora model of industrial development, generating female labor competition with men, high turnover, "disposable" labor, and multiple social consequences (Kopinak 2004; Salzinger 2003; Staudt 2008).

Maquiladora employment peaked in the year 2000, with a quarter of a million workers working in three hundred factories. The workforce has become more gender-balanced, but there is still a female majority. The official minimum wage is US$4–5 daily, and most workers generally make about twice that (Staudt 1998) although a living wage is calculated to be at least three times the minimum. Inflation and peso devaluations have meant that wages have not kept up with cost of living increases (Staudt and Vera 2006). In the early twenty-first century, Ciudad Juárez lost approximately fifty thousand lower-skill maquila jobs when several plants moved to China.

Mexico has a multiparty political system, although the Institutional Revolutionary Party (PRI) won all national presidential elections for seventy-one years from 1929 to 2000. In the early 1980s genuine party competition emerged, primarily in the north, when the National Action Party (PAN), the conservative opposition, won the municipal presidency in Ciudad Juárez and the governorship in Baja California Norte. More competitive multiparty democracy made little difference for women, as they were rarely candidates, and women's public policy issues were rarely raised. In the 1990s, however, as more women were elected, a new center-left party emerged, and some parties put gender quotas in place, as critical masses of women deputies developed coalitions across party lines in Mexico's Congress. This produced occasional symbolic legislative victories, some denouncing gender violence (Rodríguez 2003). Moreover, Mexico has what the United Nations (UN) calls "women's machinery," a gender unit to provide advocacy and accountability in government: the Instituto Nacional de la Mujer (INMUJER). Although INMUJER has made violence against women a priority, it has not yet had an impact on the flawed state and local police institutions that are widely characterized as behaving with impunity throughout the country (see selections in Bailey and Chabat 2002). Citizens rarely trust the police. Their agencies are plagued with corruption, investigations are neglected and unprofessional, and forced confessions are common in jail, leading to conviction in trials without juries. The State of Chihuahua, in which Ciudad Juárez is located, appears to be a special case of superimpunity (Washington Valdez 2006).

Mexico has a federal system of government, and law enforcement occurs at the state level for state-defined crimes. Mexico's democratization has been accompanied by decentralization, strengthening the power and authority of governors, whom Victoria Rodríguez calls the "modern viceroys" of Mexico (1997:25). In the State of Chihuahua, local authorities (the governor, the attorney general, the state judicial police, and public investigators) are responsible for the investigation and prosecution of serious crimes. The PAN controlled the State of Chihuahua under the six-year term of Governor Francisco Barrio Terrazas, from 1992 to 1998, although Mexico's president still belonged to the PRI. In 2000, two years after the PRI governor Patricio Martínez was elected, the PAN won the presidency for six years. The PRI and the PAN thrive on making one another look bad. One sign of their lack of cooperation is that at the state level, PRI and PAN administrations give different official figures for the number of femicides. However, both administrations downplayed the issue, calling the numbers comparable to those for murder in other cities and therefore "normal."

Along with fast-paced industrialization and long-overdue democratization, serious drug cartelization of Ciudad Juárez began in the early 1990s. When supply paths moved from sea and air routes through Florida to land routes across the Mexico-United States border (Payan 2006), the region became a gateway to supply the largest drug-consuming country in the world, the United States. The cartels compromised the already weak police institutions at the municipal and state levels, both threatening and corrupting them.

Despite these grim facts, there are many successful examples of cross-border, transnational organizations. These range from business and official government cooperation and well-established environmental, health, and labor NGOs to informal networks. Examples are diverse (Staudt and Coronado 2002): the International Boundary and Water Commission (official agencies on each side of the border, more than a century old, that focus on water allocation, boundary demarcation, and the environment, among other issues); FEMAP and the FEMAP Foundation (focused on family planning, health, microenterprise, and energy-efficient fuels); faith-based shelters for immigrants and refugees; and chambers of commerce. Factors that bode well for the success of such organizations include Mexican heritage and Spanish-language capability; commitments to shared stakes in cooperation; and policies, laws, and subsidies that legitimize, encourage, and fund border cooperation.

In addition, there are significant public subsidies for business groups in both the United States and Mexico, such as contracts to chambers of commerce to attract new businesses and government-paid staff who are responsible for assisting business development, but there is no such encouragement for human rights organizations. Obstacles to cross-border, binational cooperation include economic inequalities (an approximate tenfold wage differential), fears, and stereotypes. There are long waits and document checks at the international ports of entry for people who meet with their counterparts on the other side (Staudt and Coronado 2002); these have become more onerous since 9/11.

The United States national tragedy of September 11, 2001, hardened policies around immigration and border control. Official U.S. discourse sees borders as weak spots, as vulnerable to terrorism, and as threats to national security. In 2006 four candidates for Texas governor framed their campaigns primarily in terms of border security. Ironically, the City of El Paso ranks as the second or third safest big city in the United States, as measured in terms of "serious" crimes, rather than as a site of lawlessness and chaos. Undocumented immigrants often try to maintain a low profile, which may reduce crime levels. In 2006 the Texas governor made funds available to western Texas border county sheriff departments, in a program called Operation

Linebacker, to set up checkpoints to monitor residents outside the city limits and to refer immigrants engaged in unlawful behavior to the Border Patrol. Over a thousand residents have been sent to Mexico (Grissom 2006), although most are identified as nonviolent, deported for crimes such as driving without a license.

Anti-immigrant rhetoric in the 2006 U.S. elections was shrill and polarizing, and the U.S. Congress authorized a border "fence" (*muro de odio*, wall of hate, as it is sometimes called in Mexico) to be built along seven hundred miles of the two thousand–mile border, supplementing the nearly one hundred miles of already extant fencing. Occasionally, the U.S. Department of Homeland Security issues color-coded alerts that bring traffic on ports of entry to a near halt, despite the fact that the United States is Mexico's largest trading partner and Mexico is the second-largest trading partner of the United States. Close economic interconnections are at odds with the shrill anti-immigration rhetoric. After the Texas gubernatorial elections, in which candidates used harsh border-security language, the governor and one of his opponents issued reports and press releases about the benefits that immigrants bring to the state of Texas (2006), largely to appease the business community that supports access to plentiful, low-cost immigrant labor.

At the border the majority of people do not support anti-immigrant and militarized border solutions. As local newspaper surveys show, their views are similar to those among Hispanics (Pew Research Center/Pew Hispanic Center 2006). Many citizens and residents on the U.S. side of the border are linked to friends, relatives, and coworkers across the border. Border businesses depend on customers from Mexico, whether at up-scale malls or in smaller shops that benefit from pedestrian traffic across the border.

## Women and Feminist NGOs: From Work to Violence Agendas ✦

Women's nongovernment organizations exist on both sides of the border, although few are explicitly self-defined as feminist. Yet many pursue feminist agendas, seeking to expand opportunities, raise wages, and reduce gender inequalities in law and society. In the early 1970s several NGOs gained widespread attention: the Centro de la Orientación de la Mujer Obrera (Center for the Orientation of Women Workers; COMO) focused on women workers (Peña 1997), while FEMAP concentrated on women's health and reproductive rights. Neither organization explicitly addressed violence against women, perhaps illustrating Sonia Alvarez's (1998) warning that NGO-ization causes women's and feminist organizations to lose the critical edge they had as independent (but resource-poor) civil-society organizations.

As awareness of women's murders spread, Ciudad Juárez became a stain on the international map. Portillo's documentary (2001), explored theories about the killers, and exposed police complicity. It gained widespread audiences when it was televised on the nationwide PBS *Point of View* series in the United States. The University of California, Los Angeles (UCLA), and Arizona State University West, among others, hosted major conferences on femicide in 2003 and 2004. The Mexico Solidarity Network sent fund-raising caravans with testimonials from the victims' mothers. Notable intellectuals like Alma Guillermoprieto and Elena Poniatowska gave speeches and wrote essays about femicide. Popular bands, like Los Tigres del Norte, wrote and performed songs about *las muertas*.

Networking spread far and quickly. Hilda Solís, a U.S. Congresswoman from Los Angeles with Juarenses in her constituency, led a U.S. congressional delegation to the border with assistance from the Washington Office on Latin America (WOLA). Amnesty International also became active on this issue and published *Intolerable Killings* in 2003. Eve Ensler, the creator of *The Vagina Monologues* (1998), a play performed annually on or near "V-Day" (February 14) in thousands of locations around the world, authorized the use of her play for antiviolence work. Ensler added a monologue on femicide in Juárez in 2003, complementing other monologues on Bosnian mass rape, so-called South Korean comfort women during World War II, and the war in Iraq.

From 2003 to 2006 Mexico's federal government stepped in, under the pretext that organ trafficking might be occurring, which constitutes a federal crime. President Vicente Fox of the PAN, the first non-PRI president in seventy years, appointed a federal prosecutor and a federal investigator, both of them women. Like other female appointees at the state level before them, they wrote reports and engaged with other institutions and activists. Yet these appointments offered largely symbolic pressure rather than concrete institutional change.

In late 2003 activities in border, national, and transnational networks peaked in preparation for V-Day, February 14, 2004. Thousands of visitors from around the world converged on El Paso–Ciudad Juárez for performances of the *Vagina Monologues* in Spanish and in English, on both sides of the border. Mexico City and Hollywood movie stars joined those thousands for a frenzy of media coverage. It proved a public relations disaster for Mexico's northern border political and economic establishment. Invariably, existing tensions among NGOs about representation, fundraising, and distribution became more aggravated (Gaspar de Alba 2003; Wright 2006). Some activists gave priority to femicide, while others sought to bring attention to other issues raised by the *Vagina Monologues*, especially interpersonal violence.

A PRI governor, Reyes Baeza, was elected in 2004, promising change and appointing a female attorney general. There is now some evidence of institutional change, especially in the form of public affairs–oriented press releases after murders, and businesses have pledged to improve public security. But these changes are motivated by the need to clean up the city's image rather than by outrage at the deaths of women, although politicians no longer publicly blame the victims. At the federal level, the government has begun to acknowledge that women are being killed at high rates in other cities as well. International human rights organizations have recently highlighted femicide in Guatemala, where the absolute numbers exceed those in Ciudad Juárez.

As femicide has received greater attention, however, the issue of domestic violence has been pushed aside, although it is a serious, ongoing problem for women and police institutions are similarly unresponsive. If a third of the femicides involve rape and mutilation—as both activists and government reports acknowledge—and are considered possible serial killings, the other two-thirds of cases are seen as "normalized" domestic-violence murder, common in Mexico and other countries. The numbers alone suggest that domestic violence and its potentially lethal consequences deserve serious attention.

Domestic Violence in Ciudad Juárez, a City of Migrants ⚜

With all the organizing attention and media frenzy directed at the sexualized killings of women, there has been little focus on domestic violence and domestic-violence homicide, which also constitutes a form of femicide. Since 1993, when most people began to count the number of female murders in Ciudad Juárez, the government has disputed the data, saying that the figures are exaggerated, that such deaths are "normal" — simple crimes of passion or lovers' quarrels. Activists and Amnesty International counted 370 murdered women during the "decade of impunity" from 1993 to 2003 (AI 2003). Many women have also disappeared, with unofficial estimates ranging from the hundreds to thousands, but it is not known whether these disappearances are voluntary departures, forcible human trafficking, or bodies dumped in the desert and not yet found.

The spectacle of femicide was horrifying for the victims' mothers, human rights and feminist activists, and most decent people. The highly publicized speculations about who the killers might be, noted earlier, caused some panic. Whether they were the victims of serial killers or partners, however, all the women suffered premature and tragic deaths. All violence against women, including domestic violence, demands attention and action. Our experience working on the border suggests that migrant and immigrant women face special risks.

Violence against women has been defined and measured in multiple ways. It can be physical, sexual, psychological, and verbal; it can occur over a lifetime, over a year, or perhaps only once (although that incident may be fatal). Domestic violence, which has only been defined as a crime in recent decades, is vastly underreported. Most studies rely on women's self-reports. Throughout the Americas it is estimated that a quarter to a half of women report experiencing some type of violence at some point in their lives (Morrison and Biehl 1999; Moser and McIlwaine 2004). Violence is an everyday threat to women, in homes or on the streets.

In Mexico, INMUJERES conducted a nationwide survey of violence against women and found high levels of abuse; half of the women had experienced at least one type of violence, including psychological, and a tenth had experienced physical violence within the last year (INMUJERES and INEGI 2003). The researchers reported these data in many ways (such as by rural and urban differences, by age levels, and by state), but they did not disaggregate it down to the municipal level. Thus activists in Ciudad Juárez lacked basic information on the incidence of violence. Good data often spurs action, making collective struggle possible and proving the need for policy change.

From 2004 to 2005 we collaborated with a large health-oriented NGO, FEMAP, in research and workshops with a representative sample of 404 women aged fifteen to thirty-nine in Ciudad Juárez (Staudt et al. 2005). Over half of the women were migrants from north-central Mexico. They lived in households with earnings of less than US$100 weekly and had been educated only at the *primaria* (grade 6 or less) level. The majority were fearful of and sad about their living conditions. They were aware of domestic violence's illegality and were critical of abusers who used excuses like alcohol, drugs, and "women's mistakes" as justifications for violence.

We asked about many kinds of violence but report here on physical (27 percent) and sexual (12 percent) violence. To the extent that the random sample matches that age group in the population, we estimate that about one hundred thousand women in Ciudad Juárez are at risk for physical violence. Only 20 percent of women we surveyed reported their injuries to the police, whom few women trusted. As we looked more closely at violence, we found that several key factors are connected: migration and the lack of social support, low income, limited education, and extensive psychological abuse are all highly associated with physical violence. These factors limit survivors' ability to exit dangerous relationships and put them at risk for future serious injuries and even death.

Yet women are not passive victims in response to violence. In the individual surveys we also asked women about the strategies they used in response to physical violence. Our examination of a subsample with violent experiences revealed that the most common response was to return the attack, followed by communication with others about the attack along with searches for help or shelter with parents and friends. Of course, newer migrants in Ciudad Juárez are less likely to have family and friends available nearby, and this situation is aggravated for immigrants crossing international boundaries to new lands.

Violence against women is not only a feminist issue but a serious public health and safety problem. Hundreds of women have been killed in Ciudad Juárez over a decade, some of them raped and mutilated before death, and thousands have been beaten and raped. Migrants inside Mexico are at special risk because they are strangers who lack the social capital of friends and extended family should they seek support after abuse, and they must survive in a large, alienating, crime-ridden city with unreliable law enforcement institutions. Noncitizen immigrant women in El Paso are also at risk. Most have crossed the international border from Mexico, and they, too, lack social capital and economic resources. As noncitizens, they may not know their rights or how to pursue them in their new homeland.

The United States has long been home to many immigrants and naturalized citizens, and continuing transnational movements have led to the presence of an estimated 12 million undocumented people (Passel 2006) who lack legal status and the rights of citizens. Since the 9/11 attacks, U.S. policies have stressed the need for border security to stop terrorists, which in turn has fueled anti-immigrant sentiment and provoked actions not only by the government but also by private groups who are impatient with the government's inability to "control the borders."

In El Paso County, the U.S. Census reports that 80 percent of the population is Hispanic, and most Hispanics at the Mexico–United States border are Mexican-heritage citizens and residents. Seven of ten El Pasoans speak Spanish in their homes, and 27 percent are foreign-born. Some of these are naturalized citizens, others are legal permanent residents (LPRs), and yet others are undocumented.

The border economy is integrated, and many people visit relatives and shop on both sides of the border. About seven hundred thousand people cross legally from Mexico to the United States every day for shopping, school, and work (Orrenius 2001). According to the Bureau of Transportation statistics (U.S. Department of Transportation 2006) 7,613,546 pedestrians and 15,971,739 personal vehicles with about 29,180,824 passengers made authorized annual crossings through El Paso's international ports of entry during 2005.

The El Paso and Ciudad Juárez police departments are situated in two sovereign countries, and neither can enter the other's jurisdiction unless invited. Yet both Mexico and the United States are friendly neighbors, having signed several treaties on major issues, such as trade and drugs, but also on detailed concerns, such as insect control. No binational human rights treaty or infrastructure is in place, but both cities have long cooperated over stolen cars, with notification mechanisms in place for instant action. The Coalition against Violence has repeatedly asked publicly about matching cooperation concerning the murders of women. In 2003 a 1–800 number was made available for those who wanted to provide information, but to little avail, although there has been some limited mutual training on professional practices, such as securing evidence sites.

Immigrant and Hispanic women tend to have lower levels of education, lower incomes, more children, and greater language barriers when compared to other ethnic groups (Gondolf with Fisher 1988). As Manuela Romero and Tracy Yellen report, the El Paso Police Department receives nearly 28,000 domestic violence–related calls annually, of which 5,800 result in investigations and 2,900 in arrests (2004:27). El Paso's Center against Family Violence estimates that only 10 percent of the domestic-violence cases are reported.

Abusers and criminals use the border to escape local pursuit and incarceration, in both directions. In 2006 one of the alleged killers who brazenly left eight tortured victims in a cotton field was identified in Colorado and returned to Mexico. In El Paso alleged abusers often cross into Mexico after hurting or killing their partners. Occasionally they are located, such as a husband who hung himself in Chihuahua after murdering his wife in El Paso in 2006. El Paso's battered women's shelter opens its doors to abused women survivors from Cuidad Juárez who say their husbands made threats to leave their dead bodies in the desert, "just like the others" (Staudt 2008).

## Domestic Violence among Immigrants ✦

Like women migrants in Ciudad Juárez, immigrant women in the United States lack the social capital of extended family and friends in their new country, and economic stress can aggravate tensions that lead to violence in households. Previous studies have noted cultural patterns among immigrants that make some forms of domestic violence seem normal. Language barriers may prevent the victims from seeking help; they are often ignorant about the laws intended to protect them from abuse and may fear deportation (Ammar et al. 2005).

Our experiences with NGOs that supply assistance to immigrant survivors of domestic violence illustrate the depth of the problem. In one case a husband locked an undocumented immigrant wife in the house for weeks until she escaped. In another case an abuser preyed on immigrant women, often beating them, and assumed that because they were immigrants, they would have no criminal recourse. In other cases undocumented women feared the loss of their citizen children if deported.

The depth of the problem is illustrated by the following anonymous vignettes taken from letters written by undocumented immigrant women who applied for assistance under VAWA from a faith-based NGO in which one of us (Gabriela) served.

- *Abusers tend to exercise economic control over their victims.* "He would get home drunk and gave me only 10 pesos [about $1] a day, with which I could only afford one kilo of beans and one kilo of tortillas."
- *Victims/survivors get mixed messages from law enforcement.* An abused woman said that *la migra* (Border Patrol agents) showed up at her house, trying to find her husband, who was involved with drugs. The agents put a gun to her forehead and threatened to deport her if she failed to tell them where her husband was. All this happened in front of the woman's two-year-old girl. She had not reported her husband's abuse and was not receiving any help. When she finally sought help, her lawyer told her that she should not be afraid of the police because, under VAWA, her deportation was cancelled. When the agents showed up again, she asked them for their badges and told them what her lawyer had said. But the agents left: they did not care about the domestic violence; they were only interested in their drug case.
- *Children of abused spouses suffer as well.* "He arrived home and started beating up my mother a lot. At that time, my mother was only four or five months pregnant. I tried helping her out by telling him to stop, but he wouldn't. He then kicked me and threw me against the wall. He was drunk and he fell asleep. A few hours later, in the afternoon, I heard my mother calling me . . . she was lying in the restroom. She had had a miscarriage due to the beating she had received that day. I helped to wrap up the fetus in towels and then placed it in a plastic bag."

GOVERNMENT REMEDIES

As a result of the women's movement in the late 1960s and early 1970s, state and local governments in the United States strengthened laws against domestic violence and rape. Over a thirty-year period, with pressure from civil rights and feminist groups, the federal government supplied monetary support and, with increasing professional accountability, police and sheriff departments in city and county governments came to view violence against women as a priority. Violence is not only a crime statistic but also a behavior that drives and intensifies other crimes. Civil and criminal remedies withstood court challenges, and gradually a complex and bureaucratized system was put in place, with protective orders, criminal charges and convictions, and programs to re-educate serial batterers.

Yet justice depends both on reporting crimes and on "street-level bureaucrats" (Lipsky 1980), government agents such as police and judges who have discretionary authority that may benefit or burden crime victims (Staudt forthcoming). In the federal system, despite extensive population movements among states, professionalized law enforcement capable of handling violence against women has effectively advanced in some states, while others lag behind.

In 1994 the U.S. Congress passed and President Clinton signed the first Violence against Women Act (known as VAWA I), which elevated the importance of enforcing laws on domestic violence, designated more than $1 million in state grants for the expansion of shelters and social services, and established a national hotline, research programs, and educational programs for judges and police officers (Orloff and Little 1999). Significantly, VAWA allowed spouses and children of U.S. citizens or immigrants who are legal permanent residents to petition for legal permanent residency and employment authorization *without* the assistance of their abusive spouse.

In 2000 Congress revised this law and authorized $3.3 billion for a five-year program. Under VAWA II battered spouses and children could obtain legal residency in the United States without having returned to their country of origin to obtain a visa. The revised law also created visas (known as T and U visas) for victims who have suffered substantial physical or mental abuse as a result of certain serious crimes. In 2005 VAWA III was authorized, allowing victims of domestic violence to petition for VAWA benefits even if the abuse did not take place in the United States (Family Violence Prevention Fund 2006; WomensLaw.org 2006; DMRS 2006).[3]

### BUREAUCRATIC COMPLEXITY

In El Paso antiviolence, faith-based, and civil rights organizational staff have been able to acquire training to assist immigrant women to apply for protection under VAWA provisions. To qualify for legal permanent residence, a victim of domestic violence must document: (1) Marriage or divorce within two years of application from a U.S. citizen or LPR, or from a nonimmigrant authorized to work in the United States; (2) battery or extreme cruelty; (3) a good-faith marriage (some abusers are bigamists, but if the victim can prove the marriage was in good faith, she qualifies to apply); (4) good moral character; and (5) U.S. residency. Although the criteria seem clear, there are personal barriers that prevent victims of domestic violence from seeking help and that prevent organizations who want to do so from providing victims with adequate assistance.

Several laws contradict VAWA's provisions to protect immigrants from domestic abuse. Title IV of the 1996 welfare reform (Personal Responsibility and Work Opportunity Act), for example, restricts noncitizens from receiving supplemental security income, temporary assistance for needy families, and food stamps. The Illegal Immigration Reform and Immigration Responsibility Act of 1996 imposed harsh penalties on undocumented immigrants. By expanding the definition of "aggravated felony" to include a wide range of relatively minor crimes, the law allows the immigrants convicted of a crime in this category to be deported (Family Violence Prevention Fund 2006; Sacks and Kolken 1999).

Today, VAWA III is being implemented in the United States in a context of hypernationalism and even xenophobia, resulting in part from the terrorist attacks of 9/11, but also reflecting resistance to the rapid pace of immigration, legal and illegal, during the last two decades. There are now efforts to make illegal migration an aggravated felony, turning undocumented immigrants into deportable felons. Although laws that limit services to illegal immigrants make some exceptions for crime victims, contradictory policies make it difficult to train those who provide legal assistance to give accurate advice that will not endanger those who seek help.

## NGO SERVICE PROVIDERS

NGOs provide public services in many areas. But they face chronic funding problems, relying on charitable contributions, fees for services from clients, and reimbursements from different levels of government for services provided. Sonia Alvarez (1998) has expressed concern that, as NGOs become professionalized, they lose contact with their grass-roots constituencies and become dependent on government (or international) funding, rather remaining autonomous actors in civil society. Yet professional training is necessary for NGOs to help undocumented immigrants access their rights under laws that are bureaucratically complex, and VAWA offers a prime example. Theoretical arguments do not capture what is happening on the ground. Many activists are volunteers, donating their own funds and time beyond their other paid work. Their commitment ebbs and flows, dependent on crises and leadership that frames those crises. Nongovernmental service providers are committed year-round, but they are often wary of those whose passionate advocacy may threaten the precarious funding that allows the NGOs addressing violence against women to survive. Faith-based NGOs bring religious legitimacy, but they are rarely motivated to take critical feminist stances. Justice for women requires that both activists and service providers work hand in hand, maintaining their critical edge.

Several government agencies and NGOs are committed to stopping domestic violence against women on both sides of the Mexico–United States border. El Paso may be one of the safest big cities in the United States (judged by levels of "serious" crimes, rather than counting "misdemeanor" assaults such as domestic violence), but it is home to many immigrants and to poverty. El Paso's per capita income is 60 percent of the average U.S. per capita income, and El Paso County is the third poorest county in the United States, with levels of relative poverty common to many counties along the border (Sharp 1998). Many El Paso nonprofit organizations provide critical public services to serve low-income and immigrant communities.

Whatever their status (migrants, immigrants, residents, and/or citizens), border women must acquire some legal literacy to obtain justice. If women decide to report domestic violence, they will have to deal with very different government agencies on both sides of the border. On the Mexican side, victims can either call the police or go directly to government agencies with documentation about their injuries and/or with requests for counseling. But in Ciudad Juárez, Casa Amiga, the city's only shelter for battered women, offers only ten places.

On the U.S. side of the border fear of deportation keeps many immigrant victims from calling the police (in the city) or sheriff's deputies (outside the city limits). Perpetrators threaten to call la migra or to take away the victims' children if they call the police to report the abuse. Through VAWA the existing agencies are able to help victims seek civil remedies, called protective orders, and food and shelter for themselves and their children.

Still, several problems emerge. Many abused women are living in so-called free unions with their abusers, which disqualifies them from receiving VAWA. If abusers are undocumented, women are not eligible for VAWA. To petition for VAWA benefits, victims must fill out ten double-sided forms in complex, fine-print English, Spanish, and "legalese." Some do not even know how to read or write, and they must disclose very personal information to someone else who can fill out the forms. Once benefits are approved, it takes about three months to get a work permit, several weeks to get protection from deportation, and about two years to obtain a permanent resident visa. In the meantime, the victims and their children must stay at a shelter if there is space, all of this providing they are not prevented by other laws from receiving VAWA protections.

Finally, staff and volunteers at these nonprofit agencies are not always well trained. Volunteerism can have both good and bad effects in a poverty-stricken community. Motivations for volunteers' involvement vary; some are ideological, perhaps feminist; others are meeting internship and service-learning requirements in their university courses. Some staff and volunteers ignore the loopholes through which they can get more benefits for their clients, or may make mistakes on the forms that victims must complete to apply for VAWA benefits, so the applications are rejected. Each permit needs to be renewed every year, for up to five years, so the process must be repeated, and although the first application is free, every renewal costs about $180.

Migrant women in Ciudad Juárez have a difficult enough challenge reporting violence, but once they cross the border into El Paso, their isolation and vulnerability are aggravated. Law-enforcement institutions are in place to respond to domestic violence, but those institutions are intimidating, and often biased against immigrants. Narrow criteria used to authorize protection leave many outside. Nonprofit NGOs serve women without asking for their immigration status, yet they face severe resource and staff constraints. The feminist movement has focused on femicide, not on migrants and immigrant women, and their attention has begun to shift from Ciudad Juárez to places like Guatemala, which have even more horrifying femicide statistics.

Concluding Thoughts on the Obstacles
to Justice on the Border ⸙

Many women face violence from their partners and on the streets, but their ability to seek justice is complicated by conditions on the Mexico–United States border. Women on both sides of the border suffer domestic violence, but their legal systems, for different reasons, make it difficult to obtain justice. Many women do not report violence for various reasons: shame, increased risks of abuse, economic dependency, and poor or repressive police response. Border zones are magnets for opportunities and threats: job opportunities, amid obscene wage inequalities; criminals and victim/survivors crossing the border to evade and to seek justice; routes for trafficking drugs and other goods. Migrant women are often isolated, and when they cross the border, language and cultural barriers as well as sovereign (but often ineffective) legal and law enforcement institutions make it difficult for them to seek justice.

Mexico's northern border region resembles other borders in the Americas, and when feminists act at borders, they face special challenges. We have described the extreme violence against women in the Mexico–United States border region of Ciudad Juárez/El Paso. We have documented the serious difficulties women and NGOs face in confronting domestic violence, which may account for many of the deaths reported as femicides, and put many women at daily risk. Feminist, human rights, and nonprofit NGOs have made the public aware of femicide, which is now an international scandal. Yet activists remain much more interested in the murders than in protecting women from everyday domestic violence. Few are willing to commit the kind of time and dedication needed to sustain the everyday antiviolence work of NGOs.

Feminist and human rights activists must increase their efforts to enlist social and government institutions to protect abused women in transnational border settings. To succeed, NGOs must further expand their cross-border constituencies and create coalitions for change. Activists need to think about how to reframe their discourses in language that can engage allies at various levels of the federal systems in both Mexico and the United States. Human rights groups need to include the specific problems of border justice in their own strategies and practices.

On the United States side of the border, institutions are in place to respond to survivors of domestic violence, but they do so in a heavily bureaucratized way that limits the support available to victims/survivors and strains the capabilities and commitment of the NGO staff and volunteers who must not only navigate conflicting laws and the shifting legal terrain but also sustain their funding. Borders divide women by serving as pretexts to deny them justice. We hope for the day when people in good-neighbor countries, like Mexico and the United States, can move as freely across borders as people do in the European Union and when treaties and other cooperative practices address these issues. But most important, we hope for a day when social norms no longer tolerate violence and murder as "normal" means of control over women.

# Notes ⚡

1 Among border residents, 1.5 million live in Mexico's fifth-largest city and 700,000 live in the twenty-first largest city in the United States.

2 This section and the section on NGOs are highly condensed from Staudt forthcoming.

3 The victim must be currently residing in the United States. If living abroad, the abuser must work for the U.S. government, be a member of the U.S. military, or have subjected the victim to some abuse in the United States (WomensLaw.org 2006).

# 10

## Feminist Activism and the Challenges of Democracy ✦

*Jane S. Jaquette*

In the two decades since the transitions in the Southern Cone and Peru, women's movements and feminist activism have not disappeared but have fragmented and diversified (Chinchilla and Haas 2006), making it more difficult to grasp their impact, measure their successes and failures, and assess their implications for democracy.[1] Women's movements are viewed, and view themselves, as having a strong stake in democratic institutions. Women's movements have raised new issues, strengthened civil society, and pressed Latin American democracies to become more inclusive. And women have gained greater access to positions of power. But feminists have also had to develop new strategies as the democratic institutions and practices continue to change, presenting new opportunities and challenges, and women's movements have had less impact on the quality of democratic practice than many expected (Montecinos 2001).

### Difference and Autonomy ✦

One way to gauge the impact of these shifts on feminist thought is by tracking how two concepts at the heart of feminist debates in the early 1990s—maternal citizenship and autonomy—have taken on new meanings, reflecting ongoing debates about what Latin American feminism is and what its political priorities should be.

The debate over maternal feminism was initially provoked by the activism of the Mothers of the Plaza de Mayo: in emphasizing their role as grieving mothers, were they bringing formerly private concerns into the public arena, changing the content of politics and thereby changing gender power relations, as difference feminists argued? Or were they actually reinforcing women's traditional roles, as egalitarian feminists feared?[2] The conflict between egalitarian and difference feminisms is no longer a subject of heated debate. Many have concluded that, in the Latin American context, egalitarian and difference approaches to women's rights are complementary rather than opposed (e.g., Jelin 1998b:177–79; Minow 1990).[3] For example, both difference and egalitarian arguments have been used to argue the case for gender quotas: women should be granted *equal* representation in part because they will bring *different* issues and perspectives to public policy. However, an egalitarian skeptic might reply that, as Marcela Ríos Tobar's account of Michelle Bachelet's presidency suggests, the persistence of gender stereotypes may be useful, but not always benign.

More important, perhaps, is that "difference" has now acquired a much broader meaning in Latin American feminist analysis. Feminists argue that the inclusion of women helped open the door to the political recognition of many formerly marginalized groups, such as Afro-Brazilians, indigenous peoples, youth, and gays and lesbians, as Jacqueline Pitanguy argues in the essay by Flávia Piovesan. Pluralist democracies do not define citizenship as homogeneous; they are a departure from the universalist projects of state building in the past, in Latin America as elsewhere. Pluralist democracies are inclusionary (Young 2000) and receptive to identity politics, although, as Virginia Vargas points out in her essay celebrating pluralism, identity cannot exhaust the meaning of citizenship. Social movements have encouraged the tendency to move toward a politics of "recognition" as distinct from the politics of "redistribution" that characterized much of the twentieth century (Fraser 2003). The debate is not over, however. Martha Gimenez (2004) argues that, given the failure of "neoliberal globalization" to lessen inequalities in Latin America, it is time for feminists to return to a Marxist analysis, while Vargas calls for going beyond the "univocal" paradigms of the past, including Marxism and, implicitly, feminism itself.

The term *autonomy* has also taken on a range of meanings. Originally used to describe the feminist rejection of ties to political parties (e.g., Barrig 1994), it was soon adapted to describe how women's and feminist groups were distancing themselves from the state. Autonomy was debated by participants in the regional *Encuentros* and as a defense of those who distanced themselves from government gender units, such as the women's ministry in Chile (e.g., Schild 2000) and the National Council in Brazil (Pitanguy 2005; Macaulay 2006). When Peru's president Alberto Fujimori portrayed himself as a champion of feminist causes during the 1990s, appointing a number of women to his administration and supporting women's reproductive rights, Peruvian feminists sounded the alarm about the need for autonomy to resist co-optation (Blondet 2002; Barrig 2001).

Sonia Alvarez's critique of the "NGO-ization" of women's movements in Latin America (1999) saw autonomy as an alternative to dependency on foundations, governments, and foreign-assistance agencies that used their financial clout to impose their agendas on women's organizations. Alvarez expressed concern about the increasing professionalization and bureaucratization of women's organizations, which moved them further away from their cross-class origins, and found it troubling that NGOs were becoming service providers rather than advocates for change.

Victoria Schild (2000) argued for autonomy on the grounds that women's groups were becoming complicit in the "neoliberal project," allowing the state to slough off its responsibility to provide social services. Schild criticized the emergence of "neocitizens," who are defined "in the context of market rationality, individual choice, personal responsibility, control over one's own fate and self-development." To a liberal democrat, individual choice, personal responsibility, and control over one's fate seem like defensible, even admirable, goals. But Schild's point is that women do not in fact have the range of choices liberalism assumes and that the neoliberal model makes women responsible for "their own failures, and, ultimately, their own poverty" (Schild 2000:282). Susan Berger, agreeing with Schild, thinks that social movement activists have been encouraged "to work with and within the state to achieve so-called common goals," so that the state can "withdraw from servicing society." She criticizes the state for co-opting much of its opposition by "discursively pilfer[ing] the concerns of social movements" to maintain stability and "state control over civil society" (2006:6).

Individual autonomy is rarely praised by Latin American feminists who tend to reject individualism as part of their critique of neoliberal capitalism. In their essay, however, Teresa Valdés and Alina Donoso argue that individual autonomy is a criterion of citizenship that is especially important for women who have lived under patriarchy and, in many cases, under authoritarian rule. Their concept of active citizenship is not based on women's roles as mothers, but on their standing as individuals: "Autonomy depends on multiple, complex processes, such as individuation, the construction of identities, and empowerment." To be full citizens, individuals must have sufficient economic resources to be able to make their own decisions. In a region that is traditionally patriarchal and has the worst indices of inequality in the world, this implies a role for the state in labor relations, managing markets and redistributing wealth. Valdés and Donoso emphasize the importance of social responsibility in any definition of citizenship. But autonomy implies choice: citizens take up their social responsibilities voluntarily; they are not coerced.

Closer analysis suggests that Schild's and Berger's arguments are not limited to neoliberalism, but constitute a critique of capitalism itself. If there is a viable alternative economic system waiting for citizens to develop the political will to demand that it be put in place, then "autonomy"—refusing to participate in democratic governments based on capitalism—can be understood as a rational strategy. But it is not clear that such an alternative exists, and therefore that autonomy is politically justifiable on strategic or ethical grounds. Further, if governments persistently failed to involve women in their projects and ignored the discourses of social movements, they would surely be accused of excluding or marginalizing them. Nor is it convincing to argue that asking women to assume individual responsibility is bad in itself. Women may lack the resources to exercise choice, but an ideology that denies the importance of individual choice fails to grant the moral autonomy central to any concept of citizenship.

Taking individual responsibility can and should include joining with others to press for the kinds of structural changes that address poverty and exclusion in ways that markets alone clearly fail to do. Markets are particularly hard on women, not only because of persistent sex discrimination but also because women, not men, are expected to provide the unpaid labor necessary to reproduce the family. Whatever responsibilities governments may have assumed in the past (and Latin American governments were never able to provide social services to the majority of their citizens), they did not address the burden of care work on women. The availability of domestic help has largely kept this issue off the feminist agendas of the region, which has had negative consequences for feminist cross-class alliances and finessed a fundamental issue of gender power relations.

## Practicing Democracy: Civil Society, Social Movements, and the State in a Globalized Era ✦

Discussions about autonomy and difference have occurred largely among feminists. But they are part of two larger debates: one on the relations between civil society and the state, and the other on the impact and future of the antiglobalization movement. Women's organizations form part of civil society, which can be conceived of as either a partner or a competitor to the state. In the former model, civil-society groups raise new issues, make the state more accountable, and expand the concept of citizenship. Pluralism in this context offers an opening to formerly marginalized groups, including indigenous movements that are seeking both voice and autonomy within the state.[4]

Vargas's celebration of the pluralist dynamic of the World Social Forum (WSF) demands a different model because the nation-state constitutes too narrow a field for the emancipatory possibilities she envisions. Her idealism is shared by many today, from political theorists such as Richard Rorty to students of global civil society, including Manuel Castells and John Keane (see also Juris 2008). In Keane's view, global civil society accepts differences, bridges societies with different moral values, and resists "intellectual imperialisms." Global civil society does not promote one set of values; in fact, it has only one "universal principle," which is that it cannot tolerate intolerance (2003:203).[5]

The politics of global civil society, as Vargas and others experience it, are emotionally demanding and intellectually innovative; they are also open-ended rather than directed toward achieving outcomes in ways that many feminists find compelling. Marguerite Waller, evoking chaos theory, speaks of the "unboxed, 'chaotic,' interactive terrain that transcultural collaboration both requires and creates" (2005:130). Moya Lloyd describes her involvement (in a local campaign) as a "messy, unstable, infinitely reversible, yet generative dynamic" (2005:1). These images are consistent with Hannah Arendt's view that politics should be dialogic rather than instrumental (1969). When Vargas calls for going beyond the ideologies of the past, it is not because she has a clear vision for the future, or because she believes that global civil society is an answer in itself. It is obvious that the wsf is not the solidary and nurturing utopia that difference and maternal feminists have held out as their image of a feminist future.

Contemporary critics have questioned the "Tocquevillean" ideal of civil society that seems to equate political freedom with market choice, a position that some have argued reinforces a narrow neoliberal view of democracy (Howell and Pierce 2001). But new critiques are beginning to cut deeper, raising questions about whether a civil society based on social movements and postauthoritarian ngos has helped or hurt democratic consolidation (e.g., Armony 2004). In *Latin America's Elusive Democracies*, Bernardo Sorj argues that Latin America has experienced democratic consolidation, "but not the way people expected." Identity and social movement politics have have "fragment[ed] social representation," creating the paradox of "growing egalitarian expectations accompanied by deepening social inequity" (2007:8–10).

Although the crisis in political representation can be partly explained by the rise of a "market-centered discourse," which has weakened traditional concepts of citizenship, Sorj maintains it is also the result of a widening gap between ngos and political parties; the ubiquity of human rights discourse; and the "moralistic" disassociation of values from interests (8). Civil society has captured the "social imagination," and its liberatory ideals are often celebrated in contrast to "the inhumanity of the market and the State" (61). But social movements (including those organized around ecology, feminism, race or ethnicity) "lack a vision of national society," causing public policy to focus on "increasingly splintered targets." Nongovernmental organizations may mobilize public opinion, but they cannot create a clearly defined social mandate.

Like Beatríz Kohen, Sorj finds the judicialization of social conflict a symptom of the decline in political parties. But he fears that the legal strategies used by "single-cause" groups will divide court systems that are already weak and can only gain legitimacy by acting in ways that are perceived as "fair." He criticizes human rights litigation for simply filling "the gaps created by the deficiencies—and sometimes simply the repression of—old social rights." Moreover, both human rights discourse and religious fundamentalism are based on moral demands, and these are by definition "absolute and nonnegotiable." This makes it difficult for political parties to form projects that will attract majorities, and "driv[es] a wedge between morals and politics, . . . rights and interests" (9).

Sorj echoes criticisms made by others. Ariel Armony (2004) has emphasized that NGOs cannot claim to be representative or internally democratic and that not all civil-society groups have goals that are congruent with democracy. Nancy Hartsock (1990) maintains that postmodernist politics creates fragmentation and resistance rather than transformation. Carina Perelli (1994) has argued that when interest groups in posttransition Uruguay imitated the moralistic discourse of the Madres, they undermined democratic politics. The fact that moral demands cannot be compromised allowed each individual or group "to further [its] own private interests at all costs, regardless of what others have to pay" (146). Far from naturally democratic or egalitarian, civil society can be described as a "terrain mined by unequal relations of power" (Alvarez, Dagnino, and Escobar 1998:18).

Sorj faults several characteristics of women's participation that many feminists have praised. Autonomy fails to recognize the "context of a community substratum of shared values" (2007:17). A pluralist concept of citizenship "erodes . . . the sense of being part of the same world, of shared problems, values and institutions," while identity politics denies "a core premise" of citizenship, "the sense of belonging to a world of 'equals'" (49). These criticisms will draw feminist responses, as will Sorj's assertion that the blurring of the distinction between public and private is dangerous, because the private sphere "is the main bulwark against authoritarian and totalitarian tendencies," a standard conservative defense of "the family" that fails to distinguish between, say, totalitarian surveillance and the state's "crossing the threshold" to confront domestic violence and ignores the totalizing effects of social control that are taught and enforced in the family.

Without space for pluralism and identity politics, it will be impossible to create the conditions of equality that give real meaning to the idea of "belonging to a world of equals" in countries that are neither socially nor racially homogeneous. Sorj is right to see in the judicialization of conflict the need to strengthen political institutions, but he seems to miss the point that living under the rule of law means that citizens will regularly seek to have their views reflected in the justice system as a coequal branch of government, not as a mere appendage to executive power. As Kohen writes, when citizens "challenge or modify the way laws are interpreted" or hold governments accountable, courts begin to take themselves more seriously." Both "civil society and democratic institutions are strengthened and citizens gain a sense of their own abilities to act."

Finally, Sorj's view that human rights are simply the "old social rights" expressed in a new language is provocative but misleading. Human rights claims are based on an individualist understanding, while the "old social rights" are collective, an important distinction relevant to different approaches to democratic citizenship (Caldeira 1998). Nor is it possible to dismiss the kind of autonomy indigenous peoples are now demanding as part of the "old" categories of justice (Marcos 2005).

Yet Sorj is making some important points that many feminists too easily dismiss or ignore. Institutions are important; and democratic polities need strong parties to link representation to concrete government actions backed by a mandate that makes it possible for the state to act. The nation-state is still the only political context in which debates over policy can result in effective action, not only because capable states can enforce laws but also because a unifying nationalism makes it possible for citizens to engage in democratic negotiation and compromise over issues of redistribution and recognition without feeling mortally threatened. Moralizing political discourse denies the reality of interests, including women's gender interests.

In the name of social justice and cultural integrity, many feminists have become active opponents of economic globalization. Chandra Mohanty calls on women to unite to "make sense" of a world "indelibly marked by the failure of postcolonial capitalist and communist nation-states to provide for the social, economic, spiritual, and psychic needs of the majority of the world's population" (2005:xi). Manuel Castells has called the World Social Forum "the most important movement [today]" because it is "changing public opinion all over the world," forcing states to recognize that they must address problems of inequality and environmental breakdown that markets cannot address on their own (Castells and Ince). Like Mohanty, Martha Gimenez (2004) sees women's resistance to globalization as the one issue around which women can organize globally.

But social movements, including women's movements, have not been very effective in bringing about more just societies. At the global level, civil society can remain highly speculative and fluid (as it is performed, say, in the WSF) precisely because global civil society lacks the means to implement its visions. At the local and national levels, however, social and political institutions, particularly political parties and governments, are critically important to democratic representation and government performance. Global pluralism can provide new ideas and change perceptions, but the appeal of spontaneous, "messy" politics underestimates the value of accountable institutions that can deliver public goods, including personal security, social services, and legal fairness—and address issues of redistribution as well as growth.[6] Bridges need to be built, and acknowledged as valuable, between women inside and outside the state and political parties; between feminist activists and women who do not share the same class interests; and between women and men, despite the persistence of sexism.

A focus on the value of institutions suggests that the results of the processes of NGO-ization are not all bad for women. Professionalization can be elitist, of course, and women's organizations that turn to service over advocacy can become dependent and welfarist, or be co-opted into clientelist relations with particular leaders or regimes. But women's organizations that focus on addressing the gaps between what the state can do and the concrete changes that are needed may provide services that states are not yet (and may never be) able to provide, and they can do so without losing their feminist edge. Service and advocacy are not necessary opposites. Effective advocacy must be based on experience, and advocacy, although it can change laws, cannot ensure that laws are implemented. Organizations that are not professionalized cannot be politically effective over the long term in a functioning democracy. This kind of organizing is not as exciting as going to the streets, although it may provide the infrastructure needed when the time comes to do so. But without such efforts, feminist visions of improving women's rights and achieving their full citizenship will certainly go unfulfilled, and the pressures that civil society can exert on states to provide economic justice will surely be weakened.

Many second-wave feminists began their activist lives on the Marxist left. Socialism offered a single, transformational answer to all social ills: development, redistribution, women's liberation, social services, and community. It was, and remains, an intellectually coherent and in many ways a morally compelling worldview. But socialism in that total sense is no longer an option, not because people are hopelessly selfish or misled by false consciousness, but because they are different from one another, as pluralists argue, and because markets produce more goods and services than state-run economies, while millions still lack the material means to live decent and dignified lives.

Politics today is a process of negotiation and compromise over outcomes that ultimately only states can provide. This process needs the generative dynamism, plural perspectives, and utopian idealism of social movements, both local and global. But it also requires respect for "politics as usual," for organizations and institutions, and for the predictability that makes it possible for people to plan and hope. Feminists must be committed to the institutional means, as well as the utopian ends, of social justice.

## Notes ⸎

1 Venezuela has been a democracy since 1958, so it did not experience "bureaucratic-authoritarian" military rule or transition politics that made the experiences of Argentina, Chile, and Brazil seem comparable. Peru was always recognized as a different case, because its military government was on the left and repression occurred in the context of civil war and under civilian governments. Elisabeth Friedman (2000) has put feminist politics in the Venezuelan case in the comparative transitions framework.

2 On motherhood and citizenship, see Ruddick 1989 and Chuchryk 1989. On the shift "from maternalism to women's rights and power," see Rakowski 2003.

3 Teresa Caldeira finds the lack of a debate between "egalitarian" and "difference" feminism in Brazil due to the lack of appreciation for individual rights as compared to social or collective rights, and "as a consequence, the notion of gender-specific rights to difference becomes legitimated but not as a critique of liberal notions of equality as fairness. Rather they are uncriticized developments of a patriarchal-paternalist tradition" (1998:96).

4 Of the countries focused on here, only Peru has a large indigenous population, although indigenous rights are a political issue for the Mapuche in Chile. Venezuela has a small indigenous population, but Hugo Chávez claims solidarity with indigenous movements across the continent. On indigenous movements and human rights, see Stavenhagen 1996. On the conflicts between indigenous gender complementarity and gender equity, see Barrig 2006. On feminism within indigenous movements, see Marcos 2005.

5 Answering the question Vargas raises about whether the WSF can exclude anyone, Keane maintains that global civil society can accept any position but not any behavior: it is legitimate to allow people to be pro-life or antigay, but these people cannot exclude others from the dialogue.

6 Arguments in favor of institutionalization have been barred from much feminist thinking. Mary García Castro and Laurence Hallewell agree with Bernardo Sorj that civil society activism has not changed the lives of the poor or created a "Third Estate" within the existing power structure, but has resulted in competition among groups and become bogged down in bureaucratic rigidity. But, unlike Sorj, they lament the loss of "Marcuse's dream . . . an attack on the productive ethic

of the market and an unrepressed sensuality oriented toward pleasure" (2001:33). Although morally satisfying, this kind of resistance, by individuals who are not themselves marginalized and who could contribute politically and materially to any reform process, is costly to those who are poor and marginalized. Steven Levitsky argues the need for institutions: "Where institutions are weak, politics becomes a Hobbesian world of uncertainty, short time horizons, and low levels of mutual trust and cooperation. There is a sense that 'everything is possible' and social and political actors routinely pursue objectives through extrainstitutional means" (2005:65).

☙ Bibliography

Abal Medina, Juan Manuel, Julieta Suárez Cao, and Facundo Nejamkis. 2003. "Reglas similares, resultados distintos: Las instituciones políticas argentinas y brasileñas en perspectiva comparada." In *La Argentina de Kirchner y el Brasil de Lula*, ed. Carlos Chacho Álvarez. Buenos Aires: Prometeo.

Abramovich, Víctor. 2006. "Acceso a la justicia y nuevas formas de participación en la esfera política." In *Acceso a la justicia como garantía de igualdad: Instituciones, actores y experiencias comparadas*, ed. Haydée Birgin and Beatríz Kohen. Buenos Aires: Biblos.

Abregú, Martín. 2007. "Derechos humanos para todos." *Escenarios alternativos* 11.

Acosta Vargas, Gladys. 2004. "La Convención sobre la Eliminación de Todas las Formas de Discriminación contra la Mujer y la Convención sobre los Derechos del Niño: Hacia la ciudadanía plena para niños, adolescentes y mujeres." In *Derechos universales realidades particulares*, ed. Eleanor Faur and Alicia Lamas. Buenos Aires: UNICEF.

AFM (Articulación Feminista Marcosur). 2007. "Diálogos feministas, Nairobi 2007: Celebrar la diversidad; Construyendo estrategias globales." www.mujeresdelsur .org.uy/df/df07 (accessed October 23, 2008).

———. 2005. "Nota de prensa desde el barco de las mujeres," Foro Social Mundial 2005, Porto Alegre, Brasil. www.mujeresdelsur.org.uy.

———. 2002. "Documento de la campaña contra los fundamentalismos." Foro Social Mundial 2002, Porto Alegre, Brasil. www.mujeresdelsur.org.uy.

Aguilar, Delia D., and Anne E. Lacsamana, eds. 2004. *Women and Globalization*. Amherst, N.Y.: Humanity Books.

———. 2000. "Translating the Global: Effects of Transnational Organizing on

Local Feminist Discourses and Practices in Latin America." *Meridians: Feminism, Race, Transnationalism* 1 (1): 29–67.

AI (Amnesty International). 2003. "Intolerable Killings: Ten Years of Abductions and Murders of Women in Ciudad Juárez and Chihuahua," August 11. www .amnesty.org.

Alvarez, Sonia E. 1999. "Advocating Feminism: The Latin American Feminist NGO 'Boom.'" *International Feminist Journal of Politics* 1 (2): 181–209.

————. 1998. "Latin American Feminisms 'Go Global': Trends of the 1990s and Challenges for the New Millennium." In *Cultures of Politics/Politics of Cultures: Revisioning Latin American Social Movements*, ed. Alvarez, Evelina Dagnino, and Arturo Escobar, 293–324. Boulder, Colo.: Westview.

————. 1994. "The (Trans)formation of Feminism(s) and Gender Politics in Democratizing Brazil." In *The Women's Movement in Latin America: Participation and Democracy*, ed. Jane S. Jaquette, 13–64. Boulder, Colo.: Westview.

————. 1992. "Feminisms in Latin America: From Bogota to San Bernardino." *Signs* 17 (2): 27–54.

————. 1990. *Engendering Democracy in Brazil: Women's Movements in Transition Politics*. Princeton: Princeton University Press.

Alvarez, Sonia. E., et al. 2003. "Encountering Latin American and Caribbean Feminisms." *Signs* 28 (2): 537–79.

Alvarez, Sonia E., Evelina Dagnino, and Arturo Escobar. 1998. "The Cultural and the Political in Latin American Social Movements." In *Cultures of Politics/Politics of Cultures*, ed. Alvarez, Dagnino, and Escobar, 1–29. Boulder, Colo.: Westview.

Americas Watch. 2000. "Criminal Injustice: Violence against Women in Brazil." In *International Human Rights in Context: Law, Politics, Morals; Text and Materials*, 2nd ed., ed. Henry Steiner and Philip Alston. Oxford: Oxford University Press.

Ames, Barry. 2002. *The Deadlock of Democracy in Brazil*. Ann Arbor: University of Michigan Press.

Ammar, Nawal H., et al. 2005. "Calls to Police and Police Response: A Case Study of Latina Immigrant Women in the USA." *International Journal of Police Science and Management* 7 (4): 230–44.

Anzaldúa, Gloria. 1987. *Borderlands/La Frontera: The New Mestiza*. San Francisco: Aunt Lute Press.

Araujo, Alesandra Noguiera. 2005. "A atuação do Juízado Especial Criminal de Belo Horizonte nos casos de violência contra a mulher: Intervenções e perspectives." Master's thesis, Federal University of Minas Gerais, Rio de Janeiro.

Araújo, Clara. 2004. "Las cuotas para mujeres en el sistema legislativo brasileño." In *La aplicación de las cuotas: Experiencias latinoamericanas*. Stockholm: International IDEA.

————. 1999. "Cidadania incompleta: O impacto da lei de cotas sobre a representação política das mulheres no Brasil." Ph.D. diss., Federal University of Minas Gerais, Rio de Janeiro.

Archenti, Nélida. 2002. "Los caminos de la inclusion política, acciones afirmativas de género." In *Hombres públicos, mujeres públicas*, ed. Silvia Vázquez. Buenos Aires: Fundacion Friedrich Ebert, Fundacion Sergio Karakachof.

Arendt, Hannah. 1998 [1958]. *The Human Condition*. Chicago: University of Chicago Press.

———. 1995. *Men in Dark Times*. New York: Harcourt, Brace and World.

———. 1969. On Violence. New York: Harcourt Brace.

Armony, Ariel C. 2004. *The Dubious Link: Civic Engagement and Democratization*. Stanford, Calif.: Stanford University Press.

Arteaga, Ana María. 1998. *El ejercicio del control ciudadano: Hacia una ciudadanía activa de las mujeres*. Santiago: CEDEM.

Articulación de Mujeres Brasilera. 2005. "Carta abierta a Fray Beto," Foro Social Mundial 2005, Porto Alegre, Brasil. www.articulacaomulheres.org.br.

Astelarra, Judith. 1990. *Participación política de las mujeres*. Madrid: Centro de Investigaciones Sociológicas.

Auth, Pepe. 2005. "Estudio sobre las elecciones parlamentarias Santiago." *Colección Ideas 57*. Santiago: Fundación Chile Veintiuno.

Auyero, Javier. 2003. *Contentious Lives: Two Argentine Women, Two Protests, and the Quest for Recognition*. Durham, N.C.: Duke University Press.

Ávila, Betânia. 2003. "Pensando o Forum Social Mundao: A través do feminismo." *Revista estudos feministas* 11 (2).

———. 2001. "Feminismo y ciudadanía: La producción de nuevos derechos." Mujeres al Timón: cuadernos para la incidencia política feminista, no. 2. Lima: Flora Tristán, AGENDE, Equidad de Género.

Bailey, John, and Jorge Chabat, eds. 2002. *Transnational Crime and Public Security: Challenges to Mexico and the United States*. La Jolla: University of California, San Diego, Center for U.S.-Mexican Studies Press.

Bakker, Isabella. 2003. "Neoliberal Governance and the Reprivatization of Social Reproduction: Social Provision and Shifting Gender Orders." In *Power, Production, and Social Reproduction: Human In/security in the Global Political Economy*, ed. Bakker and Stephen Gill, 66–82. New York: Palgrave Mcmillan.

———, ed. 1994. *Strategic Silence: Gender and Economic Policy*. London: Zed.

Barrancos, Dora. 2001. *Inclusión/exclusión: Historia con mujeres*. Buenos Aires: Fondo de Cultura Económica.

Barreiro, Line. 1996. "Las recién llegadas: Mujer y participación política." In *Estudios básicos de derechos humanos IV*, ed. Y. Azize et al. San José, Costa Rica: Instituto Interamericano de Derechos Humanos.

Barreiro, Line, Oscar López, and Lilian Clyde Soto. 2004. "Sistemas electorales y representación femenina en América Latina." Serie Mujer y Desarrollo no. 54. Santiago: CEPAL (Women and Development Unit).

Barrig, Maruja. 2006. "What Is Justice? Indigenous Women in Andean Development Projects." In *Women and Gender Equity in Development Theory and Practice*, ed. Jane S. Jaquette and Gale Summerfield, 107–34. Durham, N.C.: Duke University Press.

————. 2001. "Latin American Feminisms: Gains, Losses, and Hard Times." *NACLA Report on the Americas* 34 (5): 29–36.

————. 1998. "Female Leadership, Violence, and Citizenship in Peru." In *Women and Democracy: Latin America and Central and Eastern Europe*, ed. Jane S. Jaquette and Sharon L. Wolchik, 104–24. Baltimore: Johns Hopkins University Press.

————. 1997. "De cal y arena: ONGs y movimiento de mujeres en Chile." Unpublished manuscript.

————. 1994. "The Difficult Equilibrium between Bread and Roses: Women's Organizing and Democracy in Peru." In *The Women's Movement in Latin America: Participation and Democracy*, ed. Jane S. Jaquette, 151–76. Boulder, Colo.: Westview.

Barsted, Leila Linhares. 2006. "A violência contra as mulheres no Brasil e a Convenção de Belém do Pará dez anos depois." In *O progresso das mulheres no Brasil*, 248–289. Brasilia: UNIFEM, Ford Foundation. www.mulheresnobrasil.org.

————. 2001. "Lei e realidade social: Igualdade x desigualdade." In *As mulheres e os direitos humanos*. Rio de Janeiro: Cepia.

Baynes, Kenneth. 2002. "A Critical Theory Perspective on Civil Society and the State." In *Civil Society and Government*, ed. Nancy L. Rosenblum and Robert C. Post, 123–45. Princeton: Princeton University Press.

Beck, Ulrich. 2004. *Poder y contrapoder en la era global: La nueva economía política mundial*. Paidós Estao y Sociedad. Barcelona: Paidós Libreria.

Benería, Lourdes. 2003. *Gender, Development, and Globalization: Economics as If People Mattered*. New York: Routledge.

Benítez, Rohri, et al. 1999. *El silencio que la voz de todas quiebra: Mujeres y víctimas de Ciudad Juárez*. Chihuahua: Azar.

Bergallo, Paola. 2007. "Equidad de género: Perspectivas para su exigibilidad judicial." In *La aplicación de los tratados sobre derechos humanos en el ámbito local: La experiencia de una década*, ed. Víctor Abramovich, Alberto Bovino, and Christian Courtis. Buenos Aires: Centro de Estudios Legales y Sociales.

Bergallo, Paola, and Cristina Motta. 2005. "Los derechos humanos de las mujeres." In *Informe sobre género y derechos humanos; Vigencia y respeto de los derechos de las mujeres en Argentina*, 23–52. Buenos Aires: ELA.

Berger, Susan A. 2006. *Guatemaltecas: The Women's Movement, 1986-2003*. Austin: University of Texas Press.

Bhabha, Homi. 1994. "Narrating the Nation." In *Nationalism*, ed. John Hutchison and Anthony D. Smith, 306–11. New York: Oxford University Press.

Birgin, Haydée. 2000. "El género en el derecho y el derecho en el género." In *Rompiendo la indiferencia: Acciones ciudadanas en defensa del interés público*, 155–208. Santiago: Ford Foundation.

Birgin, Haydée, and Beatríz Kohen. 2006a. "Introducción: El acceso a la justicia como derecho." In *Acceso a la justicia como garantía de igualdad: Instituciones, actores y experiencias comparadas*, ed. Birgin and Kohen, 15–25. Buenos Aires: Biblos.

———. 2006b. "Justicia y género, una experiencia en la ciudad e Buenos Aires." In *Acceso a la justicia como garantía de igualdad: Instituciones, actores y experiencias comparadas*, ed. Birgin and Kohen, 233–53. Buenos Aires: Biblos.

Birgin, Haydeé, and Gabriela Pastorino. 2005. "Violencia contra las mujeres." In *Informe sobre género y derechos humanos: Vigencia y respeto de los derechos de las mujeres en Argentina*, 291–336. Buenos Aires: Biblos.

Blay, Eva. 2002. "Mulher e igualdade: Cidadania e género. *Socialdemocracia brasileira* 1 (2): 58–63.

Blofield, Merike. 2006. *The Politics of Moral Sin: Abortion and Divorce in Spain, Chile, and Argentina*. New York: Routledge.

Blondet, Cecilia. 2002. "The 'Devil's Deal': Women's Political Participation and Authoritarianism in Peru." In *Gender, Justice, Development, and Rights*, ed. Maxine Molyneux and Shahra Razavi, 277–305. Oxford: Oxford University Press.

Böhmer, Martín, and Verónica Matus. 2000. "Nuevo énfasis en la defensa del interés público: Una mirada hacia el futuro." In *Rompiendo la indiferencia: Acciones ciudadanas en defensa del interés público*, ed. Angelika Rettberg, 489–520. Santiago: Fundación Ford.

Bonino, María. 1998. *Hacia la construcción de un índice de compromisos cumplidos en educación de mujeres en la V Conferencia Internacional de Educación de Adultos: Un instrumento para monitorear los acuerdos de la Conferencia*. Santa Cruz de la Sierra: Taller Internacional Seguimiento a Beijing y Hamburgo Educación-Género-Ciudadanía REPEM.

Bonner, Michelle D. 2007. *Sustaining Human Rights: Women and Argentine Human Rights Organizations*. University Park: Pennsylvania State University Press.

Caldeira, Teresa P. R. 1998. "Justice and Women's Rights: Challenges for Women's Movements and Democratization in Brazil." In *Women and Democracy: Latin America and Central and Eastern Europe*, ed. Jane S. Jaquette and Sharon L. Wolchik, 75–103. Baltimore: Johns Hopkins University Press.

Caro, Pamela, and Alejandra Valdés. 2000. *Control ciudadano en educación y género, monitoreo de acuerdos internacionales*. Santiago: CEDEM.

Castañeda, Jorge, and Patricio Navia. 2007. "The Year of the Ballot." *Current History* 106 (697): 51–63.

Castells, Manuel. 1999. "Los efectos de la globalización en América Latina por el autor de 'la era de la información.'"*Insomnia*, June 25.

Castells, Manuel, and Martin Ince. 2003. *Conversations with Manuel Castells*. Cambridge: Polity.

Castro, Mary García, and Laurence Hallewell. 2001. "Engendering Powers in Neoliberal Times in Latin America: Reflections from the Left on Feminisms and Feminisms." *Latin American Perspectives* 28 (6): 17–37.

Cavallero, James L. 2002. "Toward Fair Play: A Decade of Transformation and

Resistance in Human Rights Advocacy Law in Brazil." *Chicago Journal of International Law* 3 (2).

CEDAW Committee. 1992. General Recommendation no. 19 (A/47/38). January 29.

CEDES (Centro de Estudios de Estado y Sociedad). 2005. *Ciudania y sexualidad.* Buenos Aires: Defensora del Pueblo.

CEPAL (Comision Económica para América Latina). 1999. Directorio de organismos nacionales a cargo de las políticas y programas para las mujeres de América Latina y el Caribe. Santiago, Chile.

Charlesworth, Hilary. 1999. "Feminist Methods in International Law." *American Journal of International Law* 93 (2): 379–93.

Chiarotti, Susan. 2006. "Utilizar la ley como herramiento de cambio: El CLADEM, red regional de feministas que trabajan con el derecho." In *De lo privado a lo público: Treinta años de lucha ciudadana en América Latina*, ed. Nathalie Lebon and Elizabeth Maier, 380–90. Mexico City: Siglo Veintiuno.

Chicago Council on Global Affairs. 2007. "World Public Opinion, 2007." June. www.worldpublicopinion.org.

Chinchilla, Norma, and Liesl Haas. 2006. "De Protesta a Propuesta: The Contributions and Challenges of Latin American Feminism." In *Latin America after Neoliberalism: Turning the Tide in the Twenty-First Century*, ed. Eric Hershberg and Fred Rosen, 252–75. New York: New Press.

Chuchryk, Patricia M. 1989. "Subversive Mothers: Women's Opposition to the Military Regime in Chile." In *Women, the State, and Development*, ed. Sue Ellen M. Charlton, Jana Everett, and Kathleen Staudt. Albany: State University of New York Press.

Claro, Magdalena, and Virginia Seoane. 2005. *Acción afirmativa hacia democracias inclusivas, Argentina.* Santiago: Fundación Equitas.

Cohen, Jean L. 1985. "Strategy or Identity: New Theoretical Paradigms and Contemporary Social Movements." *Social Research* 52 (4).

Comisión Nacional de Seguimiento (CNS mujeres). 1999. *El estado uruguayo y las mujeres.* Montevideo: Editorial CNS mujeres. www.cnsmujeres.org.uy (accessed October 25, 2008).

*Contrainforme 2002: Derechos humanos de las mujeres; Asignaturas pendientes del estado argentino.* www.rimaweb.com.ar/derechos/contra_informe_CEDAW.html (accessed October 25, 2008).

Coordinación Subregional Cono Sur de ONG hacia Beijing y Otras. 1996. *Plataforma Beijing 95: Un instrumento de acción para las mujeres.* Santiago: Isis Internacional.

Corporación de la Mujer, La Morada. 1999. *Reporte alternativo al III Informe Periódico del estado del cumplimiento de la Convencion sobre la Eliminacion de Todas las Formas de Discriminacion contra la Mujer por parte del gobierno de Chile.* Santiago: Facultad de Derecho, Universidad de Chile.

Corporación Humanas. 2006. "Evaluación de la paridad en el poder ejecutivo: Avances y resistencias." Unpublished report. www.humanas.cl.

Correa, Sonia. 1997. "Conferencia Internacional de Población y Desarrollo (CIPD): La dimensión de género; Antecedentes, procesos, resultados y retos para el futuro." In *Género, educación y desarrollo en América Latina*, ed. X. Erazo, L. Lagarrigue, and S. Larraín. Santiago: Servicio Universitario Mundial, Coordinación para América Latina y el Caribe.

"Corte final para el 3D: Veintitres aspirantes." 2006. *El nacional* (Caracas), August 28.

Craske, Nikki. 2003. "Gender, Politics, and Legislation." In *Gender in Latin America*, ed. Sylvia Chant with Craske, 19–45. New Brunswick, N.J.: Rutgers University Press.

De Barbieri, Teresita. 1992. "Sobre la categoría de género: Una introducción teórico-metodológica." In *Fin de siglo: Género y cambio civilizatorio*, ed. Regina Rodriguez. Santiago: Isis Internacional.

Deere, Carmen Diana, and Magdalena León. 2001. *Empowering Women: Land and Property Rights in Latin America*. Pittsburgh: University of Pittsburgh Press.

Del Campo, Esther. 2005. "Women and Politics in Latin America: Perspectives and Limits of the Institutional Aspects of Women's Political Representation." *Social Forces* 85 (4): 1697–1726.

De los Ríos, Rebecca. 1993. "Del integracionismo al enfoque de género en las concepciones sobre la salud de la mujer." Paper presented at the Seminario Internacional Presente y Futuro de los Estudios de Género en América Latina, Cali, Colombia.

De Luca, Miguel, Mark P. Jones, and María Inés Tula. 2002. "Back Rooms or Ballot Boxes? Candidate Nomination in Argentina." *Comparative Political Studies* 35 (4): 413–36.

Deng, Francis M. 1996. "Further Promotion and Encouragement of Human Rights and Fundamental Freedoms: Including the Question of the Programme and Methods of Work of the Commission on Human Rights, Mass Exoduses, and Displaced Persons." Report of the Secretary-General (submitted pursuant to Commission on Human Rights Resolution 1995/57), E/Cn.4/1996/52/Add.1. Geneva.

De Sousa Santos, Boaventura. 2006. *Conocer desde el Sur: Para una cultura política emancipatoria*. Colección Transformación Global. Lima: Universidad de San Marcos. www.democraciaglobal.org.

———. 2003. "Para uma sociologia das ausências e uma sociologia das emergências." *Revista crítica de ciencias sociales* 63:237–80.

Divine, Gloria. 1998. "Necesidades de las mujeres como fuente de acciones de interes público." In *Experiencias de acciones de interés público en el Cono Sur*. Santiago: FORJA.

DMRS (Diocesan Migrant and Refugee Services). 2005. "Ministry of the Catholic Diocese of El Paso," www.dmrs_ep.org.

Eckersley, Robyn. 1992. *Environmentalism and Political Theory: Toward an Ecocentric Approach*. Albany: State University of New York Press.

ELA (Equipo Latinamericano de Justicia y Género). 2007. *Como nos vemos las mujeres: Actitudes y percepciones de las mujeres sobre distintos aspectos de sus condiciones de vida.* Buenos Aires: -L. www.artemisnoticias.com.ar.

————. 2005. *Informe sobre género y derechos humanos: Vigencia y respeto de los derechos de las mujeres en Argentina.* Buenos Aires: Biblos. www.artemisnoticias.com.ar.

Elson, Diane. 2003. "Gender Justice, Human Rights, and Neo-liberal Economic Policies." In *Gender Justice, Development, and Rights,* ed. Maxine Molyneux and Shahra Razavi, 78–114. Oxford: Oxford University Press.

————. 1991. "Structural Adjustment: Its Effects on Women." In *Changing Perceptions: Writing on Gender and Development,* ed. Tina Wallace and Candida Marsh, 39–53. Oxford: Oxfam.

En Diversidad, Otro Mundo Es Posible. 2007. "Carta al Comité Internacional del Foro Social Mundial." Internal letter to Comité Internacional.

Equidad de Género, Ciudadanía, Trabajo y Familia. 2005. *Índice de compromiso cumplido México 1995-2003: Una estrategia para el control ciudadano de la equidad de género.* Mexico City: Equidad de Género, Ciudadanía, Trabajo y Familia.

Escobar-Lemmon, Maria, and Michelle M. Taylor-Robinson. 2005. "Women Ministers in Latin American Government: When, Where, and Why?" *American Journal of Political Science* 49 (4): 829–44.

Espina, Gioconda. 2006. "Institucionalización de la lucha feminista/femenina en Venezuela: Solidaridad y fragmentación, oportunidades y desafíos." In *De lo privado a lo público: Treinta años de lucha ciudadana en América Latina,* ed. Nathalie Lebon and Elizabeth Maier, 310–30. Mexico City: Siglo Veintiuno.

————. 2003. "Las feministas de aquí." In *Las mujeres de Venezuela,* ed. Inés Quintero. Caracas: Funtrapet.

Espina, Gioconda, and Cathy Rakowski. 2002. "¿Movimiento de mujeres o mujeres en movimiento? El caso Venezuela." *Cuadernos del Cendes* 19 (49): 31–48.

Facio, Alda. 1991. "El sexismo en el derecho internacional de los derechos humanos." In *Mujer y derechos humanos en América Latina.* Lima: CLADEM.

Facio, Alda, and Lorena Fríes, eds. 1999. *Género y derecho.* Santiago: Lom.

Family Violence Prevention Fund. 2006. "Department of Health and Human Services Violence against Women Funding." www.endabuse.org.

Faur, Eleonor, and Natalia Gherardi. 2005a. "El derecho al trabajo y la ocupación de las mujeres." In *Informe sobre género y derechos humanos: Vigencia y respeto de los derechos de las mujeres en Argentina,* 207–52. Buenos Aires: Biblos.

————. 2005b. "Sexualidades reproducción: La perspectiva de los derechos humanos." In *Informe sobre género y derechos humanos: Vigencia y respeto de los derechos de las mujeres en Argentina,* 169–206. Buenos Aires: Biblos.

Feminist Dialogues. 2005. "Global Feminist Strategies, Challenges, and Common Approaches." Conceptual Note No. 2. www.feministdialogue.isiswomen.org.

————. 2007a. "Global Feminist Strategies, Challenges, and Common Approaches." Conceptual Note No. 3. www.feministdialogue.isiswomen.org.

———. 2007b. "Global Feminist Strategies, Challenges, and Common Approaches." Conceptual Note No. 5. www.feministsdialogues.isiswomen.org.

Fernández-Kelly, María Patricia. 1983. *For We Are Sold, I and My People: Women and Industry in Mexico's Frontier*. Albany: State University of New York Press.

FORES (Foro de Estudios sobre la Administración de Justicia) and Fundación Libertad. 2005–6. "Índice de confianza en la justicia." www.foresjusticia.org.ar.

Franceschet, Susan. 2006. "El triunfo de Bachelet y el ascenso político de las mujeres." *Nueva sociedad* 202 (March–April): 13–22.

———. 2005. *Women and Politics in Chile*. Boulder, Colo.: Lynne Rienner.

———. 2003. "State Feminism and Women's Movements: The Impact of Chile's Servicio Nacional de la Mujer on Women's Activism." *Latin American Research Review* 38 (1): 9–40.

Fraser, Nancy. 2003. "Social Justice in the Age of Identity Politics: Redistribution, Recognition, and Participation." In *Redistribution or Recognition? A Philosophical Exchange*, by Fraser and Axel Honneth, 7–109. London: Verso.

———. 2000. "Rethinking Recognition." *New Left Review* 3:107–20.

———. 1997. *Iustitia interrupta. Reflexiones críticas desde la posición "postsocialista."* Bogotá: Siglo del Hombre Editores.

Friedman, Elisabeth. 2000. *Unfinished Transitions: Women and the Gendered Development of Democracy in Venezuela*. University Park: Pennsylvania State University Press.

Fries, Lorena, and Gloria Maira, eds. 2005. *Informe regional de derechos humanos de las mujeres y justicia de género*. Santiago: Corporación Humanas.

Fundación IDEAS (Chile). 1999. *Percepción de las mujeres jóvenes de las barreras de acceso al empleo y dificultades en el trabajo*. Santiago: Grupo Iniciativa Mujeres.

Fundación Konrad Adenauer and Centro de Estudios Unión por Nueva Mayoría. 1998. "Estudio auto percepción del periodismo en la Argentina." *Revista contribuciones* 1.

Fundación Poder Ciudadano. 1997. *Herramientas de acción ciudadana para la defensa de los derechos de la mujer*. Buenos Aires: Fundación Poder Ciudadano, Programa de Participación y Fiscalización Ciudadana.

Gallagher, Michael, and Michael Marsh, eds. 1988. *Candidate Selection in Comparative Perspective: The Sweet Garden of Politics*. Newbury Park, Calif.: Sage.

Gálvez, Thelma. 1999. *Indicadores de género para el seguimiento y la evaluación del Programa de Acción Regional para las Mujeres de América Latina y el Caribe, 1995–2000 y la Plataforma de Acción de Beijing*. Santiago: CEPAL.

———. 1997. *Propuestas para un sistema de estadísticas de género*. Santiago: UNICEF-INE.

Gandhi, Nandita, and Nandita Shah. 2007. "Un espacio interactivo para feministas." www.feministdialogue.isiswomen.org.

Gannon, María Isabel, and Eugenia Hola. *¿Feminismo en los sectores populares? Las organizaciones de mujeres en los sectores populares urbanos de la Región Metropolitana*. Unpublished report. Santiago: Ford Foundation.

García Frinchaboy, Mónica. 2005. "Situación educativa de las mujeres." In *Informe sobre género y derechos humanos: Vigencia y respeto de los derechos de las mujeres in Argentina*, 53–92. Equipo Latinoamericano de Justicia y Género (ELA). Buenos Aires: Biblos.

Gaspar de Alba, Alicia. 2003. "The Maquiladora Murders: 1993–2003." *Aztlán: A Journal of Chicano Studies* 28 (2): 1–17.

Gherardi, Natalia, and Beatríz Kohen. 2005. "Participación de las mujeres en cargos políticos." In *Informe sobre género y derechos humanos: Vigencia y respeto de los derechos de las mujeres en Argentina*, 53–92. Buenos Aires: Biblos.

Gherardi, Natalia, and Leticia Kabusacki. 2006. "Abortion Permitted by Law in Legal and Judicial Discourse in Argentina: The Need to Refine and Promote Main Legal Arguments to Counteract Conservative Legal Discourse." Unpublished manuscript.

Gimenez, Martha E. 2004. "Connecting Marx and Feminism in the Era of Globalization: A Preliminary Investigation." *Socialism and Democracy* 18 (1): 85–96.

Gondolf, Edward W., with Ellen R. Fisher. 1988. *Battered Women as Survivors: An Alternative to Treating Learned Helplessness*. Lexington, Mass.: Lexington Books.

Gónzalez Morales, Felipe. 1998. "Las acciones de interés público y su impacto en la cultura: algunos apuntes básicos." In *Experiencias de acciones de interés público en el Cono Sur*. Santiago: FORJA.

Goodman, James. 1998. "Transnational Integration and 'Cosmopolitan Nationalism.'" Paper presented at the colloquium "The Possibilities of Transnational Democracy," Centre for Transnational Studies, University of Newcastle.

Gorriti, Gustavo. 1990. *Sendero: Historia de la guerra milenaria en el Perú*. Lima: Apoyo.

Gray, Lorriane. 1986. *The Global Assembly Line*. Documentary film.

Grissom, Brandi. 2006. "Operation Linebacker Catches More Immigrants than Criminals." *El Paso Times*, November 20, 1A.

Grupo de Iniciativa ONG–Chile. 1997. *Foro Nacional para el seguimiento de los acuerdos de Beijing: Acta de la primera sesión; Las mujeres en el ejercicio del poder y la toma de decisiones*. Santiago.

Grzybowsky, Cándido. 2002. ¿"Es posible un mundo más femenino?" Talk at the World Social Forum, January 31–February 5.

Güell, Pedro E. 2004. "Chile Has Changed . . . but in What Ways Has It Changed?" *ReVista/Harvard Review of Latin America* (spring 2004): 4–7.

Guzmán, Virginia. 2004. *Democratic Governance and Gender: Possible Linkages*. Santiago: CEPAL.

Guzmán, Virginia, and Marcela Ríos. 1995. *Propuesta para un sistema de indicadores de género*. Santiago: Servicio Nacional de la Mujer.

Hagopian, Frances. 2005. "Conclusions: Government Performance, Political Representation, and Public Perceptions of Contemporary Democracy in Latin America." In *The Third Wave of Democratization in Latin America: Advances and Setbacks*, ed. Hagopian and Scott P. Mainwaring, 319–62. New York: Oxford University Press.

——. 1992. "The Compromised Consolidation: The Political Class in the Brazilian Transition." In *Issues in Democratic Consolidation: The New South American Democracies in Comparative Perspective*, ed. Scott P. Mainwaring, Guillermo O'Donnell, and J. Samuel Valenzuela. Notre Dame, Ind.: University of Notre Dame Press.

Harari, Sofía. 2005. "Familias y autonomía de las mujeres." In *Informe sobre género y derechos humanos: Vigencia y respeto de los derechos de las mujeres en Argentina*, 273–90. Buenos Aires: Biblos.

Hartsock, Nancy. 1990. "Foucault on Power: A Theory for Women?" In *Feminism/Postmodernism*, ed. Linda J. Nicholson, 157–75. New York: Routledge.

Hayner, Priscilla B. 1996. "International Guidelines for the Creation and Operation of Truth Commissions: A Preliminary Proposal." *Law and Contemporary Problems* 59 (4): 173–81.

Heath, Roseanna Michelle, Leslie A. Schwindt-Bayer, and Michelle M. Taylor-Robinson. 2005. "Women on the Sidelines: Women's Representation on Committees in Latin American Legislatures." *American Journal of Political Science* 49 (2): 420–36.

Heringer, Rosana, and Miranda Dayse. 2004. "ICC — Brasil: Índice de Compromissos Cumpridos; Uma estratégia para o controle cidadão da igualdade de gênero." www.cepia.org.br.

Hernández Castillo, R. Aída. 2002. "National Law and Indigenous Customary Law: The Struggle for Justice of Indigenous Women in Chiapas, Mexico." In *Gender Justice, Development, and Rights*, ed. Maxine Molyneux and Sahra Razavi, 384–412. Oxford: Oxford University Press.

Herrera Flores, Joaquín. 2004. "Directos humanos, interculturalidade e racionalidade de resistencia." In *Direitos humanos e filosofia juridica na América Latina*, ed. Antonio Carlos Wolkmer. Rio de Janeiro: Lúmen Juris.

Howell, Jude, and Jenny Pierce. 2001. *Civil Society and Development: A Critical Exploration*. Boulder, Colo.: Lynne Rienner.

Htun, Mala. 2003a. *Dimensions of Political Inclusion and Exclusion in Brazil: Gender and Race*. Washington: Inter-American Development Bank, Department of Sustainable Development. www.iadb.ng.lsds/author.

——. 2003b. *Sex and the State: Abortion, Divorce, and the Family under Latin American Dictatorships and Democracies*. Cambridge: Cambridge University Press.

——. 2001. "Advanced Women's Rights in the Americas: Achievements and Challenges." Working paper. Miami: University of Miami, North-South Center. www.thedialogue.org.

Htun, Mala, and Mark P. Jones. 2002. "Engendering the Right to Participate in Decision-Making: Electoral Quotas and Women's Leadership in Latin America."

In *Gender and the Politics of Rights and Democracy in Latin America*, ed. Nikki Craske and Maxine Molyneux. Houndmills, Basingstoke, UK: Palgrave.

Human Rights Watch. 2005. "Decisión prohibida: Acceso de las mujeres a los anticonceptivos y al aborto en Argentina." June. www.hrw.org/women.

———. 1991. *Criminal Injustice: Violence against Women in Brazil*. New York: Human Rights Watch.

IACHR (Inter-American Commission on Human Rights). 2001. "*Maria da Penha Fernandes v. Brasil 04/16/2001*: Report #54/01, Case 12.051." Washington: OAS. www1.umn.edu/humanrts/cases/commission.htm.

———. 1996. "*Raquel Martín de Mejía v. Perú*: Case 10.970. Report No. 5/96." Washington: OAS.

INMUJERES (Instituto Nacional de las Mujeres) and INEGI (Instituto Nacional de Estadística Geografía e Informática). 2003. "Encuesta nacional sobre la dinámica de las relaciones en los hogares." www.inmujeres.gob.mx.

Instituto del Tercer Mundo. 2001. *Control ciudadano 2001, No. 5*. Montevideo: Instituto del Tercer Mundo. www.socialwatch.org.

———. 1999a. *Control ciudadano No. 3*. Montevideo: Instituto del Tercer Mundo. www.socialwatch.org.

———. 1999b. *Para ejercer el control ciudadano: Monitoreo de la Cumbre de Copenhague y la Conferencia de Beijing*. Montevideo: Instituto del Tercer Mundo. www.socialwatch.org.

———. 1998. *Control ciudadano No. 2*. Montevideo: Instituto del Tercer Mundo. www.socialwatch.org.

———. 1997. *Control ciudadano No. 1*. Montevideo: Instituto del Tercer Mundo. www.socialwatch.org.

———. 1996. *Control ciudadano No. 0*. Montevideo: Instituto del Tercer Mundo. www.socialwatch.org.

Inter-American Court of Human Rights. 2006. "Case *Castro Castro v. Peru*," November 25. San José, Costa Rica: OAS.

———. 1997. "Case *Loaya Tamayo*," September 17. San José, Costa Rica: OAS.

Jaquette, Jane S., ed. 1994. *The Women's Movement in Latin America: Participation and Democracy*. Boulder, Colo.: Westview.

Jaquette, Jane, and Sharon L. Wolchik, eds. 1998. *Women and Democracy: Latin America and Central and Eastern Europe*. Baltimore: Johns Hopkins University Press.

Jelin, Elizabeth. 2003. "La escala de la acción de los movimientos sociales." In *Mas allá de la nación: Las escalas múltiples de los movimientos sociales*, ed. E. Jelin. Buenos Aires: Libros del Zorzal.

———. 1998a. *Ciudadanía y alteridad: Tensiones y dilemmas*.

———. 1998b. "Women, Gender, and Human Rights." In *Constructing Democracy: Human Rights, Citizenship, and Society in Latin America*, ed. E. Jelin and Eric Hershberg, 177–96. Boulder, Colo.: Westview.

————. 1997. "Igualdad y diferencia: Dilemas de la ciudadanía de las mujeres en América Latina." *Cuadernos de estudios políticos* 7.

————. 1996. "La construcción de la ciudadanía: Entre la solidaridad y la responsabilidad." In *Construir la democracia: Derechos humanos, ciudadanía y sociedad en América Latina*, ed. E. Jelin and Eric Hershberg. Caracas: Editorial Nueva Sociedad.

Jelin, Elizabeth, and Eric Hershberg. 1998. "Convergence and Diversity: Reflections on Human Rights." In *Constructing Democracy: Human Rights, Citizenship, and Society in Latin America*, ed. E. Jelin and E. Hershberg, 215–24. Boulder, Colo.: Westview.

Jones, Mark P. 2004. "The Recruitment and Selection of Legislative Candidates in Argentina." Paper presented at the "Pathways to Power: Political Recruitment and Democracy in Latin America" conference, Wake Forest University, Winston-Salem, N.C., April 2–4.

Jones, Mark P., and Patricio Navia. 1999. "Assessing the Effectiveness of Gender Quotas in Open-List Proportional Representation Electoral Systems." *Social Science Quarterly* 80 (2).

Juris, Jeffrey S. 2008. *Networking Futures: The Movements against Corporate Globalization*. Durham, N.C.: Duke University Press.

Keane, John. 2003. *Global Civil Society?* Cambridge: Cambridge University Press.

Keck, Margaret E., and Kathryn Sikkink. 1998. *Activists beyond Borders: Advocacy Networks in International Politics*. Ithaca: Cornell University Press.

Kohen, Beatríz. 1998a. "Fiscalización ciudadana de la gestión pública." In *Acciones de fiscalización y control ciudadano de la gestión pública*. Buenos Aires: Red Interamericana y del Caribe para la Democracia.

————. 1998b. "Poder ciudadano y la acciones de interés público: La experiencia del Programa de participación y fiscalización ciudadana." In *Experiencias de acciones de interés público en el Cono Sur*. Santiago: FORJA.

————. 1998c. "Poder ciudadano y las acciones de interés público: Un ejemplo de control desde la sociedad civil." In *Lo público no estatal en la reforma del estado*, ed. Luis Carlos Bresser Pereira and Nuria Cunill Grau. Buenos Aires: LAD, PAIDOS.

————. 1997. "Relatoría sobre acciones de interés público en Argentina." In *Las acciones de interés público: Argentina, Chile, Colombia y Perú*, ed. Felipe González Morales et al. Santiago: Universidad Diego Portales, Escuela de Derecho.

Kopinak, Kathy, ed. 2004. *The Social Costs of Industrial Growth in Northern Mexico*. La Jolla: University of California at San Diego Center for U.S.-Mexican Studies Press.

Krook, Mona Lena. 2007. "Gender Quota Laws in Global Perspective." Paper prepared for "Women in the Americas: Paths to Political Power" conference, Inter-American Dialogue, Inter-American Development Bank, League of Women Voters, Washington. March 4. www.thedialogue.org.

———. 2006. "Gender Quotas, Norms, and Politics." *Politics and Gender* 2 (1): 110–18.

Kumar, Corinne. 2005. "South Wind: Toward a New Political Imaginary." In *Dialogue and Difference: Feminisms Challenge Globalization*, ed. Marguerite Waller and Sylvia Marcos, 165–200. New York: Palgrave Macmillan.

Kurtz, Marcus J. 2004. "The Dilemmas of Democracy in the Open Economy: Lessons from Latin America." *World Politics* 56 (3): 262–302.

Lafer, Celso. 2006. Preface to *Dereitos humanos e justiça internacional*, ed. Flávia Piovesan, xxii. São Paulo: Saraiva.

Lamas, Marta. 1990. "La antropología feminista y la categoría de género." In *El género: La construcción social de la diferencia sexual*, ed. Lamas. Mexico City: PUEG.

LaRamée, Pierre. 2007. "Sex, Lies, and the Left." NACLA *Report on the Americas* 40 (3): 3.

Lázaro, Alejandra, and Ileana Fraquelli. 2003. "'Ley de cupo': ¿Avance legislativo o judicial?" In *Estrategias políticas de género: Reformas institucionales, identidad y accion colectiva*, ed. Nélida Archenti. Buenos Aires: Instituto Gino Germani de la Facultad de Ciencias Sociales de la Universidad de Buenos Aires.

Lebon, Nathalie, and Elizabeth Maier, eds. 2006. *De lo privado a lo público: Treinta años de lucha ciudadana de las mujeres en América Latina*. Mexico City: Siglo Veintiuno.

Lechner, Norberto. 2002. *Las Sombras del Mañana; La dimensión subectiva de la política*. Santiago: Lom ediciones.

———. 1996. "La transformación de la política." *Revista Mexicana de Sociología* 58 (1): 5–17.

Leon, Magdalena, ed. 1994. *Mujeres y Participación Política: Avances y Desafíos en América Latina*. Bogotá: Editores T/M.

Levitsky, Steven. 2005. "Argentina: Democratic Survival amidst Economic Failure." In *The Third Wave of Democratization in Latin America: Advances and Setbacks*, ed. Frances Hagopian and Scott P. Mainwaring, 63–89. New York: Oxford University Press.

Liebowitz, Deborah. 2002. "Gendering (Trans)national Advocacy: Tracking the Lollapalooza at 'Home.'" *International Feminist Journal of Politics* 4 (2): 173–96.

Lipsky, Michael. 1980. *Street-Level Bureaucracy: Dilemmas of the Individual in Public Services*. New York: Russell Sage Foundation.

Lister, Ruth. 1997. *Citizenship: Feminist Perspectives*. London: Macmillan.

Lloyd, Moya. 2005. *Beyond Identity Politics: Feminism, Power, Politics*. London: Sage.

Lochak, Daniele. 2005. *Les droits de l'homme*. Paris: La Découverte.

Lubertino, María José. 2006. "Nuevas constituciones para todos y todas." In *Informe final: Seminario Internacional; Reformas constitucionales y equidad de género, Santa Cruz de la Sierra*. Santiago: CEPAL.

Macaulay, Fiona. 2006. "Difundiéndose hacia arriba, hacia abajo y hacia los lados:

Políticas de género y oportunidades políticas en Brasil." In *De lo privado a lo público: Treinta años de lucha ciudadana en América Latina*, ed. Nathalie Lebon and Elizabeth Maier, 331–48. Mexico City: Siglo Veintiuno.

Mafia, Diana. 2000. "Ciudadanía sexual: Aspectos legales y políticos de los derechos reproductivos como derechos humanos." *Feminaria* 14 (26): 27–28.

Mainwaring, Scott P. 1999. *Rethinking Party Systems in the Third Wave of Democratization*. Stanford, Calif.: Stanford University Press.

Mainwaring, Scott P., and Aníbal Pérez-Liñán. 2005. "Latin American Democratization since 1978: Democratic Transitions, Breakdowns, and Erosions." In *The Third Wave of Democratization in Latin America: Advances and Setbacks*, ed. Frances Hagopian and Mainwaring, 14–62. New York: Oxford University Press.

Mantilla Falcón, Julissa. 2005. "The Peruvian Truth and Reconciliation Commission's Treatment of Sexual Violence against Women." *Human Rights Briefing* 12 (2): 1–4.

Marcos, Sylvia. 2005. "The Borders Within: The Indigenous Movement and Feminism in Mexico." In *Dialogue and Difference: Feminisms Challenge Globalization*, ed. Marguerite Waller and Marcos, 81–112. New York: Palgrave Macmillan.

Mariner, Joanne. 2005. "Latin America's Abortion Battles." *Conscience* 26 (3): 11.

Marques-Pereira, Bérengére. 1997. "Los derechos reproductivos como derechos ciudadanos." *La Ciudania en debate*, ed. Eugenia Itola and Ana Maria Portugal. Santiago: Isis International.

Márquez, Celina, and Cecilia Caione. 2007. "El NO ganó en ambos bloques." *El nacional* (Caracas), December 3, 2.

Martínez, Oscar J. 1994. *Border People: Life and Society in the U.S.-Mexico Borderlands*. Tucson: University of Arizona Press.

Martins, Luciano. 1992. "The Liberalization of Authoritarianism in Brazil." In *Issues in Democratic Consolidation: The New South American Democracies in Comparative Perspective*, ed. Scott P. Mainwaring, Guillermo O'Donnell, and J. Samuel Valenzuela. Notre Dame, Ind.: University of Notre Dame Press.

Marx, Jutta, Jutta Borner, and Mariana Caminotti. 2007. *Las legisladoras: Cupos de género y política en Argentina y Brasil*. Buenos Aires: Siglo XX, Instituto Torcuato di Tella, UN Development Program.

Matland, Richard. 2004. "El proceso de representación y reclutamiento legislativo de las mujeres." In *Mujer, partidos políticos y reforma electoral*. Lima: IDEA (Institute for Democracy and Electoral Assistance) International and Transparencia. www.idea.int.

McCoy, Jennifer L., and David J. Myers, eds. 2004. *The Unraveling of Representative Democracy in Venezuela*. Baltimore: Johns Hopkins University Press.

Medina, Cecilia. 2003. "Derechos humanos de las mujeres: ¿Dónde estamos ahora en las Americas?" In *Essays in Honour of Alice Yotopoulos-Marangopoulos*, ed. A. Manganas, 2:907–30. Athens: Panteion University.

Merz, Gabriela. 2005. *Índice de Compromiso Cumplido: Venezuela 1995–2003; Una estrategia para el control ciudadano de la equidad de género*. Caracas: Círculos Populares Femeninos.

Meyer, Mary K., and Elisabeth Prügl, eds. 1999. *Gender Politics in Global Governance*. Lanham, Md.: Rowman and Littlefield.

Miguel, Luis Felipe. 2004. "Participação eleitoral e gênero no Brasil: As cotas para mulheres e seu impacto." Paper presented at II Congreso Latinoamericano de Ciencia Política (ALACIP), Mexico City, October.

Minow, Martha. 1990. *Making All the Difference: Inclusion, Exclusion, and American Law*. Ithaca: Cornell University Press.

Minyersky, Nelly. 2001. "Derechos civiles y políticas de la mujer: Medidas de acción positiva." Asociación Abogados de Buenos Aires. www.aaba.org.ar (accessed in February 2007).

Moghadam, Valentine M. 2005. *Globalizing Women: Transnational Feminist Frameworks*. Baltimore: Johns Hopkins University Press.

Mohanty, Chandra Talpade. 2005. "Series Editor's Foreword." In *Dialogue and Difference: Feminisms Challenge Globalization*, ed. Marguerite Waller and Sylvia Marcos, xi–xii. New York: Palgrave Macmillan.

Molyneux, Maxine. 2001a. "Analyzing Women's Movements." In *Women's Movements in International Perspective: Latin America and Beyond*, ed. Molyneux, 140–62. Houndmills, Basingstoke, UK: Palgrave.

———. 2001b. "Gender and Citizenship in Latin America: Historical and Contemporary Issues." In *Women's Movements in International Perspective: Latin America and Beyond*, ed. Molyneux, 163–202. Houndmills, Basingstoke, UK: Palgrave.

———. 1985. "Mobilization without Emancipation? Women's Interests, State, and Revolution in Nicaragua." *Feminist Studies* 11 (2): 227–54.

Monárrez Fragoso, Julia. 2002. "Feminicidio sexual serial en Ciudad Juárez: 1993–2001." *Debate feminista* 13 (25).

Mongrovejo, Norma. 2006. "Movimiento lésbico en Latinoamerica y sus demandas." In *De lo privado a lo público: Treinta años de lucha ciudadana de las mujeres en América Latina*, ed. Nathalie Lebon and Elizabeth Maier, 195–207. Mexico City: Siglo Veintiuno.

Montecinos, Verónica. 2001. "Feminists and Technocrats in the Democratization of Latin America." *International Journal of Politics, Culture, and Society* 15 (1): 175–99.

Montesino, Sonia, and Josefina Rossetti, eds. 1990. "Tramas para un nuevo destino: Propuestas de la concertacion de mujeres por la democracia." Unpublished manuscript.

Moreno, María Aluminé. 2003. "Carrera de obstáculos: La participación de las mujeres." *Escenarios alternativos* 13.

Morfín Otero, Guadalupe. 2004. "Informe de gestión: Noviembre 2003–Abril 2004." In *Comisión para Prevenir y Erradicar la Violencia Contra las Mujeres de Ciudad Juárez*. Juárez, Chihuahua: CIBELES.

Morrison, Andrew R., and María Loreto Biehl. 1999. *Too Close to Home: Domestic Violence in the Americas*. Washington: Inter-American Development Bank.

Moser, Caroline O. N., and Cathy McIlwaine. 2004. *Encounters with Violence in Latin America: Urban Poor Perceptions from Colombia and Guatemala*. New York: Routledge.

Motta, Cristina. 2005. "Reconocimiento, plurinacionalidad y multiculturalismo en la Argentina." In *Informe sobre género y derechos humanos: Vigencia y respeto de los derechos de las mujeres en Argentina*, 337–50. Buenos Aires: Biblos.

NACLA (North American Congress on Latin America). 2007. "How Pink Is the Pink Tide? Feminist and LGBT Activists Challenge the Left." *NACLA Report on the Americas* 40 (2).

National Feminist Health and Reproductive Rights Network. 1999. *Jornal da rede-saúde: Informativo da Rede Nacional Feminista de Saúde e Direitos Reprodutivos* 19 (November).

National Human Rights Movement. 1998. *Primavera já partiu: Retrato dos homicides femininos do Brasil*. Brasília: Vozes.

Navia, Patricio. 2006. "Bachelet's Election in Chile: The 2006 Presidential Contest." *ReVista/Harvard Review of Latin America*, spring/summer issue, 9–11.

Nohlen, Dieter. 1998. *Sistemas electorales y partidos políticos*. Mexico City: Fondo de Cultura Económica.

Norris, Pippa, ed. 1997. *Passages to Power: Legislative Recruitment in Advanced Democracies*. New York: Harper Collins.

O'Donnell, Guillermo. 2007. Dissonances: Democratic Critiques of Democracy. Notre Dame, Ind.: University of Notre Dame Press.

———. 1992. "Transitions, Continuities, and Paradoxes." In *Issues in Democratic Consolidation: The New South American Democracies in Comparative Perspective*, ed. Scott P. Mainwaring, O'Donnell, and J. Samuel Valenzuela. Notre Dame, Ind.: University of Notre Dame Press.

Orloff, Leslye E., and Rachel Little. 1999. *Somewhere to Turn: Making Domestic Violence Services Available to Battered Immigrant Women*. Harrisburg, Pa.: National Resource Center on Domestic Violence.

Orrenius, Pia M. 2001. "The Border Economy: Illegal Immigration and Enforcement along the Southwest Border." Federal Reserve Bank of Dallas, June. www.dallasfed.org.

Palacios, Margarita, and Javier Martínez. 2006. "Liberalism and Conservatism in Chile: Attitudes and Opinions of Chilean Women at the Start of the Twenty-First Century." *Journal of Latin American Studies* 38 (1): 1–34.

Passel, Jeffrey S. 2006. *The Size and Characteristics of the Unauthorized Migrant Population in the U.S.: Estimates Based on the March 2005 Current Population Survey*. Report. Washington: Pew Hispanic Center. March 5.

Pautassi, Laura. 2005. "El derecho de las mujeres a la salud." In *Informe sobre género y derechos humanos: Vigencia y respeto de los derechos de las mujeres en Argentina*, 93–168. Buenos Aires: Biblos.

Payan, Tony. 2006. "The Drug War and the U.S.-Mexico Border: What Does Kill You, Makes You Stronger." *South Atlantic Quarterly* 105 (4): 863–80.

Peña, Devon G. 1997. *The Terror of the Machine: Technology, Work, Gender, and Ecology on the U.S.-Mexico Border*. Austin: Center for Mexican-American Studies, University of Texas.

Pereira, Javier. 2006. "Sólo uno de cada tres candidatos obtiene más de 1% de los votos." *El nacional* (Caracas), August 28, A2.

Perelli, Carina. 1994. "The Uses of Conservatism: Women's Democratic Politics in Uruguay." In *The Women's Movement in Latin America: Participation and Democracy*, ed. Jane S. Jaquette, 131–50. Boulder, Colo.: Westview.

Peruvian Truth and Reconciliation Commission. 2003. *Final Report*. Lima. www .cuerdad.org.pe.

Pew Research Center/Pew Hispanic Center. 2006. *2006 National Survey of Latinos: The Immigration Debate*. Washington: Pew Hispanic Center. www.pewhispanic .org.

Phillips, Anne. 1995. *The Politics of Presence*. Oxford: Clarendon.

Pinto, Mónica. 2006. "Cuestiones de género y acceso al sistema internacional de derechos humanos." In *Acceso a la justicia como garantía de igualdad: Instituciones, actores y experiencias comparadas*, ed. in Haydée Birgin and Beatríz Kohen, *2006 National Survey of Latinos*. Buenos Aires: Biblos.

Piovesan, Flávia, and Sylvia Pimental. 2003. *Contribuição a partir da perspectiva de gênero ao relatório alternativo sobre o Pacto Internacional dos Direitos Econômicos, Sociais e Culturais*. CLADEM. www.un.org/womenwatch/daw.

———. 2002a. "Conspiração contra a impunidade." *Folha de São Paulo*, November 25.

———, eds. 2002b. *Relatório Nacional Brasileiro sobre a Convenção sobre a Eliminação de Todas as Formas de Discriminação contra a Mulher*. Brasília. www .mulheresnobrasil.org.br.

Pitanguy, Jacqueline. 2006. "As mulheres e os direitos humanos." In *O progresso das mulheres no Brasil* 29. Brasília: UNIFEM.

———. 2005. "Reflexiones sobre la presencia en el estado del movimiento de mujeres." In *Activistas e intelectuales de sociedad civil en la función pública en América Latina*, ed. Carlos Basombrío I., 335–48. Santiago: FLACSO.

Portillo, Lourdes. 2001. *Señorita Extraviada* (Lost Girl). Documentary film.

Pribble, Jennifer. 2006. "Women and Welfare: The Politics of Coping with New Social Risks in Chile and Uruguay." *Latin American Research Review* 41 (2): 84–113.

Rakowski, Cathy A. 2003. "Women as Political Actors: The Move from Maternalism to Citizenship Rights and Power." *Latin American Research Review* 38 (2): 180–95.

Reynolds, Andrew. 1999. "Women in the Legislatures and Executives of the World: Knocking at the Highest Glass Ceiling." *World Politics* 51 (4).

Ríos Tobar, Marcela. 2003. "Chilean Feminism(s) in the 1990s: Paradoxes of an Unfinished Transition." *International Feminist Journal of Politics* 5 (2): 256–80.

Ríos Tobar, Marcela, Lorena Godoy Catalán, and Elizabeth Guerrero Caviedes, eds. 2004. *Un nuevo silencio feminista? La transformación de un movimiento social en el Chile postdictadura*. Santiago: LOM.

Ríos Tobar, Marcela, and Andrés Villar. 2005. "Mujeres en el Congreso 2006–2010." *Observatorio 2*.

Rodríguez, Victoria E. 2003. *Women in Contemporary Mexican Politics*. Austin: University of Texas Press.

———. 1997. *Decentralization in Mexico: From Reforma Municipal to Nuevo Federalismo*. Boulder, Colo.: Westview.

Romero, Manuela, and Tracy Yellen. 2004. *El Paso Portraits: Women's Lives, Potential, and Opportunities: A Report on the State of Women in El Paso, Texas*. El Paso: YWCA and UTEP Center for Civic Engagement.

Rosenberg, Marta. 2002. "Which Other World Is Possible?" *Women's Global Network of Reproductive Rights Newsletter* 75:5–8.

Rosenblum, Nancy L. 2002. "Feminist Perspectives on Civil Society and Government." In *Civil Society and Government*, ed. Rosenblum and Robert C. Post, 151–78. Princeton: Princeton University Press.

Rubin, Gayle. 1990. "El tráfico de mujeres: Notas sobre la 'economía política' del sexo." In *El género: La construcción cultural de la diferencia sexual*, ed. Marta Lamas. Mexico City: PUEG.

Ruddick, Sara. 1989. *Maternal Thinking*. Boston: Beacon.

Rule, Wilma. 1994. "Parliament of, by, and for the People: Except for Women?" In *Electoral Systems in Comparative Perspective: Their Impact on Women and Minorities*, ed. Rule and Joseph F. Zimmerman. Westport, Conn.: Greenwood.

Saba, Roberto, and Martín Böhmer. 2000a. "Participación ciudadana en la Argentina: Estrategias para el efectivo ejercicio de derechos." In *La sociedad civil frente a las nuevas formas de institucionalidad democrática Foro de la Sociedad Civil de las Américas*, ed. Martín Abregú and Silvina Ramos, 15–36. Buenos Aires: CEDES, CELS.

———. 2000b. "Participación ciudadana en la Argentina: Estrategias para el efectivo ejercicio de derechos." In *Rompiendo la indiferencia: Acciones ciudadanas en defensa del interés público*, ed. Angelika Rettberg, 123–53. Santiago: Ford Foundation.

Sabsay, Daniel. 2000. "Comentario de participación ciudadana en la Argentina: Estrategias para el efectivo ejercicio de derechos." In *La sociedad civil frente a las nuevas formas de institucionalidad democrática: Foro de la Sociedad Civil de las Américas*, ed. Martín Abregú and Silvina Ramos, 40–44. Buenos Aires: CEDES, CELS.

Sacks, Gordon W., and Robert D. Kolken. 1999. "IIRAIRA Reform." AILA advocacy issue papers. www.sackskolken.com.

Salzinger, Leslie. 2003. *Genders in Production: Making Workers in Mexico's Global Factories*. Berkeley: University of California Press.

Samuels, David. 2004. "Political Ambition, Candidate Recruitment, and Legislative

Politics in Brazil." Paper presented at the "Pathways to Power: Political Recruit-ment and Democracy in Latin America" conference, Wake Forest University, Winston-Salem, N.C., April 2–4.

Sanchís, Norma. 2006. "Las dimensiones no económicas de la economía." In *América latina, un debate pendiente: Aportes a la economía y a la política con una visión de género*, 167–97. Montevideo: REPEM, DAWN, IFC.

Santiago M, Mari. 2004. "Building Global Solidarity through Feminist Dialogues." Isis Women's Resource Centre. Manila.

Santiso, Javier. 2006. *Latin America's Political Economy of the Possible: Beyond Good Revolutionaries and Free-Marketeers*. Trans. Cristina Sanmartín and Elizabeth Murry. Cambridge: MIT Press.

Schild, Verónica. 2000. "Neo-liberalism's New Gendered Market Citizens: The 'Civilizing' Dimension of Social Programs in Chile." *Citizenship Studies* 4 (3): 275–305.

Schmidt, Gregory D., and Clara Araújo. 2004. "The Devil's in the Details: Open List Voting and Gender Quotas in Brazil and Peru." Paper presented at the Twenty-Fifth International Congress of the Latin American Studies Association, Las Vegas, October 7–9.

Schwindt-Bayer, Leslie A. 2006. "Still Supermadres? Gender and the Policy Priori-ties of Latin American Legislators." *American Journal of Political Science* 50 (3): 570–85.

Scott, Joan. 1996. "El género: ¿Una categoría útil para el análisis histórico?" In *El género: La construcción cultural de la diferencia sexual*, ed. Marta Lamas. Mexico City: PUEG.

SERNAM. 2006. *Encuenta de Opinion Pública: Paridad de género, mujer y política*. Santiago.

Sharp, John. 1998. *Bordering the Future*. Austin: Comptroller of Public Accounts, State of Texas.

Sikkink, Kathryn. 1993. "Human Rights, Principled Issue Networks, and Sover-eignty in Latin America." *International Organization*.

Slater, David W. 1988. *New Social Movements and Old Political Questions*. Ottawa: Interuniversity Centre for Research and Documentation.

Smulowitz, Catalina. 2001. "Judicialización y accountability social en la Argen-tina." Paper presented at the Twenty-Second Conference of the Latin American Studies Association.

———. 2000. "Comentario de participación ciudadana en la Argentina: Estrate-gias para el efectivo ejercicio de derechos." In *La sociedad civil frente a las nuevas formas de institucionalidad democrática Foro de la Sociedad Civil de las Américas*, ed. Martín Abregú and Silvina Ramos, 37–39. Buenos Aires: CEDES, CELS.

———. 1997. "Ciudadanos, derecho y política." In *Las acciones de interés público: Argentina, Chile, Colombia y Perú*, ed. Felipe González Morales et al., 407–37. Santiago: Universidad Diego Portales, Escuela de Derecho.

Sorj, Bernardo. 2007. *Latin America's Elusive Democracies*. Edelstein Center for Social Research. www.bernardosorj.com.

Speck, Bruno Wilhelm. 2004. "Análisis comparativo sobre financiamiento de campañas y partidos políticos—Brasil." In *De las normas a las buenas prácticas: El desafío del financiamiento político en América Latina*, ed. Steven Griner and Daniel Zovatto. San José, Costa Rica: OAS/IDEA.

Staudt, Kathleen. 2008. *Violence and Activism at the Border: Gender, Fear, and Everyday Life in Ciudad Juárez*. Austin: University of Texas Press.

———. 1998. *Free Trade: Informal Economies at the U.S.-Mexico Border*. Philadelphia: Temple University Press.

Staudt, Kathleen, and Irasema Coronado. 2007. "Binational Civic Action for Accountability: Antiviolence Organizing in Cd. Juárez-El Paso." In *Reframing the Administration of Justice in Mexico*, ed.Wayne A. Cornelius and David A. Shirk, 329–67. Notre Dame, Ind.: University of Notre Dame Press.

———. 2002. *Fronteras no Más: Toward Social Justice at the U.S.-Mexico Border*. New York: Palgrave Macmillan.

Staudt, Kathleen, and David Spener. 1998. "The View from the Frontier: Theoretical Perspectives Undisciplined." In *The U.S.-Mexico Border: Transcending Divisions, Contesting Identities*, ed. Spener and Staudt, 3–33. Boulder, Colo.: Lynne Rienner.

Staudt, Kathleen, with Enrique Suárez Toriello and Vanessa Johnson. 2005. "Antiviolence, Self-Defense, and Risk Avoidance: A Comparison of Treatment and Control Groups among Women Aged Fifteen to Thirty-Nine in Ciudad Juárez." Report to the Center for Border Health Research, El Paso, Texas.

Staudt, Kathleen, and Beatríz Vera. 2006. "Mujeres, políticas públicas y política: Los caminos globales de Juárez–El Paso." *Región y sociedad* 37 (18): 127–73.

Sternbach, Nancy Saporta, et al. 1992. "Feminisms in Latin America: From Bogotá to San Bernando." *Signs* 27 (2) (winter): 393–434.

Stokes, Susan C. 2001. *Mandates and Democracy: Neoliberalism by Surprise in Latin America*. Cambridge: Cambridge University Press.

Strayhorn, Carol Keeton. 2006. *Undocumented Immigrants in Texas: A Financial Analysis of the Impact to the State Budget and Economy*. Austin: Comptroller of Public Accounts, State of Texas.

Tamayo, Giulia. 1998. "Re-vuelta sobre lo privado / re-creación de lo publico: La aventura inconclusa del feminismo en América Latina." In *Encuentros, (des)encuentros y búsquedas: El movimiento feminista en América Latina*, ed. Cecilia Olea Mauleón. Lima: Flora Tristán.

Tanaka, Martín. 2005. "Peru: 1998–2000; Chronicle of a Death Foretold? Determinism, Political Decisions, and Open Outcomes." In *The Third Wave of Democratization in Latin America: Advances and Setbacks*, ed. Frances Hagopian and Scott P. Mainwaring, 261–88. New York: Oxford University Press.

Taylor, Vertha. 1989. "Social Movement Continuity: The Women's Movement in Abeyance." *American Sociological Review* 54 (5): 761–75.

Thayer, Millie. 2001. "Feminismo transnacional: Re-lendo Joan Scott no serrato." *Revista estudos feministas* 9 (1): 12.

TNS-Gallup Argentina. 2006. In *Información y justicia II: Datos sobre la justicia argentina.* Buenos Aires: Unidos por la Justicia and Fundación Konrad Adenauer.

Torrado, Susana. 2003. *Historia de la familia en la Argentina moderna (1870–2000).* Buenos Aires: Ediciones la Flor.

Touraine, Alain. 1985. "An Introduction to the Study of Social Movements." *Social Research* 52 (4): 776–77.

TRC Liberia. 2005. "Truth and Reconciliation Act (Liberia)," June. www.trcofliberia .org.

Tula, María Inés. 2002. "La ley de cupo en la Argentina: La participación de las mujeres en los órganos representativos de gobierno." In *Hombres públicos, mujeres públicas,* ed. Silvia Vázquez.

UN Committee on the Elimination of All Forms of Discrimination against Women (CEDAW Committee). 1992. "General Recommendation No. 19: Violence Against Women" (A/47/38). January 20.

UN Development Program (PNUD). 1995. *Informe sobre desarrollo humano 1995.* New York.

Unidos por la Justicia and Fundación Konrad Adenauer. 2006. *Información y justicia II: Datos sobre la justicia argentina.* Buenos Aires: Unidos por la Justicia and Fundación Konrad Adenauer.

UN Office of the High Commissioner for Human Rights. 1999. "Gender Integration into the Human Rights System." Geneva, Report of the Workshop "United Nations Office at Geneva," May 26–28.

UN Secretary-General. 1998. "Integrating the Gender Perspective into the Work of United Nations Human Rights Treaty Bodies." Geneva (HRI/MC/1998/6, par. 19), September 14–18. www.un.org/womenwatch.

———. 1997. *Las conferencias mundiales: Formulación de prioridades para el siglo XXI.* New York: Department of Public Information.

———. 1995. "Informe de la Cuarta Conferencia Mundial sobre la Mujer (Beijing, 4 a 15 de septiembre de 1995)" (A/CONF.177/20). October.

———. 1994. "Informe de la Conferencia Internacional sobre la Población y el Desarrollo (Cairo, 5 a 13 de septiembre de 1994)" (A/CONF.171/13). October.

———. 1985. *Estrategias de Nairobi orientadas hacia el futuro para el adelanto de la mujer (Nairobi, 15 a 26 de julio de 1985).* New York.

U.S. Department of Justice (USDOJ), Office of Justice Programs, Bureau of Justice Statistics. 2001. *Intimate Partner Violence and Age of Victims, 1993–99.* Washington: U.S. Department of Justice.

U.S. Department of Transportation, Research and Innovative Technology Administration. 2006. *Bureau of Transportation Statistics, 2006.* Washington: U.S. Department of Transportation.

Valdés, Teresa, ed. 1999. *El ICC: Una estrategia para el control ciudadano de la equidad de género*. Santiago: FLACSO.

Valdés, Teresa, Ana María Muñoz B., and Alina Donoso O., eds. 2007. *ICC: Índice de Compromiso Cumplido, 1995-2003; Una herramienta para el control ciudadano de las mujeres latinoamericanas; Brasil, Chile, Honduras, México, Nicaragua, Panamá, República Dominicana y Venezuela*. Santiago: CEDEM.

———. 2006. *1995-2003: ¿Han avanzado las mujeres? Índice de Compromiso Cumplido latinoamericano*. Santiago: FLACSO.

———. 2005. *ICC: Índice de Compromiso Cumplido; Una herramienta para el control ciudadano de las mujeres latinoamericanas; Argentina, Colombia, Ecuador, Paraguay, Perú y Uruguay*. Santiago: FLACSO.

———. 2004. *1995-2003: ¿Han avanzado las mujeres? Índice de Compromiso Cumplido Latinoamericano*. Santiago: FLACSO.

Valenzuela, María Elena. 1998. "Women and the Democratization Process in Chile." In *Women and Democracy: Latin America and Central and Eastern Europe*, ed. Jane S. Jaquette and Sharon L. Wolchik, 47-74. Baltimore: Johns Hopkins University Press.

Varas, Augusto. 2000. "Democracia, ciudadanía y defensa del interés público en América Latina." In *Rompiendo la indiferencia: Acciones ciudadanas en defensa del interés público*, 19-37. Santiago: Ford Foundation.

Vargas, Virginia. 2000. "Un tema en debate: La ciudadanía de las mujeres." Lima: Centro de la Mujer Peruana Flora Tristán. www.flora.org.pe.

Vargas, Virginia, and Lilian Celiberti. 2005. "Los nuevos escenarios, los nuevos / viejos sujetos y los nuevos paradigmas de los feminismos globales." www .mujeresdelsur.org.

Vázquez Sotelo, Roxana. N.d. "Los un@s y las otr@s: Feminismos y derechos humanos." Unpublished manuscript.

Vilas, Carlos M. 2006. "The Left in South America and the Resurgence of National-Populist Regimes." In *Latin America after Neoliberalism: Turning the Tide in the Twenty-First Century*, ed. Eric Hershberg and Fred Rosen, 232-51. New York: New Press.

Waller, Marguerite. 2005. "One Voice Kills Both Our Voices: First World Feminism and Transcultural Feminist Engagement." In *Dialogue and Difference: Feminists Challenge Globalization*, ed. Waller and Sylvia Marcos, 113-42. New York: Palgrave Macmillan.

Washington Valdez, Diana. 2006. *The Killing Fields: Harvest of Women; The Truth about Mexico's Bloody Border Legacy*. Los Angeles: Peace at the Border.

———. 2002. "Death Stalks the Border." *El Paso Times* (special insert), June 24.

Waterman, Peter. 2006. "Los nuevos tejidos nerviosos del internacionalismo y la solidaridad: Colección transformación global." Programa de Estudios sobre Democracia y Transformación Global. Lima: Universidad Nacional Mayor de San Marcos.

———. 2005. "Feminism, Globalisation, Internationalism: The State of Play and the Direction of the Movement." *Review of International Social Questions*, March 19. www.risq.org.

————. 2000. "17 tesis acerca de: El viejo internacionalismo, la nueva solidaridad global, una futura sociedad civil global." January 11. www.antenna.nl/~waterman/17tesis.

Waylen, Georgina. 2007. *Engendering Transitions: Women, Mobilization, Institutions, and Gender Outcomes*. Oxford: Oxford University Press.

Weyland, Kurt. 2005. "The Growing Sustainability of Brazil's Low-Quality Democracy." In *The Third Wave of Democratization in Latin America*, ed. Frances Hagopian and Scott P. Mainwaring, 90–120. New York: Oxford University Press.

Winslow, Anne, ed. 1995. *Women, Politics, and the United Nations*. Westport, Conn.: Greenwood.

Wise, Carol, and Riordan Roett. 2003. *Post-Stabilization Politics in Latin America: Competition, Transition, Collapse*. Washington: Brookings Institute Press.

Women's Assembly. 2005. Communiqué from meeting at the Universidad Central de Venezuela (UCV) on the exclusion of women from the list of candidates to the National Assembly, September 16.

WomensLaw.org. 2006. "Information for Immigrants: VAWA Laws and Procedures." www.womenslaw.org/immigrantsVAWA.htm.

Wright. Melissa. 2006. "Public Women, Profit, and Femicide in Northern Mexico." *South Atlantic Quarterly* 105 (4): 681–98.

Young, Iris Marion. 2000. *Inclusion and Democracy*. Oxford: Oxford University Press.

Yupanki, Samuel Abad. 1999. "Garantías constitucionales y derechos de las mujeres: Defensoría del pueblo, hábeas corpus y amparo." In *Género y derecho*, 371–406. Santiago: Editores LOM.

JUTTA BORNER has a degree in political science from the Free University of Berlin and was director of the Center for the Investigation and Documentation of Chile and Latin America (FDCL) in Berlin. She has published articles on contemporary politics in Argentina and was a member of the research team for the project Gender and Politics in Mercosur. She is a coauthor, with Jutta Marx and Mariana Caminotti, of *Las legisladoras: Cupos de género y política en Argentina y Brasil* (2007).

MARIANA CAMINOTTI has a degree in political science from the Argentine National University of Rosario, a master's degree in development management and policy from Georgetown University, and is taking her doctorate at the Argentine National University of San Martín. She is a member of the Gender and Politics in Mercosur research team and a coauthor (with Jutta Marx and Jutta Borner) of *Las legisladoras: Cupos de género y política en Argentina y Brasil* (2007).

ALINA DONOSO has a degree in sociology from the University of Chile and a master's degree in social sciences from UNGS-IDES in Argentina. From 2003 to 2006 she was a member of the Gender Studies Program at FLACSO-Chile and an investigator for the Indice de Compromiso Cumplido (ICC) project, a social watch program carried out in eighteen Latin American countries. She is a specialist in gender social indicators and was part of the Women's Initiative Group in Chile. She has studied teenage parents in the Chilean school system.

GIOCONDA ESPINA is the coordinator of the Women's Studies Program of the Faculty of Economics and Social Sciences of the Central University of Venezuela. A feminist since 1978, Espina has written several articles on the women's movement in Venezuela. Her most recent work, with Cathy Rakowski, was published in *De lo privado a lo público: Treinta años de lucha ciudadana en América Latina*, edited by Nathalie Lebon and Elizabeth Maier (2006).

JANE S. JAQUETTE received her Ph.D. in government from Cornell University; she is professor emerita and adjunct professor of politics at Occidental College and a visiting adjunct research professor at the Watson Institute, Brown University. She has written widely on women and politics, women and development, and international feminism, and has edited three books on women's movements and democratic politics in Latin America. Her most recent book, edited with Gale Summerfield, is *Women and Gender Equity in Development Theory and Practice* (2006).

BEATRÍZ KOHEN is a sociologist with a degree from the University of Durham (United Kingdom). She has done extensive work on gender and the judiciary. She has collaborated with Argentine nongovernmental organizations, including Poder Ciudadano (Citizen Power) and FARN (Environmental and Natural Resources Foundation), which are committed to bridging the gap between citizens and the legal system and to using legal tools to improve democratic participation and women's access to justice. Until 2007 she was the executive director of ELA (Latin American Group on Justice and Gender). Her most recent book, coedited with Haydeé Birgin, is *Access to Justice as a Guarantee of Equality* (in Spanish, 2006).

JULISSA MANTILLA FALCÓN is a lawyer and a professor at the Pontifical Catholic University of Peru. A specialist in gender and international law, she served as a consultant to the Peruvian Truth and Reconciliation Commission (PTRC). She has also worked with the World Bank, the Inter-American Institute of Human Rights, the International Association of Women Judges (IAWJ), and the UN University of Peace. In 2004 she received a Fulbright New Century Fellowship to do comparative research on gender and truth commissions in Latin America.

JUTTA MARX has a degree in social pedagogy from the Staatliche Fachhochschule für Sozialarbeit und Sozialpädogogik in Berlin and a master's degree in social science from FLACSO-Argentina. She was the director of the Women and Politics Program of the Friedrich Naumann Foundation in Buenos Aires. She has published *Women and Political Parties* (1992) and is the coauthor (with Jutta Borner and Mariana Caminotti) of *Las legisladoras: Cupos de género y política en Argentina y Brasil* (2007). She also directed the research team Gender and Politics in Mercosur.

GABRIELA MONTOYA wrote her master's thesis on violence against undocumented immigrant women. She has worked as a research assistant at the University of Texas, El Paso (UTEP) and at the university's Center for Civil Engagement. She has also volunteered for the Mexican Consulate, the Texas Supervision and Corrections Department, and the Women's Resource Center at UTEP. She is also a member of the binational Coalition against Violence toward Women at the Border.

FLÁVIA PIOVESAN is a professor of constitutional law and human rights at the Catholic University of São Paulo, as well as a professor of human rights in the postgraduate programs of the Catholic University of São Paulo, the Catholic University of Paraná, and Pablo de Olavide University of Seville, Spain. She has been a visiting fellow of the Human Rights Program at Harvard Law School (1995 and 2000), at the Centre for Brazilian Studies at Oxford (2005), and at the Max-Planck-Institute of Heidelberg (2007). She is a São Paulo state attorney and a member of CLADEM (the Latin American and Caribbean Committee for the Defense of Human Rights). She has written and lectured widely on international human rights and women's rights, and has been actively involved in litigation in defense of women's rights in Brazil.

MARCELA RÍOS TOBAR is finishing her Ph.D. at the University of Wisconsin, Madison, and has a master's degree in social science from FLACSO-Chile. She recently joined the Santiago office of the UN Development Programme as the program officer in charge of governance and gender issues. She previously coordinated the Democratic Governance Program at FLACSO-Chile. She was one of two women appointed to the Chilean electoral reform commission, which took up the issue of how to achieve parity for women in Chile's national legislature. She has written several articles and coedited *La transformación de un movimiento social en el Chile postdictadura* (2004).

KATHLEEN STAUDT is a professor of political science at the University of Texas, El Paso, where she founded the Women's Studies Program, and she serves as the director of the University's Center for Civic Engagement, which connects about a thousand students a year with community-based organizations in the El Paso area. She has been a member of the binational Coalition against Violence toward Women at the Border since its inception. Staudt has published extensively on women's issues; her most recent book is *Activism at the Border: Gender, Fear, and Everyday Life* (2008).

TERESA VALDÉS is a sociologist, professor, and researcher specializing in developing and analyzing sex-disaggregated data to press for greater gender equity. Valdés was the founding coordinator of the Gender Studies Program at FLACSO-Chile. She has written several articles and books on human rights, sexuality, family-gender dynamics, masculinities, and gender equity in Latin America. With Ximena Valdés, she proposed the Indice de Compromiso Cumplido (ICC) project to Chile's Women's Initiative Group.

VIRGINIA VARGAS is a sociologist and militant feminist. Founder of the Flora Tristán Center for Peruvian Women in Lima in 1978, she has written and edited several books on feminism, democracy, citizenship, and globalization from a feminist perspective and has lectured widely on these topics in Latin America and Europe. She coordinated a regional follow-up conference after the Fourth UN Conference on Women in Beijing (1995); she is a member of the International Council of the World Social Forum, representing the Articulación Feminista Marcosur, a cross-regional feminist network that draws its perspectives from the Global South. She is the recipient of a UNIFEM award for her writing and activism.

on the Elimination of All Forms of Discrimination against Women), 7, 84, 95, 172, 178

CEDAW, Optional Protocol, 25, 84, 126 n. 7

CEDAW, United Nations Committee on, 8, 25, 85, 88, 91, 93, 99, 115

CEDEM (Center for Democracy and Human Rights), Chile, 185 n. 4

CEJIL-Brazil (Center for Justice and International Law), 114, 120

CELS (Center for Legal and Social Studies), Argentina, 102, 107, 111, 112 n. 2

Center for Democracy and Human Rights, Chile, 185 n. 4

Center for the Study of Women, Venezuela, 75

Central University of Venezuela (UCV), 71, 75

Centro de la Orientación de la Mujer Obrera (Center for the Orientation of Women Workers), Mexico, 194

CEP (Centro de Estudios Publicos; Center for Public Policy Studies), Chile, 44 n. 18

CEPAL (Economic Commission for Latin America and the Caribbean), 185

CEPIA (Cidadania, Estudio, Pesquisa, Informacão, e Acão; Citizenship, Study, Research, Information, Action), Brazil, 184

Charlesworth, Hillary, 130

Chávez, Hugo, 4, 10, 11, 17 n. 3, 24, 65–80, 217 n. 4

Chicago Council on Global Affairs, 17 n. 5

child care, 86

child custody, 86

Chile, 1, 3, 4, 5, 18 n. 6, 21–26, 116, 135, 171, 173, 178, 185, 210, 217 n. 4; Con-

gress, 9, 27, 29, 33, 37, 39, 40, 41, 43 n. 4, 44 n. 26; Constitutional Tribunal, 39; domestic violence law, 25; Secretaria General de la Presidencia, 37; Servicio Nacional de la Mujer (*see* SERNAM); TranSantiago Crisis, 39, 40

Ciudad Juárez, 186, 189, 195, 196–98, 199, 200, 204, 207 n. 1

CLADEM (Latin American and Caribbean Committee for the Defense of Women's Rights), 112 n. 2, 114, 120, 127 n. 9, 164 n. 12

CLADEM-Brasil, 114, 120, 127 n. 9

Clinton, William J., 202

Coalition (Concertación), Chile, 4, 9, 22–44

Coalition against Violence toward Women at the Border, 188, 190, 199

Collor de Mello, Fernando, 4

Colombia, 18, 63, 140, 171

Comfort women, in South Korea, 195

Comisión de Derechos Humanos (Human Rights Commission, COMISEDH), Peru, 141 n. 6

Communist Party, Chile, 43 n. 12

Concertación (Coalition of Parties for Democracy), Chile, 4, 9, 22–44

Concertación de Mujeres por la Democracia (Coalition of Women for Democracy), Chile, 24, 33

CONG (Nongovernmental Coordination Committee), Venezuela, 67, 75

Consejo National de la Mujer, Argentina, 88, 99

Contraception, 92, 105, 108, 112

*control ciudadano*, 165–85

Convention of Belém do Pará (Inter-American Convention on the Prevention, Punishment, and Eradication of Violence against Women), 8, 87, 95, 102, 108, 115, 118, 119, 120, 122, 128 n. 12, 133

Copelon, Rhonda, 141 n. 6
Coronado, Irasema, 187, 188
Corporation of Catholic Lawyers, 107
Correa, Rafael, 4
corruption, 3, 34, 84, 189, 192
Costa Rica, 63, 171

DAWN Network, 163 n. 5, 164 n. 12
DC (Christian Democratic Party),
    Chile. *See* CD
De la Rúa, Fernando, 48
*delegacias*, Brazil, 18 n. 11
Delgado, Federico, 140
democratic transitions. *See* transitions
    to democracy
democratization, 25, 83, 116, 126 n. 2,
    190, 192
DEMUS (Estudio para los Derechos de
    la Mujer), Peru, 141 n. 6
devaluations, 17 n. 5, 191
DINCOTE (National Division against
    Terrorism of the Peruvian National
    Police Force), 113
discrimination, 7, 25, 27, 71, 43 n. 4,
    86, 92, 95, 97, 98, 101–3, 111, 117–19,
    125, 127 n. 8, 151, 156, 165, 170–74, 177,
    211
diversity, 147, 154–58, 156, 157
divorce, 9, 25, 26, 85- 87, 202
domestic violence, 1, 7, 12, 16, 146, 214;
    in Argentina, 87–88, 102, 110; in
    Brazil, 113–28; in Chile, 25, 28, 29; on
    Mexico-United States border, 188,
    196–200
domestic work, 87, 88, 91, 180, 181, 211
Dominican Republic, 171
double militancy, of feminist activists,
    29
drug cartels in Mexico, 192

ECOSOC (United Nations Economic
    and Social Council), 131, 141 n. 2
Ecuador, 4, 23, 63, 171

education, women's access to in Argen-
    tina, 94, 100, 103
ELA (Equipo Latinoamericano de Justi-
    cia y Género; Latin American Group
    on Justice and Gender), 11, 88, 91, 92,
    105, 109, 110
electoral campaigns, 60–61, 62
electoral systems, 46–53, 58, 60, 63 n. 5
El Paso, Texas, 190, 193, 198, 199, 202,
    204, 206; Center for Family Violence,
    188, 200
El Salvador, 43 n. 6, 171
*Elvira Bella v. Argentina Shooting Fed-
    eration*, 103
empowerment of women, 36, 39, 70,
    99, 180
Ensler, Eve, 195
European Union, 97, 207

family law, 1, 7, 9, 12, 85, 95, 101
family planning, 51, 118
FEMAP (Federación Mexicana de Aso-
    ciaciones Privadas; Mexican Federa-
    tion of Private Associations), 188, 193,
    194, 197
femicide, 16, 186–207
feminism, 6, 15, 22, 23, 28, 31, 110,
    145–64; egalitarian feminism versus
    difference, 208–9, 217 n. 3
feminist activism, 2, 6, 7, 10, 11, 13, 14, 15,
    18 n. 10, 42, 65–80, 117, 189, 190, 194,
    197, 206, 208, 216
Feministas en Acción (Feminists in
    Action), Argentina, 112 n. 2
feminist "core" in Venezuela, 67–68,
    74–79
Feminist Dialogues (Diálogos Feminis-
    tas), 158, 160–64
feminist *encuentros*: in Chile (1991), 30;
    2005, 31, 43 n. 15; Latin American
    regional, 7, 14, 30, 146, 147, 152, 160,
    163 n. 1, 173, 210; lesbian, 163 n. 1
feminist movements, 2, 5–6, 147, 163,

IACHR (*continued*)
102, 104, 113, 114, 119–21, 124, 127
n. 10, 132, 133
IC (International Council of the World
Social Forum), 153, 155, 156, 163
ICC (Índice de Compromiso Cumplido;
Index of Commitments Fulfilled),
14–15, 165–76, 179–85; indicators,
177–78
ICC (International Criminal Court), 138
ICTJ (International Center for Transi-
tional Justice), 139
IDL (Instituto de Defensa Legal; Insti-
tute of Legal Defense), Peru, 141 n. 6
immigrants, 188, 193–94, 198–204, 205
Inamujer (National Institute of
Women), Venezuela, 67, 71, 72, 75, 79
n. 2, 80 n. 5
Independent Democratic Union Party
(UDI), Chile, 34
Índice de Compromiso Cumplido
(ICC), 14–15, 165–76, 179–85
indigenous groups, 3, 13, 209, 217 n. 4
INform (Sri Lanka), 163 n. 5
Initiating Group of Chilean Women, 169
INMUJERES (Instituto Nacional de las
Mujeres), Mexico, 192, 197
Institutional Revolutionary Party,
Mexico (PRI), Mexico, 191, 192, 196
Instituto Social y Politico de la Mujer,
Argentina, 112 n. 2
Inter-American Commission on
Human Rights (IACHR), 8, 12, 48, 89,
101, 102, 104, 113, 114, 119–21, 124, 127
n. 10, 132, 133
Inter-American Committee of Eco-
nomic, Social, and Cultural Rights,
91, 94
Inter-American Convention on Human
Rights. *See* American Convention on
Human Rights
Inter-American Convention on the Pre-

vention, Punishment, and Eradica-
tion of Violence against Women. *See*
Convention of Belém do Pará
Inter-American Convention to Prevent
and Punish Torture, 126 n. 7, 134
Inter-American Court of Human
Rights, 133
Inter-American Development Bank, 115
International Boundary and Water
Commission, 193
International Center for Transitional
Justice, 139
International Committee of the Red
Cross, 139
International Convention on the Rights
of the Child, 95
International Covenant on Civil and
Political Rights, 95, 127 n. 9, 129
International Democratic Federation of
Women (Cuba), 73
International Labor Organization
(ILO), 8, 91
international human rights conven-
tions, 126 n. 7
International Monetary Fund (IMF), 4
International Social and Economic
Rights Convention, 95, 126 n. 12
International Women's Day, 67, 190
Isis Manila, 164 n. 12
ISPM (Women's Social and Political
Institute), Argentina, 103
IWHC (International Women's Health
Coalition), 185 n. 5

JP (Justicialist [Peronist] Party), Argentina, 54, 56, 64 n. 7, 64 n. 8, 83–84
judicialization of conflict, 11, 83, 84, 214

Keane, John, 212, 217 n. 5
Kirchner, Néstor, 4, 64 n. 8, 90

Labarca, Amanda, 37
labor force, women in, 25, 91, 126 n. 3,
191, 211; as ICC indicator, 179, 181

sexual rights, 42, 151, 156, 162, 163, 170, 173, 175, 176, 178, 182, 184

sexual violence, 13, 18 n. 11, 94, 98, 105, 115, 116, 118, 119, 130–32, 134, 136, 137, 138, 139, 140, 146, 187

Shah, Nandita, 159

Sharif, Sharif, 190

Shining Path (Sendero Luminoso), Peru, 13, 18 n. 12, 133, 135, 137

Sierra Leone, 135

Sikkink, Kathryn, 124

Smulowitz, Catalina, 109

social accountability, 166–69, 171, 172, 184, 185, 211

social democracy, 4, 38, 42

socialism, 79, 215

Socialist Party, Chile, 34, 42 n. 2, 43 n. 12

social movements, 5, 54, 61, 149, 217

social security systems, 27, 91, 174

Solis, Hilda, 195

Sorj, Bernardo, 213–17, 217 n. 6

Sousa Santos, Boaventura de, 157

South Africa, 104, 135, 136, 137

South Korean comfort women, 195

Special Secretariat for Policies for Women, Brazil, 18 n. 6, 128 n. 12

Spain, 104

street-level bureaucrats, 201, 202

structural adjustment reforms, 3, 6

Suplicy, Marta, 49, 50, 51

Tanaka, Martín, 18 n. 8

terrorism, 193, 199, 203

Thayer, Millie, 148

Third World Institute (Montevideo, Uruguay), 185

Toledo, Alejandro, 136

torture, 127 n. 8, 130–39

trafficking, 16, 85, 197

transitions to democracy, 1, 3, 7, 13, 21, 24, 27, 28, 29, 30, 33, 40, 47, 54, 83–85, 96, 99, 116–17, 126, 146, 179, 208, 217 n. 1

transnational feminist movement, 7, 9, 124

transparency, 40, 97

Tupac Amaru Revolutionary Movement (MRTA), 13

UCR (Unión Civica Radical; Radical Civic Union party), Argentina, 48, 54, 57, 101

UDI (Unión Democrática Independiente; Independent Democratic Union Party), Chile, 34

UNIFEM (UN Fund for Women), 185 n. 5

UNFPA (UN Fund for Population Activities), 185 n. 5

Union of Black Women, Venezuela, 77

United Kingdom, litigation strategies of, 97

United Nations, 14, 47

United Nations Committee on CEDAW, 8, 25, 85, 88, 91, 93, 99, 115

United Nations Congress on the Prevention of Crime and the Treatment of Offenders, 141 n. 3

United Nations Convention on the Elimination of All Forms of Discrimination against Women (CEDAW), 7, 84, 95, 172, 178

United Nations Decade for Women, 7, 14, 67, 68, 148

United Nations Declaration of Human Rights, 95, 129

United Nations Development Program, 8, 63 n. 3, 170

United Nations Economic and Social Council (ECOSOC), 131, 141 n. 2

United Nations global conferences, 28, 152; on environment and development (Rio de Janeiro, 1992), 7, 15, 146, 185; on human rights (Vienna, 1993), 14, 15, 118, 129, 131, 146, 147; on population and development (Cairo,

JANE S. JAQUETTE is a professor emerita and adjunct professor of politics at Occidental College.


*Library of Congress Cataloging-in-Publication Data*

Feminist agendas and democracy in Latin America /
edited by Jane S. Jaquette.
p. cm.
Includes bibliographical references and index.
ISBN 978-0-8223-4437-7 (cloth : alk. paper)
ISBN 978-0-8223-4449-0 (pbk. : alk. paper)
1. Women in politics—Latin America.
2. Women and democracy—Latin America.
3. Feminism—Latin America.
4. Democracy—Latin America.
I. Jaquette, Jane S.
HQ1236.5.L37F46  2009
320.98082—dc22   2009005183